STARTING AND BUILDING YOUR OWN ACCOUNTING BUSINESS

Also by Jack Fox:

Accountants' Guide to Budgetary Automation

GOD's Business Gamebook and Business Planning Guide

Selling Skills for Client/Server Accounting Software Professionals

Accounting and Recordkeeping Made Easy for the Self-Employed

How to Obtain Your Own SBA Loan

STARTING AND BUILDING YOUR OWN ACCOUNTING BUSINESS

Third Edition

JACK FOX, M.B.A.

John Wiley & Sons, Inc.

New York • Chichester • Weinheim • Brisbane • Singapore • Toronto

This text is printed on acid-free paper. ♾

Published simultaneously in Canada.

Library of Congress Cataloging-in-Publication Data:

Fox, Jack.
Starting and building your own accounting business / Jack Fox. — 3rd ed.
p. cm.
Includes index.
ISBN 0-471-35160-1 (pbk. : alk. paper)
1. Accounting firms. 2. New business enterprises. I. Title.
HF5627.F69 1999
6571.068'4—dc21 99-38819
CIP

Printed in the United States of America.

10 9 8 7 6 5 4 3 2 1

DEDICATION

To my wife,
Carole Olafson Fox

She opens her arms to the poor
and extends her hands to the needy.
. . . Proverbs 31:20

ACKNOWLEDGMENTS

I would like to acknowledge and express my gratitude to some of those who have contributed to this project and to my life:

God, who makes all things possible.

The people of the City of New York, who endowed the Bernard M. Baruch School of Business and Public Administration, of The City College of New York, which made it possible for people lacking monetary means to receive an excellent higher education.

The New York Times Company, for assisting with my formal education for a Masters in Business Administration, while permitting me to receive yet another practical MBA through a four-year tenure on staff.

The National Alliance of Business, Washington, DC, for the opportunity to serve as Budget Director. This helped in small measure to repay financial assistance I received by assisting programs for the disadvantaged to escape the shackles of structural unemployment and poverty.

PREFACE

"There can be no business without clients." Thus began my preface for the first two editions of this book. One of the key things I have learned in my accounting business journey since the first edition in 1984 is that the type of clients you attract and serve determines the kind of accounting or consulting business you build.

In the earlier editions, I chronicled the formation of my accounting business and how I managed, without a certified public accountant (CPA) certificate, to build a profitable and quality practice that gave excellent service and counsel to many smaller business clients.

After the success of the first edition of *Starting and Building Your Own Accounting Business* (a "celebrated guide," in the words of my publisher John Wiley & Sons, Inc.), I sold my six-year-old accounting business and founded Accounting Resources Group. Accounting Resources Group specializes in meeting the marketing and practice development needs of accountants and other solution providers. It does this by facilitating strategic partnerships with the producers of accounting software and other tools that serve the needs of the small-business and self-employed markets.

I have been devoted to the development and advancement of marketing, accounting, and data management skills, focusing on the unique demands of the self-employed. As I conducted more than 60 seminars across the country, I searched for a way to share my knowledge. I wanted to give accountants and consultants personalized, in-depth attention tailored to their individual situations.

Each entrepreneur has specific skills, interests, personality traits, hopes, and dreams that no seminar or book, no matter how good, can address. The many readers who wrote asking for advice on the challenges they faced and for solutions to their unique problems led to the publication of the second edition in 1991. Yet, there was more I wanted to do. These entrepreneurial, accounting professionals needed more knowledge, assistance, and just somebody to talk to about their accounting business.

I knew what worked and what did not work. Accounting franchises have come and gone from the scene during the time this book has been available. My warnings about the failure of the accounting franchises to deliver on their promises earned me the enmity of the franchisors (most of which have gone out of business or consolidated into other ventures) and the thanks of those who saved many thousands of dollars by heeding the book's advice and not investing in a franchise. Many of those have prospered, but going it alone is difficult in any business and accounting is no exception.

The Accounting Guild was the sound alternative I envisioned. It allows entrepreneurial accounting professionals to affiliate with an organization, yet remain very much in business for themselves. Exceptional professional support is always available and within their means. It is not a franchise and has no high initial fees or continuing royalties. It offers the best individualized practice development assistance and the opportunity to purchase tested and recommended software and hardware at prenegotiated group purchasing prices. By making The Accounting Guild available, a long span has been crossed to share my knowledge and experience. Now, I am looking at ways for groups of affiliated guild accountants to meet at local, regional, and perhaps national levels to "talk shop" and see the latest in accounting technology. A recent development is the formation of an accounting forum. To join without cost go to www. onelist.com/subscribe/accounting business.

I invite you to join me on this exciting journey. Please e-mail me at jfox1961@aol.com.

Las Vegas, Nevada
December 1999

Jack Fox, MBA

NOTE FROM THE AUTHOR

The greatest investment you can make in your accounting or consulting business, no matter what the stage, is to attend the Results Accountants' Systems Boot Camp. Just as an accounting business is not for everybody, the Boot Camp requires significant commitments, in both time and money. The program is so unique that it is considered cutting edge within the accounting industry. Results Accountants' Systems and The Accountant's Boot Camp™ has earned them the support and endorsement of some of the accounting industry's largest and most highly respected societies and institutes around the world.

Ric Payne, President of Results Accountants' Systems has said . . . "What served you well in the past will be less effective as time goes on. Your clients have many more choices and they're taking them. You must absolutely address their needs otherwise you'll lose everything you've worked so hard to build. As margins thin and competition for a finite number of clients intensifies, the demands made upon firm owners to work harder and harder will increase. You simply have to find a better way to add more value to what you do for your clients."

The better way is the Accountants' Boot Camp. The Accountants' Boot Camp uses a very different process to show the way strategies can be implemented in your business. While there are many reasons for the differences, the main reason The Accountants' Boot Camp stands out is the total focus brought to bear by co-founders Paul Dunn and Ric Payne on making certain each participant receives the real and lasting implementation which yields the results in their practice. Their abiding mission has been "to give accountants the mindset, the freedom, the systems, the resources, and the support they need to help them create extraordinary businesses for their selected clients (and in the process, for themselves)."

Results Accountants' Systems is located at 3825 Hopyard Road, Suite 150, Pleasanton, CA 94588. Telephone (800) 800-5601.

CONTENTS

1

HOW TO SUCCEED IN THE ACCOUNTING BUSINESS...IN THE NEW MILLENNIUM

THE ACCOUNTANT AS AN ENTREPRENEUR

Always do whatever you really want to do, whatever you are good at, something for which you have talent and that is and will be in demand.

The *U.S. Industry & Trade Outlook '99* predicted that employment opportunities in the accounting industry would continue to grow at a robust rate and rise to 655,000 jobs in 1999. An additional 29,000 positions will open in firms offering accounting, auditing, and bookkeeping services in 1999. The strongest gains are being experienced by the large national and regional accounting practices. Revenues for the nation's accounting firms will reach a record $72 billion during 1999.

Accounting entrepreneurship is not easy. In your own business, you will work harder than you ever have before. There will be times when you feel like throwing in the towel—critical times when mistakes in judgment are generally made, but if you like what you are doing, if you have the talent for it, you will carry on through the difficult periods and succeed in your endeavors.

A great deal of research on the personal qualities and behavior of entrepreneurs has been done, but the precise identification of entrepreneurial drive and talent remains elusive. Numerous studies have yielded important insights into entrepreneurship, yet available knowledge may represent only the tip of the iceberg. However, that said, drawing on this knowledge to assess your accounting entrepreneurial behavior may yield a substantial improvement over a mere seat-of-the-pants estimate. The key to a useful assessment lies in a realistic and thorough self-evaluation or "self-selection" by the prospective entrepreneur. Louis L. Allen, an experienced capital investor in small ventures, shared this view of the importance of the concept of self-selection:

> Unlike the giant firm which has recruiting and selection experts to screen the wheat from the chaff, the small business firm, which comprises the most common economic unit in our business system, cannot afford to employ a personnel manager . . . More than that, there's something very special about the selection of the owners: they have selected themselves . . .

But how can you self-select wisely when you are not sure what to look for? What, in this case, is important to the entrepreneurial role? The accountant who is deciding whether to start an accounting business must face this dilemma squarely.

One way to do this is to view the self-selection process as a matter of fitting entrepreneurial characteristics to the demands and pressures of an accounting business. In addition, other complex factors beyond your control, business conditions, political and regulatory climates, even providence, can undoubtedly affect the development of a new accounting business. This reality tends to lend further support to the importance of assessing and managing well the matters you can control, in particular, to assessing the likely fit between entrepreneurial characteristics and role requirements.

Today, it is a relatively easy matter to start an accounting business, but it is not so easy to define the profile of the business and the market niches in which it will specialize. The people who have started and maintained their own accounting businesses run from the sole practitioner to the principal in a large multioffice operation. The intent here is not to demean the small practitioners. They can be successful and have an extremely lucrative business, but they must adapt to current trends and conditions. They must be aware that constant evolution is necessary for business survival. When the corner grocery store had to transform itself into the supermarket, some entrepreneurs found a niche in moving from the supermarket model to the small specialty gourmet shop, and thrived as a result. Automobile dealers have found that for some, the solution to competition was multidealerships of various brand automobiles and then on to consolidation of dealerships for economies of scale. This phenomenon is going on in the accounting industry, too.

Small tax and accounting practices are facing unprecedented competitive pressures that are expected to increase in the future as national consolidators tighten their grip on the marketplace. Small firms are being warned that American Express, Century Business Services, H & R Block, and others will soon have reached critical mass in the tax and accounting industry and will turn from building market share to stealing it. In finding and retaining clients, smaller firms may find themselves competing against the kind of sophisticated marketing campaigns, deep-pocketed recruiting programs, and cutthroat pricing wars that the Big Five accounting firms wage when competing for *Fortune* 1000 targets.

Accounting entrepreneurs come from widely varying backgrounds in terms of education and experience. Most accounting businesses in this country are small when compared to the statistics for all businesses in general. Many accountants are worried that they are facing an industry Armageddon. To dispell that fear, let's analyze the accounting industry. Eliminate the Big Five firms from the equation because they operate in a *Fortune* 1000 market, far away from the Main Street clients handled by the nation's independently owned and locally operated tax and accounting practices. The Big Five accounts for about $24 billion of the government-estimated $72 billion tax and accounting business.

The remaining $48 billion represents the small business tax and accounting market. We will assume that market is served by some 390,000 CPAs at 46,500 firms, using the American Institute of Certified Public Accountants (AICPA) membership roster of 332,000 as the entire accounting universe. Non-CPAs, consultants, accounting software specialists, accountant value-added resellers (VARs), and quasi-accounting firms would probably account for an additional several hundred thousand practitioners in a significant number of firms.

Of the 46,500 firms, some 45,000 employ fewer than 10 CPAs, far too small to interest the consolidators. Of the remaining 1,500 firms, 1,200 employ from 10 to 24 CPAs. To a consolidator, those 10-to-24 CPA offices would be the most expensive to acquire in terms of revenues and take the longest to integrate. That leaves only about 300 firms with more than 25 CPAs. These firms employ about 16,000 CPAs. If each firm bills an industry average $150,000 in fees per CPA, then the three hundred firms collectively are worth $2.4 billion in revenues—or barely 5 percent of the $48 billion small-business market. Even if consolidators acquired every last one of the 1,200 firms in the costly 10-to-24 CPA category (which is not likely), they would still control only $5 billion, or a less-than-dominating 11 percent of the CPA market.

If consolidators are going to become multi–billion dollar enterprises, they will need revenues from beyond tax and accounting—from financial and insurance services, from payroll and benefits administration, and from technology and systems consulting, to name a few. Consolidation is redefining the meaning of CPA services and, in so doing, is enlarging the marketplace.

CHARACTERISTICS OF SUCCESSFUL ACCOUNTANTS

The wide variety of businesses in the accounting industry and in the entrepreneurs who run them makes across-the-board generalizations about their characteristics difficult. For example, an accounting firm specializing in accounting system computer technology differs from one that offers traditional tax and auditing services. The skills and educational backgrounds of technology consultants are different from those of predominantly financial backgrounds.

The best way to identify the characteristics necessary for success in the accounting business is to examine the knowledge and personal development needed to establish and grow a business. Some entrepreneurial skills, such as goal setting, can be developed; certain role requirements, such as the specialized knowledge of particular market niches, can be learned. Early success provides not only a valuable experience but also a platform on which to build a larger, more complex, demanding, and more profitable venture later on. Therefore, in the final analysis, you will have to judge for yourself where you are, where you are headed, and what you can do to increase your entrepreneurial potential from, say, a moderate fit to a high fit, as depicted in Exhibit 1.1.

For the entrepreneurial accountant, prospective partner, affiliate, and investor alike, evaluating the nature and extent of entrepreneurial potential is critical to future success. With the material that follows, we will help you identify any major shortcomings or potentially fatal flaws that could make your pursuit of an accounting business a program for failure. Do not expect that this guide will enable you to decide whether you are capable of building an Arthur Andersen, Ernst & Young, or PricewaterhouseCoopers. However, we do believe we can help you determine whether, in fact, you have a reasonable chance of succeeding in an accounting business that will suit your own goals, values, and needs. In developing these entrepreneurial characteristics, we examined the available research on the behavioral characteristics of successful entrepreneurs. We also reviewed the current practices of venture capitalists when assessing the personal characteristics of entrepreneurs in whom they wanted to invest. We found that venture capitalists expended considerable effort to determine whether persons wanting to start a new venture and applicants for venture capital did in fact possess the necessary characteristics. Our investigations identified 14 dominant characteristics of successful entrepreneurs:

EXHIBIT 1.1
A Matter of Fit

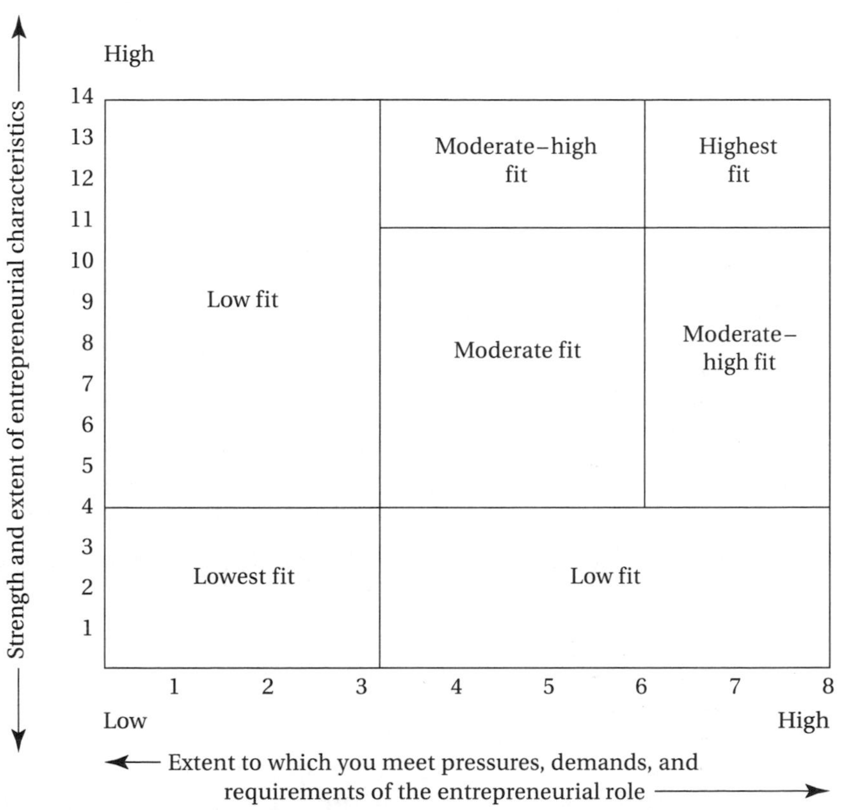

Dominant Characteristics of Successful Entrepreneurs

1. *Drive and energy.* Entrepreneurs are generally recognized as having abundant personal energy and drive, a capacity to work for long hours and sometimes in spurts of several days with less than the normal amount of sleep. Our examination of the venture capital industry confirmed drive and energy as characteristics mandated by investors and frequently observed in successful entrepreneurs—and some afflicted with manic depression.
2. *Self-confidence.* There is also general agreement that successful entrepreneurs possess a high level of self-confidence. They

tend to believe strongly in themselves and their ability to achieve the goals they have set. They believe that events in their lives are mainly self-determined, that they have a major influence on their personal destinies, and that their success depends little on luck. Researchers often cite this characteristic. Further, venture capitalists and the financial community look for a strong sense of self-confidence before placing their money but regard overconfidence, subtle arrogance, or absence of humility—all of which may suggest a lack of realism—as negative traits.

3. *Long-term involvement.* Involvement is a characteristic that distinguishes the entrepreneur—the creator and builder of a business—from the promoter or quick-buck artist. Entrepreneurs who create high-potential ventures are driven to build a business. They are not interested in getting in and out in a hurry; their commitment to long-term projects and to working toward goals that may be quite distant is total.

   One venture capitalist has said: "The lemon trees bear fruit in two or three years; the plum trees take seven or eight years." On the basis of their own experience, venture capitalists know that a successful growth business requires complete concentration on the attainment of objectives. This involvement, so characteristic of successful entrepreneurs, has been confirmed by research.

4. *Money as a measure.* Money has a special meaning for the professional accountant entrepreneur: It is a way of keeping score. Salary, profits, capital gains, and net worth are seen as measures of how well self-established goals are met. The accountant is involved in a continuous process of making money, of investing it in other companies, and then starting all over again. This cycle seems never to end, and the money accrued is a way of measuring performance.

5. *Persistent problem solving.* Accountant entrepreneurs who build new accounting businesses possess intense levels of determination to overcome hurdles, solve problems, and complete the job. They are not intimidated by difficulties. Rather, their self-confidence and general optimism seem to translate into a belief that the impossible just takes a little longer. Yet, they are neither aimless nor foolhardy in their relentless attack on obstacles that can impede their progress. Although they are extremely persistent, they are also realistic

in recognizing what they can and cannot do and how they can get assistance to solve difficult but necessary tasks.

6. *Goal setting.* Entrepreneurs have the ability to set clear goals for themselves—goals that tend to be challenging but always realistic and attainable. Entrepreneurs are action-oriented doers with a clear and direct purpose. They know where they are headed.

7. *Moderate risk taking.* The successful entrepreneur prefers to take moderate, calculated risks in which the chances of winning are neither so small that they become a gamble nor so large that they represent a sure thing. In a situation whose outcome is influenced as much by ability and effort as by chance, the successful entrepreneur prefers risks that provide a reasonable chance of success. This entrepreneurial characteristic is one of the most important because it indicates how decisions are made and implies the success or failure of the business.

8. *Dealing with failure.* Successful entrepreneurs view failure as a way of learning and understanding not only their own part but that of others in the cause of the failure so as to avoid similar mistakes in the future. Success and failure are not opposites. Rather, they are companions, like the hero and the sidekick in the old western movies. The trial-and-error nature of becoming a successful entrepreneur makes serious setbacks and disappointments a part of the learning process. The most effective accountant entrepreneurs are realistic enough to expect difficulties. They are not disappointed, discouraged, or depressed by setbacks—at least not for long. More typically, they seek opportunity in difficult times and victory in situations in which most people would see only defeat.

   Entrepreneurs are not afraid of failure. Being more intent on succeeding, they are not intimidated by the possibility of failing. Those who fear failure will neutralize whatever motivation for achievement they may possess. They will tend to engage in easy tasks in which there is little chance of failure or in chance situations in which they cannot be held personally responsible if they do not succeed.

9. *Use of feedback.* Entrepreneurs, as high achievers, are especially concerned with doing well. This concern is responsible, in part, for another entrepreneurial characteristic: the use of

feedback. Without feedback, the entrepreneur cannot know how good or bad the performance is. Successful entrepreneurs demonstrate an ability to use feedback to improve or to take corrective action.

10. *Taking the initiative and assuming personal responsibility.* Historically, the entrepreneur has been viewed as an independent and highly self-reliant innovator, a champion of the free-enterprise economy. Considerable agreement has been reached among researchers and practitioners alike that effective entrepreneurs take the initiative by placing themselves in situations in which they are personally responsible for the success or failure of the operation.

11. *Use of resources.* Several studies have shown that successful entrepreneurs know when and how to obtain outside assistance in building their companies and will follow the best advice they can afford. They are not so ego-involved that they will refuse to allow anyone else to help. This trait, at first glance, appears to be at odds with a popular stereotype of all entrepreneurs as highly individualistic loners. The willingness to take advantage of outside resources is a key characteristic that distinguishes the high-potential entrepreneur from the rest of the pack.

12. *Competing against self-imposed standards.* Competitiveness can be a misleading attribute. It is most important to distinguish between competition directed toward others, without any objective measure of performance, and an internalized kind of competition with a self-imposed standard.

13. *Internal locus of control.* The accountant entrepreneur does not believe that the success or failure of a new business depends on luck or fate or other external, uncontrollable factors. Rather, the belief is that personal accomplishments as well as setbacks lie within one's personal control and influence.

14. *Tolerance of ambiguity and uncertainty.* Entrepreneurs have long been viewed as having a special tolerance for the ambiguous and for making decisions under conditions of uncertainty. In contrast to the professional manager, they are able to live with modest-to-high levels of uncertainty in job security. Job permanency is considerably lower on the entrepreneur's list of preferences as compared with a managerial counterpart. This toleration for insecurity is generally recognized as an important characteristic.

Dominant Characteristics Analysis

These dominant characteristics of successful entrepreneurs were abstracted from the literature on entrepreneurship in general, entrepreneurship among accountants, research with venture capitalists, and personal experience. They constitute what is currently believed to be the most significant aspects of entrepreneurial behavior, but the biggest gap in existing knowledge is how to measure and identify many of the personality-oriented characteristics accurately and consistently.

Probably no single entrepreneur possesses all 14 characteristics to an extremely high degree. Theoretically, more are better than fewer, but weaknesses can be offset by strengths. Thus, it is important to recognize strengths and weaknesses with respect to each of the characteristics.

By the same measure, the absence of several key characteristics, many modest ratings, and few, if any, high ratings, suggest a low suitability for high-potential, high-pressure entrepreneurship.

Role Demands and Requirements

It is not enough to possess an intense level of entrepreneurial characteristics. Certain conditions, pressures, and demands are inherent in the role requirements that are important to the fit of the entrepreneurial task and to the eventual success or failure of the venture. Exhibit 1.2 describes perceptions based on years of observation of the characteristics and role models of accountants.

Although successful entrepreneurs may share several characteristics with those who succeed in other careers, their preference for and tolerance of the combination of requirements unique to the entrepreneurial role are major distinguishing features. Research has suggested eight dominant role requirements.

EXHIBIT 1.2
Perceptions of Characteristics and Role Demands

Dominant Role Requirements

1. *Accommodation to the venture.* The accountant entrepreneur lives under almost constant pressure—first to survive, then to tread water, and always to grow and withstand the thrusts of competitors. The accountant's time, emotions, and loyalty

are top-priority demands in a high-potential accounting venture—demands that are important to decisions relating to marriage, raising a family, and community involvement. To do all these things well is not a realistic expectation for most people. The cooperation and understanding of your spouse is essential and cannot be overemphasized. Many owners of small businesses share the same concerns as the accountant, and all are probably concerned as much by personal and family matters as by the profitability of the business.

2. *Total immersion and commitment.* Launching and building an accounting business is not a part-time proposition. Sure, you can start a sideline activity preparing taxes or do some freelance accounting work, but that is not an accounting business. Building a profitable accounting business requires total immersion in and commitment to that end. The managerial role can be delegated; the entrepreneurial role cannot. Building a new business or expanding an existing one is a way of life. Unless it is a way in which you can thrive, it can be intolerable.

3. *Creativity and innovation.* The entrepreneurial role has long been recognized as a prime source of innovation and creativity. Recent studies of entrepreneurial careers have identified the "career anchors" with which it is associated: creativity and innovation. Managers, however, find their career anchors in competence and efficiency, while college professors prefer autonomy—control over their time.

4. *Knowledge of the business you want to launch.* Venture capitalists, among others, stress the importance of the track records, the business experience and accomplishments, of the entrepreneurs and the teams in which they invest. Most strongly prefer that a potential venture be headed by an individual who has a thorough operating knowledge of the business to be launched. This is especially true for those considering an accounting business enterprise. Work for the type of firm you would like to someday start yourself. You will probably meet your future partners while working for another firm. Some of the clients with whom you work closely may decide to follow you to your own firm.

5. *Team building.* High-potential ventures are rarely sole proprietorships. One-person operations are extremely limited in upside potential.

6. *Economic values.* Accountant entrepreneurs must share the key values of the free-enterprise system: *private ownership, profits, capital gains,* and *responsible growth.* These dominant economic values need not exclude social values, but the realities of the competitive market economy seem to require a belief in or at least a tolerance of them.

7. *Ethics.* Historically, the accountant entrepreneur has possessed what is referred to as situational ethics. In situational ethics, right and wrong are defined by the needs and demands of the situation rather than by some external, rigid code of conduct applied uniformly, regardless of the conditions and circumstances.

8. *Integrity and reliability.* Integrity and reliability are essential qualities for the aspiring accountant who is trying to raise conventional venture capital and/or debt financing. A reputation for dependability, reliability, and honesty is essential.

Prognosis for Professional Accounting Aptitude

Except in the area of personal values, no tests or other instruments exist that can help you to assess your fit to a particular role requirement. Induction and inference, coupled with hard-nosed reality testing with those who know you well, are required to arrive at realistic self-assessments in relation to these requirements. Do not be dismayed if you do not meet them all. Perhaps nobody does. It is more important to understand the implications of these role demands, your own attraction or aversion to them, and alternative ways of compensating for deficiencies.

The accounting professional can look forward to an increasingly significant role in the country's economic future. The past years of economic upheaval have emphasized the growing value of professional support at the small- and medium-sized business level. Business has learned that out-of-date, inadequate, and labor-intensive accounting systems will no longer do. Intuit's QuickBooks is being used in millions of business that had once relied on a bookkeeper or accountant to do the necessary write-up work. CPAs, non-CPAs, and consultants are being increasingly sought for their expertise in systems design and analysis and for their abilities in many accounting specialties. Accounting has emulated medicine in the development of various and effective specialties to cater to the increasing sophistication of the small to medium-sized business market.

Government studies indicate that the demand for auditing and write-up accounting services in small to medium-sized businesses will continue to decrease. The result will continue to be dramatically shrinking profit margins for these activities. The price of the average audit has declined to about 2 cents per $10,000 of corporate revenue from 3.3 cents in 1985, and this trend shows no sign of abating.

Declining audit revenues are being more than offset by increasing revenues from value-added consulting services. To be competitive, CPAs are shifting their focus toward helping clients understand all areas of business performance rather than financial matters alone. The accountant is becoming more of a coach than a scorekeeper.

In the future, the success of the nation's CPAs will be based not on laws and regulations but on the CPAs' ability to become market-driven. On the judicial front, the United States Supreme Court ruling against the State of Florida's regulators is one that may affect the relationship among accounting firms, management consulting firms, and state regulatory boards throughout the country. That ruling "allows employees of American Express Tax and Business Services (a consolidator) to use their CPA credentials and grants this firm the right to advertise that it employs CPAs." Although the ruling went against the Florida State Board of Accountancy, the board still may assert jurisdiction over CPAs in regard to technical standards.

Other recent key trends are the large-scale mergers and separations within the accounting industry, which will influence the direction of accounting practice in the twenty-first century. High-profile mergers, such as the 1998 consolidation of Coopers & Lybrand and Price Waterhouse, aim to give clients more services and firms higher revenues and greater efficiency. Along with hoped for economic and management gains, the equally high-profile separation of Arthur Andersen and Andersen Consulting produced a degree of friction and contentiousness.

At the turn of the century, just four years after the first public accounting certificate was issued, CPAs numbered 500 nationwide. Getting its start at a time when more Americans than ever had direct stakes in the country's burgeoning industries, the new profession filled a need of the investing public for standardized financial reporting. Today, there are more than 332,000 CPAs who are members of the AICPA and over 65,000 CPAs who are not members of the AICPA.

Public accounting continues to offer a wide range of career paths: the Big Five national and international accounting firms (which together employ more than 20,000 CPAs), large national and regional firms, medium-sized partnerships, professional corporations, and small firms (which employ from 1 to 25 accountants). Large regional firms to medium-sized local firms offer new accountants the experience of a varied practice, the advice of older partners, association with a professional group, and the opportunity for specialization. A drawback is that sometimes the assignments are so specialized that the accountant is denied the opportunity of working with a wide range of companies and receives only narrow experience. The medium-sized CPA firm provides interesting work with experienced professionals and a chance to specialize or to vary assignments.

The professional corporation offers its members many of the advantages of the medium-sized partnership and certain corporate advantages: tax benefits, profit-sharing opportunities, and insurance options. Small partnerships offer staffers and partners many incentives to demonstrate individual initiative and creativity, while sole proprietorships allow the independent thinker the greatest amount of flexibility along with the drawback of working alone. Sole practitioners or those in small partnerships often describe the satisfaction of working in a less structured environment, setting their own time schedules, choosing their own clients, and making their own decisions.

However, those accountants who strike out alone to form a small partnership or sole proprietorship ultimately face the most demanding challenges. To establish themselves, they must first choose the type of practice, carefully select its location, physically set up the office, personally develop the business contacts, skillfully manage the business, and continue to update their professional knowledge of accounting and chosen specialties.

CAPABILITY, CREDENTIALS, AND CREDIBILITY

Life is a series of decisions. Some people meet those decisions with enthusiasm and anticipation; others avoid making decisions. The avoiders fool only themselves, because a decision not made is, in fact, a decision to do nothing.

CPA—To Be or Not to Be

If you hold a CPA certificate, all to the good. However, do not allow the lack of a certificate to keep you from launching a successful accounting business. The CPA certificate in and of itself does not guarantee success. To build a successful accounting business, you must be hardworking, self-motivated, and self-confident. You must enjoy working with people and excel at sales. You must be able to plan and effectively execute those plans and be able to make firm, no-nonsense and mostly correct decisions. You must have sufficient financial resources. You must have the desire to be a trusted and respected member of your community. You should be strong and sincere.

Accounting—Business's Intimate Confidant

An independent accountant (CPA or non-CPA) retained by a business is usually more involved in its day-to-day operations and is more knowledgeable about its financial condition than almost anyone other than senior management. Clients give their accountants access to sensitive business information and frequently ask them how they can cut costs, increase margins, and improve profitability. Unlike the business's lawyers, who as a rule are consulted only for a specific legal problem, the independent accountant is involved with the company on a continuing basis.

Moreover, the independent accountant has access to internal financial data that are closely guarded by owners and top management. The accountant is often privy to information that is given to no one else, not even the board of directors.

Technology Revolution

The accounting profession, in addition to being business's most intimate confidant, is now also at the forefront of a technology revolution. The issue is productivity in the workplace. In the early 1980s, as chronicled in the first edition of *Starting and Building Your Own Accounting Business,* accountants ushered in the era of the personal computer (PC). Working with small businesses and select groups of corporate managers, accountants established powerful PCs as the business management tool of choice. This created new software industries in spreadsheets and small business accounting. This was a revolution of efficiency whose purpose was to automate and simplify business transactions so that more data were available to the managers who most needed them.

Reengineering Revolution

The revolution that is going on right now is one of reengineering. Reengineered processes go beyond simply automating a manual task via a computer, but rather focus on creating information. Instead of just putting data on a big server, the new processes distribute information to the workers who need it most, helping them communicate with co-workers, customers, and clients. The need to broadly distribute information, when combined with increasing competition, a global economy, and the need to downsize operations to maintain profitability, forces corporations both large and small to take a fresh look at their organizational structures, missions, and processes. Like technology, reengineering began in the mission-critical area of accounting. As in the past, accounting professionals are on the business frontier, offering solutions, directing change, and enhancing both the level and the value of services they give to clients.

Accounting Allies

Accounting professionals who are leading the reengineering process have powerful new allies. Microsoft Corporation, the world's largest personal computer software company, and a host of accounting software developers and publishers have established strong relationships with the accounting industry. The goal of these software allies is to give accounting professionals the tools and support they need to be the architects of change for both the accounting industry and for their clients. As the accounting industry has grown, increasing competition and the effects of technology have changed the roles of accounting professionals, increasing the impact of the profession on its clients and creating opportunities for growth.

Business Value Chain

Successful professional accountants have moved up the value chain in the services they offer to clients. Today's technology usurps the lower value functions, like bookkeeping, traditionally performed by CPAs. The software for data input and routine transactions is easy for the clients to use themselves. As clients master new technology, with the professional accountants' assistance, they begin to expect more value from the dollars they spend for accountants. The small to medium-sized business clients rely heavily on their professional accountants and consultants for sophisticated business advice. The professional accountant and consultant is knowledgeable about the client and the client's business. The accountant knows what the client's business objectives are and can suggest ways to reach those objectives.

ACCOUNTING INDUSTRY'S FUTURE

This move up the value chain is reflected in the decline of revenue from traditional accounting services—tax, auditing, and write-up—and the explosive growth of consulting. Professional accountants have come to realize that they cannot serve clients by performing rudimentary bookkeeping and tax services. The future of the accounting industry is not in compiling the numbers, but in interpreting the numbers and using them to help clients identify successful business strategies.

CPA Vision Project: The AICPA-Sponsored Insight into the Future

The core purpose of the AICPA Vision Project is to make sense of a changing and complex world. The AICPA's vision of the profession's future is that CPAs will be sought out as trusted professionals who enable people and organizations to shape their future. Although the findings may be meaningful, they do represent a rather proprietary view that the future of the profession rests solely on the CPA. MBAs, CMAs, Microsoft Certified Professionals, and other financial experts will also play significant roles as the business community's trusted professionals.

Future Forums and Research Results

As part of its Vision Project, the AICPA conducted grassroots future forums around the country. The forums found that in the future, accounting professionals will deliver value:

- By communicating the total picture with clarity and objectivity
- By translating complex information into critical knowledge
- By anticipating and creating new opportunities
- By designing pathways that transform vision into reality
- By redefining missions, core purposes, and visions

- With knowledge and insight
- With increased education and training
- With increased use of technology and communications skills
- With increased opportunities to command higher compensation
- Through increased need for networking

Top Future Issues

The Vision Project identified the following as the issues that will determine the future success of CPAs:

- Future success relies on public perceptions.
- The profession must become market driven.
- The profession must become less focused on auditing/accounting and devote more attention to value-added consulting.
- Specialization is critical.
- Accounting professionals must become conversant in global business.

Top Future Services

The Vision Project found the following to be the five core services:

1. Assurance
2. Technology
3. Management Consulting
4. Financial Planning
5. International

Future Professional Accountants' Competencies

The following five competencies are critical to future success:

1. Communications skills
2. Strategic and critical thinking
3. Focus on client and market
4. Interpretation of converging information
5. Technological fluency

You can keep track of this important project by visiting the CPA Vision Project's Web site at www.cpavision.org.

The independent accountant must possess the capabilities shown in Exhibit 1.3.

EXHIBIT 1.3
Independent Accountants' Required Capabilities

- An independent accountant's education should be broad, not narrow. Small to medium-sized business problems cross functional boundaries and involve all aspects of a business. Being knowledgeable in several areas is more important than concentrating on one.
- Small-business experience is essential. The independent accountant/consultant must be able to sense what information is needed to solve a problem and fit that data into an answer that suggests a remedy. It is never too early for the independent accountant to start building small-business knowledge. One simple way is to be alert to patterns and appropriate solutions to problems encountered on jobs.
- Being able to understand the problems of owner–managers from their perspective will help accountants recognize clients' constraints and priorities as well as see the problem as a whole and the ramifications of a possible remedy.
- An accountant's breadth of experience can bring out alternative solutions that the client may not have considered. Accountants should not be hesitant about suggesting alternatives.
- Independent accountants and consultants must develop the ability to communicate with clients in terms they can understand. Accounting may be called "the language of business," but not everybody is fluent in this language. Accountants should translate their views of any problems into operational terms that clients can understand, especially if the client has no accounting staff to interpret technical language.
- Accountants must know that it is not theory but implemented solutions that clients need. Clients usually do not have the resources to implement solutions by themselves. While they are concerned about consulting fees, they will be more concerned with a job that does not meet its goals. Thus, the accountant must be willing and able to see the job through to its successful conclusion.

ACCOUNTANTS' RESOURCE REQUIREMENTS

According to surveys, clients expect their accountants and consultants to have experience in serving their type of business. The first resource for the accountant or consultant serving small business is at least 5 to 10 years of problem-solving experience in addressing the needs of this segment.

The second resource is the perspective of a manager rather than a technician. In other words, the accountant must be able to see problems from a business rather than a technical point of view. The accountant must also be able to discuss these problems and their solutions in managerial terms. The third resource is attitude, that is, having both pride in your work and the desire to assist client companies to be more effective, efficient, and adaptive to changing conditions.

Helping clients serve market needs economically is a social benefit and the accountants' professional responsibility.

Compliance versus Problem Solving

Unfortunately, too many CPAs are content to confine their relationships with clients to compliance and attestation services. If CPAs do not believe that they are key members of problem-solving teams for sophisticated small-business clients, the whole relationship between practitioners and their clients will be severely weakened. This is now being demonstrated with the acquisition of CPA firms by non–CPA-owned consolidators. After consolidators acquire a CPA firm, the certified activities of attestation are spun off to a separate entity so that the consolidator can operate the firm unfettered by CPA rules, regulations, and requirements.

Improving Problem-Solving Capabilities

Other resources that may be used to improve an accountant's ability to solve client problems include continuing professional education courses, management advisory services' publications, Web sites, and The Accounting Guild's business consulting practice aids. Another resource may be consultants outside the accounting firm. Indeed, few independent accountants have staff expertise in all areas, and the need for outside consultation should be evaluated when accepting an engagement.

Developing an Effective Marketing Strategy

Small to medium-sized businesses are a lucrative market for independent accountants and consultants. Tapping that market calls for a well-planned strategy. Your first step is to prepare an analysis of your firm's needs. Gather relevant information that will be reviewed and discussed by the firm's management and key staff members. Exhibit 1.4 lists the major areas to include in the analysis:

EXHIBIT 1.4
Checklist: Developing Effective Marketing Strategy for a Small to Medium-Sized Business

- ❑ 1. Strengths of the firm, particularly relating to the nature and breadth of the needs of small to medium-sized business clients
- ❑ 2. Weaknesses of the firm, again stressing small to medium-sized business client services
- ❑ 3. Special markets already served by the firm
- ❑ 4. Additional target markets that could be developed
- ❑ 5. Analysis of the firm's leaders to determine their attitudes toward practice development
- ❑ 6. Analysis of the technical and experience qualifications of the firm's staff to serve the ever-expanding needs of small to medium-sized business clients
- ❑ 7. Availability of resources, including staff, for the small to medium-sized business practice development effort and improvement of the firm's ability to deliver a broad range of small to medium-sized business services
- ❑ 8. Attitude of the firm's leaders toward both the need to break down barriers between areas such as audit, tax, and consulting services and special recognition for those staff members responsible for the success of the practice development program, such as additional time allocated for these activities and additional compensation

Opportunities and Preparation

A wealth of opportunities await the accountant who plans carefully and prepares adequately to serve small to medium-sized business clients. These clients come in many different sizes, shapes, structures, and stages of development. They, in turn, require varied services from their business advisors. The professional accountant who understands these diverse needs and is prepared to fulfill them will have a distinct advantage in attracting clients in this market.

As successful as the Big Five accounting firms have been, they have made few inroads into the core constituency of most local accounting firms: America's small to medium-sized businesses. Instead, the Big Five have relied on their established client base—the nation's large companies—to form their consulting practices. Therefore, large accounting firms have little insight into the concerns, problems, and hopes of smaller businesses. That potentially large market opportunity remains mostly untapped.

Reengineering Business Models

During the past several years, accountants have experienced a deterioration of their traditional core practice areas of accounting and auditing, and their tax practice revenues have grown only slightly. As most accountants know, their revenue picture is being eroded by the proliferation of lower-cost, alternative sources that provide tax, audit, and accounting services.

It seems that every few years, a new threat looms on the horizon. In the 1980s, low-cost tax preparers took away much of the CPAs' lower-end tax business. During the 1990s, tax and accounting software further eroded the revenue stream. Because they tend to be small and dependent on a few sources of revenue, most of the 47,000 independent CPA firms in the United States are vulnerable to competitive threats.

Emerging Threats to Independent Accountants

Recently, financial and travel services giant American Express has been making a strategic push into the accounting marketplace. By the end of 1998, American Express had acquired approximately 60 local CPA firms, and it planned to increase its acquisitions to a nationwide network of more than 270 firms. The company intends to provide accounting, tax, and consulting services with increased efficiency so that each of its CPA firms will serve 10 times the number of clients of a comparable independent firm. In addition, other consolidators (as these financial services firms have been termed) are increasingly following the lead of American Express into this market.

Extending Core Competencies

Faced with increasing pressures, accountants and consultants have few choices but to extend their core competencies. In this effort, they may choose industry specialization or even decide to develop specialties, such as budget and business planning and business valuation services.

The greatest potential reward by far for accountants and consultants lies in their ability to leverage relationships with current clients to provide strategic business advice.

MICROSOFT CORPORATION: A STRATEGIC PARTNER

Microsoft Corporation has always had a strong relationship with accounting professionals. The accounting industry is one of their highest priority industry-specific solutions markets. To exploit this market, Microsoft has been focusing on three sets of services to accountants and consultants:

1. The development of core technologies that lead to open, cost-effective business solutions
2. Strong support of the delivery channel for those solutions
3. The enhancement of communication systems that enable accountants to build better client relationships

Microsoft's Core Technologies

Microsoft serves as an engine for accounting solutions. Its role is to develop core technologies that run on the widest possible range of hardware systems and tools that work together seamlessly in a vast array of modular configurations. The core technologies, such as OLE, a broadly used technology for sharing data between applications, and MAPI, which allows independent software vendors (ISVs) to write applications that are automatically mail enabled, are used by thousands of software developers.

Microsoft also has two broad product lines: the Microsoft® BackOffice suite and the Microsoft® Office Professional suite of applications. The latter includes Microsoft® Word for Windows®, Microsoft® Excel for Windows®, and other programs that can be used off the shelf or customized by independent suppliers and developers.

Microsoft solves very few problems itself. Its primary role is to enable the ISVs by providing a technology engine. In today's client–server environment, this technology engine powers the development of accounting and business application software that is very flexible, very modular, and applicable to the broadest range of business requirements.

Aligning with Strategic Partners

Independent software vendors create the accounting industry software. At the client site, teams of knowledgeable VAR/installers integrate it into new and legacy (existing) computer systems. Professional accountants or business consultants assist the VARs to customize the technology and the software for specific client solutions.

> Our relationships with these professionals, the ISVs who develop software, the VAR/installers who implement it, and the accountants and consultants who customize it, are the reason that Microsoft is today a leading provider of key technologies for accounting solutions. For our part, these solution providers recognize that we are willing to support them, both technically and with marketing assistance. They know we will invest heavily to insure the success of a platform, and will do it with an eye toward being in the industry for the long term.[1]

One of the most comprehensive efforts designed to foster professional relationships between a software provider and accountants is the Microsoft Solution Provider program which is outlined in Exhibit 1.5.

[1] From a sponsored Microsoft Supplement, "Putting Microsoft® Technology to Work for You."

EXHIBIT 1.5
The Microsoft Solution Provider Program

Formed in 1992, the Solution Provider program now supports more than 70 percent of the high-end and 90 percent of the midrange accounting software ISVs. The ISVs offer value-added services that include integration, consulting, custom and turnkey application development, technical support, and training.

The Solution Provider Program is Microsoft's primary network for the distribution of Microsoft's technology, technical information, and expertise to their business partners. Members of the program receive marketing support through referrals and participation in regional seminars hosted by Microsoft. The members also receive technical information through a TechNet CD-ROM program and development tools through the Microsoft Developer Network CD. Plus, Microsoft backs them with high-quality technical support, 24 hours a day if they require it.

Members also receive the training they need to become Microsoft Certified Professionals in new technology areas and to hone their technical skills so that they can provide higher levels of accounting and computer consulting services to clients. To help ensure that they are familiar with all applications, each member receives Microsoft Office Professional, Windows for Workgroups, Windows NT Workstation, or Windows 98, and the Microsoft BackOffice suite of products. Members also receive beta test copies of new versions for software they develop and support.

Accountant Value-Added Reseller

Career challenges and opportunities have never been greater for accounting professionals. Success in today's information systems environment requires skills that go far beyond knowing write-up accounting, tax compliance and preparation, auditing, and generally accepted accounting principles. The accounting professional must know how, or affiliate with a team that knows how, to install and service network file and print servers and to support new and increasingly sophisticated multivendor enterprise environments.

Education and Certification

Effective accounting professionals need a comprehensive understanding of open systems architecture, client–server computing, and the Internet as much as they need to understand that assets equal liabilities plus net worth.

The necessary advanced skills are available at colleges, universities, and training seminars and centers as well as through Microsoft's Education and Certification. The training and certification programs demonstrate how organizations can maximize the use of Microsoft desktop operating systems and applications, Microsoft Windows NT® and the Microsoft BackOffice™ family of server software, and Microsoft development tools and technologies. Through education and certification, the professional accountant and business consultant will gain the knowledge, skills, and validation necessary to be recognized as an expert with accounting solutions using Microsoft products and technologies.

Education

The Microsoft Official Curriculum comes from Microsoft's staff of course designers, product developers, and support engineers to ensure that you get the industry's most timely and reliable course offerings related to Microsoft's advanced technology products and integration techniques. The official courses are offered through:

- Microsoft-authorized training sites
- Microsoft Solution Provider Authorized Technical Education Centers (ATECs)—commercial training organizations offering Microsoft Official Curriculum over consecutive days
- Microsoft Authorized Academic Training Program (AATP) institutions—offering Microsoft Official Curriculum over an academic term

These professional education centers deliver consistent, high-level, hands-on technical training on the full range of Microsoft productivity, networking, operating system, and application development products. All Microsoft Solution Provider ATECs and AATP sites have met stringent guidelines to receive their Microsoft authorization. These guidelines govern curriculum, class sizes, training facilities, and, most important, the educational and technical expertise of the Microsoft Certified Trainers.

Online Training

The Microsoft Online Institute allows the participant to access online Internet classes of a combination of self-paced computer-based learning materials and instructor guidance.

Self-Paced Training

Microsoft Official Curriculum is also available in self-paced training formats for those who prefer to learn on their own, at their own pace. These materials are available in book, computer-based training (CBT), and mixed-media (book and video) formats. The training materials are widely available wherever Microsoft Press® books are sold. Additional self-paced training materials are developed by third-party companies partnering with Microsoft.

Microsoft Certification

The Microsoft certification is worth pursuing. It is becoming an increasingly valuable credential and evidence of the accounting professional's capability and credibility in the accounting marketplace. The designation is a valuable symbol of your competency and will complement other esteemed honors, such as the MBA and CMA. (See Exhibit 1.6.)

Microsoft's exams and corresponding certifications were developed to validate the professional's mastery of critical competencies to design and develop, or implement and support, solutions with Microsoft products and technologies. Those who become Microsoft Certified Professionals are recognized as experts and are sought after industry-wide. (See Exhibit 1.7.)

To become certified, one must pass certification exams that provide a valid and reliable measure of technical proficiency and expertise. Microsoft exams are performance-based and reflect how Microsoft products are actually used in practice.

EXHIBIT 1.6
Microsoft Certification Designations

Microsoft Certified Professional Systems Engineer

Qualified to effectively plan, implement, maintain, and support information systems with Microsoft Windows NT Server and the Microsoft BackOffice integrated family of server software.

Microsoft Certified Professional Solution Developer

Qualified to design and develop custom business solutions with Microsoft development tools, technologies, and platforms, including Microsoft Office and Microsoft BackOffice.

Microsoft Certified Professional Product Specialist

Demonstrated in-depth knowledge of at least one Microsoft operating system. Candidates may pass additional Microsoft certification exams to further qualify their skills in a particular area of specialization.

Microsoft Certified Professional Trainer

Instructionally and technically qualified to deliver Microsoft Official Curriculum through Microsoft authorized education sites.

EXHIBIT 1.7
Benefits of Becoming a Microsoft Certified Professional

- **Industry recognition** of your knowledge of and proficiency with Microsoft products.
- **Access to technical information** directly from Microsoft.
- **Dedicated online forums,** allowing Microsoft Certified Professionals to communicate directly with Microsoft and one another (an excellent source of referrals and prospecting).
- **Subscription to *Microsoft Certified Professional* magazine,** a career and professional development magazine created especially for Microsoft Certified Professionals.
- **Microsoft Professional logos** and other materials to let you identify your Microsoft Certified Professional status to colleagues, clients, and prospective clients.
- **Invitations to Microsoft conferences,** technical training sessions, and special events.
- **Microsoft TechNet or Microsoft Developer Network** (depending on one's certification) membership or discounts.
- **No-charge product support incidents** with the Microsoft Support Network—7 days a week, 24 hours a day.
- **Eligibility to join the Network Professional Association,** a worldwide independent association of computer professionals.

A MAJOR BENEFIT FOR THE ACCOUNTING PROFESSIONAL

One of the most meaningful rewards for professional accountants is the sheer enjoyment experienced when solving a client's complex and frustrating problem by applying solid business judgment and experience.

Most clients soon forget their accountant's help in arriving at the numbers on a financial statement or a tax return, but they remember and appreciate the accountant's contribution in resolving a critical management concern of the fragile, small enterprise.

Small and medium-sized business clients need an advocate who can offer objective counsel when making a major decision. The successful professional accountant and consultant of today and many tomorrows is striving to fill that need.

VISION

Your accounting firm is the lengthening shadow of you and the other people who share your vision. The vision starts with the founder's dream of what he or she is trying to build. People act on what they think, feel, and know. If associates and employees share the dream and the vision of the owners, they will make great efforts to accomplish that dream. Tom Watson, the founder of IBM, said, "We were not just doing business. We were building a company."

Is it all worth it? What is the reward for working so hard and taking risks? The answer: self-fulfillment—the joy of being your own master and calling your own shots. Do not find excuses when facing obstacles of running your own accounting business. Find innovative solutions. Remember that sooner or later, the one who wins is the one who thinks she can!

2

STRUCTURING YOUR ACCOUNTING BUSINESS

SOLE PROPRIETORSHIPS

To the free-thinking professional, an individual accounting business presents many possibilities. Easily formed and free from the obligations of partner association, single proprietorship can result in considerable personal gratification to the accountant entrepreneur who is sufficiently motivated to make it work.

However, the solo practice lacks the "review" emphasis that contributes to the quality of the work of a partnership. Moreover, a problem common to the individual practice is the limited ability to stay up to date with massive amounts of information—tax laws, procedural obligations, and theoretical professional data—all of which affect the profession directly. Because a successful small practice is usually a busy one, an independent's time for completing required continuing professional education (CPE) units and for acquiring new knowledge in other ways can be constrained.

Another factor to be considered is one's own need for affiliation. This personality characteristic has been found by researchers to be dominant in most entrepreneurs. The high need for affiliation is common for entrepreneurs regardless of the type of enterprise. It can be very lonely running one's own accounting business without some form of peer affiliation.

Although many solo practices employ staff, being the only owner presents logistical challenges as illustrated by this quote:

> "Now here, you see it takes all the running you can do to keep in the same place," said the Cheshire Cat to Alice in Lewis Carroll's *Through the Looking Glass.* "If you want to get somewhere else, you must run at least twice as fast as that."

OVERCOMING ISOLATION

The solo practice may be what you were seeking at the outset, with its promise of no interruptions, no small talk at the water cooler, no meetings, no pitching in to help cover the phones, and no one to psych you up for the big presentation—no one at all. We are told that we have to be careful what we ask for because we may get it. One may end up asking himself, "So how come I don't feel so good?"

Psychologists and anthropologists have always known that if you take the man or woman out of society, you risk taking society out of the man or woman—leaving them feeling empty, alienated, depressed, and ultimately ineffective. Even such a strong-willed character as polar explorer Robert Byrd found the burdens of isolation nearly fatal. Working alone in a meteorological observation post, he found himself prey to hallucinations and morbid fantasies and became heedless of his health and safety.

As a solo accountant, you are not likely to encounter the type of alienation that would make you succumb to hallucinations, but the perils of isolation can pose a serious threat to your personal health and your business success. (See Exhibit 2.1.)

EXHIBIT 2.1
What Solo Accountants Missed after Leaving a Group Practice

This is what accountants answered when queried about what they missed most after leaving a medium-sized to large firm:

- Office socializing—29 percent
- Access to assistants, secretaries, and other support—27 percent
- Being part of a team—15 percent

The first step in overcoming isolation is to understand what you have lost by leaving a larger firm: the daily social interaction, input from colleagues on problems, the affirmation of doing daily work that pays immediate dividends, and the enthusiasm sparked by a boss's praise. Starting on your own is such a radical change that you must think about what you formerly took for granted and what will be absent. A suggestion for a smoother transition is to build some sort of substitute for what you had at the firm you are about to leave.

Support Groups

Before your departure, set up a small informal support group that is made up of colleagues in your business community. The individuals in the support group should be fellow entrepreneurs, preferably not in the field of accounting. Academic participation from the local college or university school of business would be a positive contribution. They would be expected to provide advice on what to expect from the transition period through the start-up phase. It is also likely that you can provide insights to the others and may also get some new clients in the process.

Create Structure

One of the greatest perks of the single proprietorship is the freedom to work when, where, and how you like. This flexibility, however, can also lead to problems for people who work best in a structured environment. Without external stimulation or support, it is easy for someone to become listless and unmotivated. One must exert an unbelievable amount of self-discipline to avoid falling into bad habits. Schedules and routines make good bulwarks against sloth and lassitude. You do not have to lock yourself back into the 9-to-5 time period or slave away for 10 hours a day (except during tax season), but establishing regular business hours is a good idea.

Also try to set aside an hour each day to do something outside your office, do some errands, run some laps, or visit the library. Do something that will not only put you in contact with people in your community but will also help rejuvenate you for the rest of your workday.

Form Professional Support Groups

Feelings of loneliness may be compounded by a loss of confidence. When you do not have someone to bounce ideas off of or a person to challenge the soundness of a decision, it is harder to be certain that you are right. Office colleagues offer positive reinforcement by reacting to ideas and questioning judgments. Accountants who work alone may have difficulties finding solutions to business problems. Teams, however, come at problems from multiple perspectives. Solo accountants may not see all the parameters they face, and any solution based on limited information is not going to be the best solution.

You have to find a way to get input on complex problems. When you are working alone, the real loss comes when you make key decisions. Arguing ideas with others brings synergy into your decision-making process. Alone, the tendency for flawed decisions dramatically increases. One way to overcome this crippling lack of perspective is to forge professional connections.

Set up a networking group of various self-employed professionals by asking your stockbroker, attorney, and others from different fields (do not invite competitors) to dinner. You will find that many of the topics discussed, such as business management and financing, are specific to the self-employed and not just to their particular work. If you are thinking about establishing your own group instead of joining an existing group, it is important not to turn the meetings into cheap, one-sided consultations. Stay focused on larger strategic issues and decisions, and be willing to put in what you expect to get out. The goal should be to help each other and not just oneself.

Trade Associations

Your participation in trade associations, such as your state and local chapters of the American Institute of Certified Public Accountants (AICPA) or the Institute of Management Accountants (IMA) as well as the trade associations for your special market niches, will also help keep you informed of important developments in the field of accounting and the fields in which you specialize. For example, if you have targeted home or commercial builders as a market niche, you should attend the local home builder trade association meetings and events and consider joining as an associate member.

The Accounting Guild

This unique Internet-based membership organization helps computer knowledgeable accountants to acquire and advise clients in establishing and maintaining accounting, recordkeeping, and other business systems. The Guild networks the accountant in a strategic alliance of other professional accountants, computer distributors, integrators, computer hardware manufacturers, and accounting software publishers who serve as associate members. The virtual online organization gives the individual affiliated accountant the ability to provide small to medium-sized business consultation and implementation of automated business accounting systems through the wholesale purchasing of resale products and cooperative services, such as configuration, installation, and service with other guild members when expertise beyond their individual capabilities is required. A valuable dialogue service allows you to post questions on the Web site or by e-mail with other affiliated accountants in your area or around the nation. With this service, you get the benefit of sharing collective experience on any subject of interest while diminishing your sense of professional isolation.

Volunteer Work

Getting involved in volunteer work can also help to strengthen the bond between you and the members of your community. It gives you the opportunity to become active and well known outside your local business community. You will be surprised at how making someone else feel better can do wonders for your own spirits. Your social life can also reap unexpected business benefits because you never know when inspiration—or a good connection—will strike. The sole proprietorship accounting practice may be what you select for just a season. Keep in mind that Arthur Andersen began his practice as a sole proprietor.

SMALL PARTNERSHIPS*

Small partnerships frequently offer new accountants the opportunity for professional independence and affiliation with peers. Partnerships can give professionals the opportunity to broaden their expertise in accounting areas into which the sole proprietor may consider it a luxury to penetrate. For instance, two partners may favor different aspects of the profession: One may prefer to handle tax procedures, whereas the other may enjoy serving clients in a consulting capacity. Partnerships also provide the opportunity to expand. Unlike the sole proprietorship, which is restricted in size for obvious reasons, the ability of a partnership to enlarge is almost unlimited. Many of today's large accounting firms began as two- or three-member partnerships.

The establishment of a partnership, of course, can sometimes be difficult. Accountants who wish to enter into partnerships should know and understand their prospective colleagues well before

* The discussion of LLCs and corporations includes legal aspects, but the partnership discussion focuses exclusively on working relationship issues.

agreeing to "hoe the same row." After the business has been established is not the time to discover an inability to get along. Bear in mind also that professional rules bar partnerships between CPAs and non-CPAs. One of the best ways to ensure the success of a partnership is to get experience as a sole practitioner, build a practice, and then merge with another sole practitioner. Remember that sole practitioner status and partnerships are not mutually exclusive. (See Exhibit 2.2.)

EXHIBIT 2.2
Checklist: Partnership Considerations

Accountants experienced in partnerships recommend that prospective partners ask themselves the following questions before making a commitment:

- ❑ Do we share professional objectives?
- ❑ Are our skills complementary? Do the professional strengths of one fill the gaps in weak areas of the other?
- ❑ Do we relate well to others?
- ❑ Do we relate well to each other?
- ❑ Are our lifestyles too different for us to share common interests?
- ❑ Do we really like each other?
- ❑ Do our spouses get along well?
- ❑ How much work can each of us provide?
- ❑ What promises can we make concerning the probability of obtaining clients?
- ❑ Are we making equal financial investments?
- ❑ Do we share the same codes of ethics and morals?

Sometimes, professionals who are not ready to enter into partnership decide instead to form a trial partnership, often referred to as a loose association. Such an arrangement provides the professional atmosphere of the partnership without the legal obligations. In such instances, two or more accountants may rent office space together and share overhead expenses. Participants do not usually share clients or workloads but are available to one another to compare notes and exchange ideas on technical problems. If successful, a loose association can provide the basis for forming a permanent partnership.

LIMITED LIABILITY COMPANIES

Limited liability companies (LLCs) are hybrids that combine the best advantages of corporations and partnerships. The owners of an LLC have the corporate benefits that protect their personal assets from business debts as well as the tax advantages of partnerships. Unlike corporations, LLCs provide greater flexibility in management and organization of the accounting business and reduce paperwork and recordkeeping. One drawback is that in many states LLCs have a limited life of 30 years, so they may not be the choice for you if you have succession considerations and want your business to survive well into the future.

CORPORATIONS

A corporation is the most formal type of business structure. It is a separate legal entity owned by stockholders, and it offers many benefits. Anyone who operates a business may incorporate, whether you are a one-person practice or an accounting giant. The two most common forms for accountants are the general corporation (or C corporation), which is for profit-making ventures that can have an unlimited number of stockholders/owners. A stockholder's liability is usually limited to the amount of investment in the business and no more. Professional corporations are formed by a group of the same type of professionals who provide services for which a professional license is required. CPAs cannot share ownership in the practice with non-CPAs (the major reason for Arthur Andersen's divesting the consulting part of the practice into a separate entity, Andersen Consulting). You may decide to set up your own separate entities to perform certain non-CPA functions and share ownership with non-CPAs.

No easy formula is available to help you decide what type of structure you should choose for your accounting business. Once armed with reliable information from your attorney and the risks involved in each choice, you can make an informed decision about how to structure your accounting business.

3

CHOOSING A LOCATION

Site-seeking accountants are naturally drawn to locations with unique business potential or access to the kind of lifestyle and cultural setting in which they feel most at home. Ideally, the best place to locate an accounting business is one that serves professional and personal needs equally well.

Achieving the ideal becomes a formidable task for many accountants who quickly find that every location option carries its share of compromise and occasional sacrifice. Veteran accountants stress that newcomers who wish to avoid big city trappings by setting up shop near suburban communities or small towns may forgo the income potential and professional stimulation usually available to practitioners situated in thriving urban centers.

Location often plays a critical role in determining the kind of work the accountant will perform. A matter of miles can mean the difference between a practice geared toward compilations and tax work and one that is involved in budget preparation, business valuation, forensic accounting, and auditing. In one area, a practice may get most of its clients from small businesses—retailers, service vendors, doctors, and dentists. In another area, customers may be large firms, government contractors, and others requiring specialized professional assistance.

HOME OFFICE

The accountant who is looking for an office location that feels like home should consider an office at home. Estimates put the number of people maintaining a home office (SOHO—small office–home office) at over 39 million, and their ranks are growing every day. More people are making a living by working out of a home office than ever before.

Those 39 million represent 39 percent of total U.S. households and contain at least one person doing income-generating work at home. SOHO workers typically fall into one of two camps: corporate employees and telecommuters for whom the SOHO is an extension of their "real" workplace or small-business owners whose only office is in their home. Many home-office workers share the same setup and maintenance problems. Primary among them is the need to maximize productivity while minimizing the space required to get the job done. Exhibit 3.1 provides a checklist to determine your suitability for a home office.

EXHIBIT 3.1
Checklist: Are You Suited for a Home Office?

You may be well suited to locate your accounting business in a home-based office if you meet seven of these 10 characteristics:

- ❑ 1. **You are self-disciplined**—able to set goals on a week-to-week basis and push yourself to meet them.
- ❑ 2. **You can resist distractions**—the family, the dog, the untended garden.
- ❑ 3. **You can set limits on others.** When your neighbor stops by for coffee or your mother calls to chat, you tell both that you are at work.
- ❑ 4. **You find work pleasant rather than onerous.** You do not need others to prod you to complete tasks.
- ❑ 5. **You have a logical mind.**
- ❑ 6. **You enjoy details.** You feel an almost compulsive need to do work in small, correct steps.
- ❑ 7. **You prefer autonomy to subordination.**
- ❑ 8. **You can tolerate solitude.** Better yet, you actually thrive on it in daily doses.
- ❑ 9. **You are not afraid to take the risk of generating your own work.** You can tolerate the insecurity of not having a conventional paycheck.
- ❑ 10. **You have a sense of adventure.** You think it is exciting to enter an area of accounting in which the potential has barely been explored.

Physical Infrastructure

Before building your SOHO, take stock of your physical surroundings. It may seem insignificant, but even something like a poorly insulated window can cause enormous problems later on. Plan your space carefully; once you get your office furniture and equipment in place, it will be difficult to shift it around. The best thing to do is to set aside an entire room for your office. That way, you will have a space in which you will be interrupted less, and you can close the door on your work at the end of the day.

Check the windows. Leaky windows bring drafts and, in the worst case, allow rain to trickle in—certain disaster for your personal computer (PC). Check the baseboards and ceiling for leaks and gaps too. Check for insects and rodents, both of which have annoying habits of crawling into PCs and gnawing on cords. Ideally, you should place your PC in front of a wall, away from any glare. If you must work near a window, consider a glare filter for your monitor.

Your home office should be a well-lit room with comfortable, ergonomic furniture. Whenever possible, it should be situated in a garage, attic, or isolated part of the house. Those who work from home need greater self-discipline than their conventional office counterparts. The 9-to-5 routine no longer means as much, but it helps to focus on the tasks at hand and a time to call it quits for the day. With PCs, access to computer networks, and the Internet with e-mail, you can pretty much work around the clock. The most difficult thing is having a sense of boundary and cutting it off.

Do not forget physical security issues! Is the proposed location vulnerable to theft? Virtually no location is immune to this problem, which makes it all the more important that the equipment be insured. Equally if not more important, your data must be secured through frequent backups, which you should then store in a separate safe location, such as a bank safe deposit box. It is easy to get lazy about backups, but remember that your computer is worth only a fraction of the value of your data.

Electricity

Another important issue is electricity. Make absolutely certain that the outlets in your office space are grounded and deliver a smooth, steady current. To find out how good your electrical supply is, have a qualified technician check the wiring, current flow, breaker boxes (to ensure that the outlets in your office can handle the current flow you will need), and grounding of your outlets. Although surge protectors, line conditioners, and an uninterruptible power supply (UPS) are standard for safe computing, they only treat the symptoms. Only an electrician can cure the disease by fixing your existing wiring. Do not let a power interruption turn into a business interruption.

All equipment will fail eventually, so it makes sense to take precautions up front to limit the damage when something does go wrong. Here are five simple steps to prevent equipment failure from short-circuiting your accounting business at a home or commercially located office:

1. You have heard it before and you will hear it here: Back up your computer work—twice for critical files. What you use to back up depends on the volume of your work, but always make copies of your work.

2. Before your equipment warranties expire, find a reliable service organization. Referrals are usually the most credible source.

3. Only you know how badly your business will suffer from the loss of a computer, fax machine, printer, or other piece of equipment, but consider an on-site service contract. Prices vary, but a few hundred dollars a year can save you the aggravation of unhooking and hauling a misbehaving component into a service center.

4. Particularly if you live in an area prone to thunderstorms and other phenomena that can cause power surges and outages, invest in a UPS and a surge protector. A UPS will keep your system powered long enough to save your work and shut the system down in the event of a power outage. Surge protectors will prevent spikes in the electric current from damaging your equipment.

5. Participate in a computer users' group. Most cities have local branches of computer users' groups that meet either online or in person to share tips on everything from getting the most out of different software programs to configuring hardware and coping with equipment problems. Chances are, the problem that will confound you at the most inopportune moment has plagued someone else in the past. So, why not benefit from their experience?

Telephone Service

Next to clean, well-grounded power, telephone service is the second most important service you will need in your office. Most of us take telephone lines for granted. After all, you plug your phone in and it works, doesn't it? Well, not always—especially when you are dealing with modem or fax transmissions. Although a standard telephone is remarkably immune to static and interference, it can still slow down, choke, and die if there is too much noise, even with all the error correction in the world. Unlike wiring, however, it is not absolutely necessary to check your lines for noise at the outset, but if you have problems with Internet, fax, or data communication, you will want to call in the phone company. It is important to have enough lines to do business. While those who only occasionally use their home office will do fine with just one line, most others will probably need two or more. Get at least one line for data, Internet, and fax, and another for voice. You should separate your home and work phone numbers, bringing your requirements to a minimum of three lines.

Exhibit 3.2 provides a convenient checklist for determining when it is most beneficial to work somewhere other than home.

EXHIBIT 3.2
Checklist: When Not to Work Out of the Home

- ☐ 1. *The need to "team."* If you have any associates, partners, or staff, you will need to work together on many projects. Your success will be based on a combination of your ideas and collaboration. Separate home offices will not provide easy access to one another, and having the office in one home could lead to undue hardship and sacrifice on the part of the person providing the home.
- ☐ 2. *An ambitious business plan.* Capturing market share that is there for the taking—but only for a short time—means pursuing new business at top speed. You have to hit your early sales targets to move forward. Working apart from your associates or isolating yourself from support staff will slow you down.
- ☐ 3. *Client expectations.* Clients get frustrated when they cannot get quick answers. Working from home and not having access to a partner when needed makes for longer response time. There is also a tendency on the part of

clients to deprecate a business that is located in the practitioner's home and to feel that the home office accountant is inferior to one working in a "real" office.

❑ 4. *Focus.* It is easy to get distracted at home. As a start-up or expanding accounting business, you cannot afford to take your eyes off the ball, even for a few minutes.

❑ 5. *Personal issues.* Home has been a haven for most of us. Working long, intense days tends to make home an escape where you can pull back and approach work the next day with a fresh attitude. It is tough to get away when you know the business is down the hall. That can lead to burnout. In addition, you will have to alter your home to meet work requirements, which could be as expensive as renting an office and lead to work dominating your home life even more.

SMALL TOWN IN A RURAL AREA

Small-town locations can provide independent or partner accountants excellent opportunities to establish useful and highly personal accounting businesses. Seasoned practitioners, however, caution that unless a town or the area around it shows an obvious trend toward economic development, the choice is often impractical.

An examination of current data on the area can be helpful. Positive speculation on the use of an area's natural resources, energy development, farming, and real estate activity by authoritative sources may provide a sound reason to establish your office in an economically placid area. (See Exhibit 3.3.)

EXHIBIT 3.3
Checklist: Yellow Pages Listings Related to an Accounting Business

A basic method of market/location research is to take a look in the Yellow Pages. Check the listings that relate to your accounting business: your competition and the support systems, equipment supplies, and services you require:

❑ Accountants
❑ Accountants—Certified Public

- ❑ Accounting and Bookkeeping Systems
- ❑ Advertising—Direct Mail
- ❑ Attorneys
- ❑ Audio-Visual Equipment—Dealers
- ❑ Banks
- ❑ Bookkeeping Services
- ❑ Business and Trade Organizations
- ❑ Business Consultants
- ❑ Business Forms and Systems
- ❑ Computers—Dealers
- ❑ Computers—Networking
- ❑ Computers—On-Site Service and Repair
- ❑ Computers—Software
- ❑ Computers—Supplies and Peripherals
- ❑ Computers—Training
- ❑ Conference Centers
- ❑ Copying Services
- ❑ Data Systems—Consultants and Designers
- ❑ Desktop Publishing
- ❑ Electrician Services
- ❑ Financial Planning Consultants
- ❑ Graphic Designers
- ❑ Incorporating Services
- ❑ Insurance Brokers and Consultants
- ❑ Inventory Services
- ❑ Letter Shop Services (also see Advertising—Direct Mail)
- ❑ Library Research Services
- ❑ Mailing Lists
- ❑ Management Consultants
- ❑ Marketing Consultants
- ❑ Market Research and Analysis
- ❑ Messenger Services
- ❑ Office Furniture and Equipment
- ❑ Payroll Preparation Services
- ❑ Pension and Profit-Sharing Specialists
- ❑ Printing Services

- ❑ Professional Organizations
- ❑ Publicity Service
- ❑ Public Relations Counselors
- ❑ Real Estate Brokers and Consultants
- ❑ Secretarial Services
- ❑ Security Consultants
- ❑ Stock and Bond Brokers
- ❑ Taxes—Consultants and Representatives
- ❑ Tax Return Preparation and Filing
- ❑ Telemarketing Services
- ❑ Telephone Answering Services
- ❑ Training Programs
- ❑ Travel Agencies

If you find more Yellow Pages listings for farm equipment than for computer sales or service, it may be an indication of the business environment. In large markets, the competition may be fierce, and a good way to succeed is to specialize. However, if you enter a smaller market, be prepared to generalize. Do not be fooled by an area's basic demographics. Small, rural farming communities have a need for sophisticated computer services and many accounting specializations. Some farming operations are comparable to medium-sized to large business enterprises in terms of revenues, tax assistance, and financing. Small towns offer something big cities often lack—client loyalty. In the smaller market, you have to be expert enough to serve both the home-office client and the larger enterprise. You will not have the luxury of needing just one or two areas of expertise.

Accountants who have started businesses in small towns report on the pros and cons. Some say they have found local residents skeptical of newcomer accountants; others report appreciative acceptance. An advantage of the small-town practice is that it permits personal involvement with the community and its members.

Others report that building a client base is extremely difficult in small-town locations. Many prospective clients avoid local practitioners because they believe that a higher degree of expertise can be obtained by traveling the extra distance to a nearby larger city. It is also important for accountants who are considering a semirural area to determine what kind of support is available. Is access to computer repair available? Is staff support readily available for client work? After establishing their practices, some accountants have found themselves swamped with nontechnical paperwork that leaves little time for professional development.

INDUSTRIAL AND URBAN-SPILLOVER AREAS

Midway between bustling city centers and small towns are heavily populated spillover areas in which many small businesses thrive, manufacturers churn out goods, and distributors distribute. Some accountants believe these outlying areas have the best potential for a new accounting business. They cite as advantages the variety of prospective clients, proximity to other professionals and support services, and probability of available and affordable housing.

Some accountants who have established businesses in urban outlying areas report initial difficulties in attracting clients. They warn newcomers to prepare for long waits before an adequate amount of work is forthcoming. Unlike the small town, in which the new accounting business is usually visible to community inhabitants, in the spillover location the new practitioner frequently seems almost anonymous and invisible. However, an accounting business is not nearly as dependent on exact location as a retail establishment or restaurant and, with effective, proactive marketing, the accountant will get the business he or she wants.

Although at first the going is often rough, accountants who are willing to persevere can usually build a healthy business within one to two years. Normally, accountants find their initial clients during tax season and through applied marketing to target market niches. After that, it is a matter of marketing, marketing, marketing.

Another phenomenon of a spillover area is that within a few years of growth the area becomes part of the nearby urban area. There is a good probability that the accountant might have made a wise choice by buying an office at what may turn out to have been a very attractive price.

DOWNTOWN AND FINANCIAL DISTRICT LOCATIONS

Accountants who choose to locate their businesses in downtown areas, specifically those sites close to or in financial districts, face a particularly demanding challenge. These urban centers—in which banks, insurance and stock brokerages, large corporations, and professional firms thrive—produce an atmosphere of quick-paced competitive pressure.

Although every practitioner must develop specific market niches regardless of location, the downtown accountant is more likely to specialize. Because so many accountants operate in the city, small practitioners often try to develop a particular expertise and establish a good reputation in regard to that specialty. When an accountant is successful at a specialty, referrals from attorneys, present and former clients, other accountants, and financial advisors will follow.

SOURCES OF LOCATION RESEARCH

Whatever the accountant's preference, the decision to locate should be backed by sound market research. A number of tools are available for this purpose.

Real Estate Reports

Real estate reports that deal with regional commercial and residential construction activity—building costs, wage rates for construction tradespeople, market activity based on deed recordings, and trends in housing and office-space costs—are published in locations throughout the United States. Frequently, these reports are sponsored by interested members of the business community, such as banks, investment corporations, builders, and commercial real estate firms, with a direct stake in the future of the area.

For the site-seeking accountant, these kinds of reports can be useful in projecting costs of office space and the emergence of new businesses while providing a fair idea of residential and commercial prices. These publications may be found in local public libraries and, in many instances, commercial real estate offices. Many metropolitan areas have a weekly business journal containing extensive commercial real estate sections and special reports.

Chambers of Commerce Reports

The accountant may also wish to consider the reports published by city, county, and state chambers of commerce. These often have valuable, detailed information on population growth, types of local businesses (including accounting businesses), average income data for residents, and sales revenue by various business categories abstracted from tax reports.

Important Contacts

An accountant with a potential location in mind should not depend entirely on published data. Statistics and census tracts, although helpful, may also be misleading. Knowledgeable individual sources often provide a key to the flexibility of an area—or lack of it.

CPA, Public Accounting, and Related Societies

State societies and their local chapters can be helpful to accountants who are uncertain about a particular location. By speaking with members, new practitioners can learn a great deal about an area's professional atmosphere and its need for new accountants.

Educational Institutions

Local colleges and universities are excellent sources of information about their region as well as information on continuing education programs, seminars, and teaching opportunities. Teaching accounting-related courses on a part-time basis is an excellent way to acquire new clients and earn extra income during your start-up transition period.

Bankers

During informal interviews, local bankers may offer valuable insight into your location plans and give you a good indication of the availability of Small Business Administration (SBA) loans for purchasing or constructing your own office facility. Interviewing local bankers is a way to market your new business, while you are seeking location and financing information.

Commercial Real Estate Brokers

Representatives of local commercial real estate firms can give advice on office-space availability, suitable commercial buildings for sale or lease-purchase, and local housing costs. The brokers/agents are excellent referral sources, so again you are getting added value from your location research.

MOVING OUT OF A HOME OFFICE

Despite some undeniable appeals of working from one's house, some home-based accountants inevitably find that there comes a time in the business's life when they need to move out. In some cases, the continued success of the business or the sanity of the accountant may depend on such a move. Although the decision to move might make sense, implementing it can be a time-consuming and costly endeavor.

There can be compelling personal and business reasons to move out of the house. Personal reasons include concerns about the intrusion of family on business and the intrusion of business on family. The need to put more space between your personal and professional lives may also be involved. This separation can be important for many accountants who are borderline workaholics. When they are very busy or cash flow is tight, it is hard not to work all the time. You walk by your home office and your work calls out, "Get in here." And even though is 11 o'clock at night, you go in and work. Such long days and nights will ultimately be counterproductive to the success of your business and your life.

Moving out of the house for business reasons is a different matter. Usually, your accounting business is growing and clearly in need of more space for equipment and employees. It is very difficult to get people to work in your basement. If you feel you have outgrown your home office, then you probably have.

Once you have made the decision to move out of the home office or into a new commercial office, your first step is to decide what is required of a new space. You must look at the exact needs of your business. Ask yourself what makes sense now and in the not-too-distant future. If you are currently in a 500-square-foot space at home and your business is consistently growing, you may want to find a space two or three times larger so there is room to grow even more. Make sure that you are getting a great deal, however, before committing to much more space than you need immediately.

Consider your timetable for hiring additional staff. If you are looking just for an office for you and space for a part-time secretary, consider space for a conference area and a training area with computers for teaching accounting and related software to clients. Always give yourself some extra breathing room. Files invariably grow, and you will probably end up adding some furniture (e.g., a comfortable reading chair to replace the one in the living room that you use now).

Economic Factors

After determining your space needs, figure out how much you want to spend. Estimate an ideal monthly payment and then a maximum cost your business can afford. This will help focus the search and give you a place to start when you take the next step into the sometimes confusing world of commercial real estate.

Call two or three commercial real estate firms in the area. Tell them how much space you need, and ask for an estimate of what it will cost. (Do not tip your hand by telling them how much you can afford, since they may surprise you by explaining that you can get what you want for less). They will likely answer you with a question about what class of space you want. Ask for estimates on all three major categories—classes A, B, and C.

If you expect to be seeing clients in your new office, there is good reason to consider class A space. This type of space will be clean, modern, well maintained, and prominently located. This space projects a professional image to your clients and becomes part of the way they define your firm—but it will cost you. Class A space runs around $15 to $20 per square foot in a midsize city, $25 in a larger city, and over $40 in a major metropolitan area.

One accountant related that when he was working at home, he always worried that it would be awkward if a client visited. As a result, he spent his first year in business meeting all his clients at their offices or in hotels over breakfast or lunch. When he moved into his new office in an attractive, suburban complex of two-story buildings, he felt it made a difference in the success of his business. "I believe I won engagements I wouldn't have gotten because I was in that office," he said.

Other accountants have a different type of practice and do not need to project such an upscale image. "I don't have clients coming to me very often. So I don't need a class A look," said another accountant. He was happy with class B space, which typically is a bit older and worn around the edges but is perfectly serviceable, often possessing a touch of character lacking in modern buildings. These spaces can save you money as well. Class B space is usually $4 to $5 less expensive per square foot than class A space. Depending on the size of your space, you may save more than $200 a month with class B.

Class C is the least expensive major category, running under $6 per square foot in a midsize city. Often, however, it is typically in older industrial or mill space or above retail shops in less desirable parts of town. Class C space can offer the attraction of high ceilings and large windows, along with the annoyance of poor acoustics and inadequate electrical wiring.

After determining your specifications, look at the numbers the commercial real estate agents gave you and compare them with your estimates. If you are in the ballpark, great. Even if you are not, do not despair. There may be ways to get the space you need for less.

Consider Office Options

Even small spaces can be prohibitively expensive in major cities. One effective way to keep your monthly costs down is to share an area with another person. Another option may be moving into an executive suite, which is a building that rents small individual spaces with a number of shared amenities, such as a receptionist or secretary, waiting area, conference room, kitchen, and office equipment. Space in these buildings costs more, but if you need some of the amenities on a regular basis, it can be a lot cheaper than paying for them yourself. Executive suites also offer a range of square footage, which is good for a growing accounting firm.

Whatever you end up with, remember that many cities across the country are suffering from a glut in the commercial real estate market. Let this soft market work for you.

Small-Business Incubators

Small-business incubators, where available, offer flexible space and leasing options, often at below-market rates. They can serve as stepping stones for accountants eager to fly the coop but unable to raise the capital needed to fund their location while maintaining monthly overhead costs. These "mother hen" facilities help fledgling businesses reduce the risk of business failure by providing access to equipment, advice, and services that tenants might otherwise be unable to afford during their early (and most vulnerable) years.

More than 80 percent of businesses that have been incubated are still in operation, and the majority continue to increase revenues and create jobs, according to a study conducted by PricewaterhouseCoopers. Incubation programs are usually sponsored by local governments, economic development agencies, and universities.

One of the major benefits to an accountant fortunate enough to become a part of an incubator is the ready number of prospective clients who are co-tenants and would be most receptive to engaging a neighbor for accounting services.

There are more than 600 incubators located throughout the United States and Canada with more than 10,000 tenants. Similar to venture capitalists, many incubators have selection criteria. Some accept a variety of professions; others concentrate on industry niches.

Consider the Costs

It is easy to determine your monthly costs for new space. Take one-twelfth of the annual lease rate for the space and add any expenses for telephone and utilities that you estimate you will incur. Add to this the costs of any additional services or equipment you need in the new office (such as a dedicated data line or fax line or payments on new computer equipment). It is then up to you to decide whether your accounting business can afford the new space.

Somewhat harder to pin down, however, are the one-time fees associated with moving. The first of these is the actual cost of the move. Even doing the move by yourself with some willing friends, you have the cost of the truck rental. Add in a security deposit and possibly the last month's rent to your new landlord. Tack on the cost of hooking up phone lines or starting other utilities and any expenses to renovate, paint, or otherwise prepare the office for your arrival.

Incidental Considerations

Some new furniture may be in order. When you move in, you will probably buy a new desk, a good chair, and filing cabinets—all the things you did not have at home. You might have the cost of printing new letterhead and business cards, as well as writing to your clients and prospective clients telling them about your move. It is highly recommended that you put a minimum of two or three months' worth of overhead aside when you move in, just to give yourself some comfort level in your new location. If establishing such a safety net presents a problem, it may be an indication that you do not have the necessary resources to move.

All of these expenses can quickly add up to a considerable sum of money if your practice is operating on a tight cash flow. One way to conserve cash is to lease equipment rather than buy it. You may pay 20 percent or more for the equipment by leasing it than if you bought it outright, but you have immediate cash to meet other obligations.

When considering what to spend money on in a new office, don't overdo it. The tendency is to go too far and buy things that are going to increase your break-even point and weigh you down. You must ask yourself what you *have* to have, not what you want to have. Take a slow and steady approach. If you feel strongly that you are going to need a particular item, get it and see how it works out, rather than getting all the things you think you might need. One possible exception is your computer system. It is best to get the most powerful solution available for your needs. This will extend the time you have to replace it.

One big intangible concerning the location of your office involves the fear that it somehow will not work out. Many accountants, instead of facing that fear, close their eyes and try to rush through it. But you need to acknowledge that the fear is there and do things to minimize it, such as planning well to avoid putting impossible burdens on your business and yourself. As with all business decisions, it is important to focus on what your accounting business needs, not just what you want.

After deciding on the geographic location of the new business, the accountant faces the question of the appearance of the building and the office space. Accountants should be careful to select quarters that reflect the position of public trust they represent. Exterior as well as interior design should be used to project an image of professionalism, good taste, and respectability. Experienced accountants often advise fledglings to lease space in well-known professional buildings in which the prospective client is likely to seek specialized services.

Small-town or suburban offices should be as visible as possible—on a main street, in a shopping center, or near municipal buildings. Any site in which there is heavy pedestrian traffic is likely to be a sound choice.

CAVEAT

All of your talents must come into play in the decision to locate your accounting business: your individual good judgment, intelligent buying, skillful negotiation, and wise application of funds. Well used, these attributes will ensure the quality and success of your new accounting business.

4

ACCOUNTING OFFICE LOGISTICS

ESTABLISHING YOUR OFFICE

Finding the location and office site is just one of the first steps in establishing your office. Once that is accomplished, it will still take another two to three months before you can open your door.

The numerous details of building a new business—legalizing the lease, purchasing computer equipment and software as well as furniture and office supplies, creating attractive decor, hiring an assistant, and sending out announcements—can overwhelm almost anyone. Attention to details at the outset can save time later when your primary concern should be professional client service. The time spent setting up the business gives you an excellent opportunity to flex managerial muscles.

Landlords and Leases

Negotiation of a lease for office space is usually the accountant's first order of business after finally deciding on the office location. Striking an equitable agreement on lease terms, costs, and optional provisions takes a bit of bargaining. Those unfamiliar with leases should keep in close touch with their attorneys. The basic "bone of contention" is the rent. Is it consistent with the area and/or building norms? Will the landlord allow a discount for leasehold improvements? What extra services are covered by rent? Who handles office maintenance, painting, and refuse collection?

Those experienced in negotiating leases often recommend that prospective lessees press landlords for the right to sublet and an option on the use of adjacent space for expansion. Lessees should also be aware of lease renewal terms, penalties for early termination, required deposits, total floor space dimensions, and exact areas of the building covered. All amenities should be fully listed, and any common-area charges included in the lease. Some accountants have been surprised to find that they are paying rent for hallways between offices and elevators.

Space Requirements

The space required can be estimated in relation to the number of persons who will be working there. A small accounting business with two partners, a receptionist/assistant, and a staff assistant will generally take 1,000 to 1,500 square feet. This allows each partner a roomy office of 250 square feet and leaves 350 square feet for the staff and reception area plus additional space for a library, files, duplicating and other office equipment, and sufficient work surface for assembling reports and returns. If the accountants plan to specialize in consulting and/or training, ample space should be allocated for a conference room and/or training room.

Layout and Design

The professional office should be attractive, yet as functional as possible. The reception area, which generally measures approximately 100 to 150 square feet, must provide visitors with comfortable seating, either cushioned chairs or a sofa. Because it most likely forms the prospective client's first impression, the reception area should reflect the accountant's taste and personality. Suitable art, live plants, a table for professional publications, and a handsomely framed CPA certificate or diploma will give the waiting client a picture of a professional even before introductions are made. Some accountants have found that an automatic coffee maker or a cooler with cold drinks are a welcome addition.

Plan Ahead

Adjacent to the reception room, but preferably out of sight, is the work area. This space, 150 to 250 square feet, contains files of client records, the assistant's desk, copier, printer, client–server computing equipment, and shelves for reference books and other materials and supplies. Follow the cardinal rules of efficient space design: minimize, consolidate, and store. Create a floor plan of your space, and make a detailed list of everything you will need (computer equipment, furniture, books, plants, etc.). Then, map out how it will all fit together. Take accurate measurements of the area and the furnishings. Your goal is to obtain a snug but comfortable fit without wasting precious inches.

Streamlined, ergonomic chairs are not only better for your health, but they take up less room than traditional office seating. Tiered equipment stands and modular desks are more space efficient than old-fashioned, bulky office desks. Desks equipped with file cabinets, drawers, keyboard and mouse trays, and other compartments also prevent clutter.

Make use of valuable wall space by installing sturdy shelves over your desk area. Wall-mounted articulating lamps and tiered peripheral and accessory storage pieces are also useful.

Store Items Efficiently

Categorize the things you need by how often you will use them: daily, occasionally, or rarely. Then, store those items in relation to their use. Remember, your computer can also serve as your fax machine, universal address card file, personal organizer, calculator, and CD player.

The professional's office is itself a matter of personal taste. Generally speaking, large desks of fine wood, carpeted floors, paneled walls, comfortable seating, and tastefully arranged personal objects are favored.

Consider Color and Lighting

Avoid jarring and dark colors that can overwhelm a smaller space. Hospital white, however, produces glare. Choosing one color and installing furniture that complements the shade creates a continuous flow rather than an abrupt end. Windows always make a room seem larger by bringing the outside in. If you have installed blinds or curtains, keep them open during working hours.

Adequate lighting in all office areas is highly conducive to good working conditions. How well you see is also an important part of the ergonomic picture. Experts say the ideal lighting arrangement is a combination of indirect overhead and tabletop task lighting. Indirect overhead lighting is soft and does not cause glare. Task lights are designed to illuminate your immediate work area.

The most common problem is that typical office lighting is much too bright. The easiest remedy is to remove a bulb or two from your overhead fixture and position your computers so no light falls directly onto the screen.

Training Room Space

To capitalize on the growth in the service and training market niches, the accountant would be wise to plan to include space to accommodate training classes. Most clients do not want to enroll their accounting department staff or bookkeeper in a semester of computer and accounting software classes at the local college. They just want one day of courses focused on their specific needs. Offering training can be a very profitable niche and is examined in detail in Chapter Six dealing with market niches. The training room can also be used for staff training and meetings and offered to local accounting society chapters as a meeting place. Software publishers may also be potential renters for space on an ad hoc daily basis for training, and this facility rental income can significantly offset occupancy expense.

Data Superhighway

Ensure your connection to the data superhighway by evaluating all the advantages of wireless and digital cellular communications. The factor that will have the most profound effect on your new office is the quality of phone lines. As long as most older offices are serviced by old-fashioned copper telephone wires, you will not be able to send huge data files back and forth, let alone multimedia files that combine video and sound, nor will you be able to carry out multiple tasks on one line.

At this time, most long distance phone lines are high-speed fiber-optic lines that carry voice, data, and video signals simultaneously. However, most lines from local switching stations into the office are the old-fashioned copper kind. While many large companies have built private fiber-optic superhighways by buying access to phone lines from the gatekeepers, universal access is years away. Locating to a new building is no guarantee of fiber-optic access because of the dependency on the system that provides service to the building.

The existing copper lines can carry more data if outfitted with Integrated Services Digital Network (ISDN) capability, which many local phone companies now offer at extra charge. For accountants and the staff who talk on the phone while using the computer, telephone headsets are critical. They prevent you from injuring your neck. Because they leave your hands free, headsets allow you to move, which is a primary principle of ergonomics.

FURNITURE POSITIONED FOR SUCCESS

Ergonomics—the science of how people interact with their work environment—has become more than a buzzword as evidence mounts that desk jobs are not as benign as they once seemed. Many ergonomists believe tailoring the office to human physiology can improve productivity and the prospects of continued good health. The ergonomists say that the most important item in your office, and one not to skimp on, is the chair.

A good ergonomic chair lets you sit with your thighs parallel to the floor and your feet flat on it. The seat should be horizontal but slope away at the forward end so there are no sharp edges cutting into the backs of your knees. The seat and back should adjust to your height, and the latter should support your lower back where your spine curves in. Although the best chairs are expensive, the benefits make the investment worthwhile.

Buy good-quality chairs. Cheap ones do not work. The top office furniture makers all build their own versions of ergonomic chairs. If you love the chair you already have and it does not violate any basic ergonomic principles, you might consider modifying it with inexpensive accessories. You can purchase foam or inflatable pillows to fill the lumbar curve in your lower back and footrests to anchor your feet.

Computing in Comfort

Because the computer has become the brain of most accountants' offices and the alleged cause of numerous cases of repetitive stress injuries, its position and accessibility have become crucial.

Ergonomists have determined that the top of the monitor should be at eye level or slightly below. Ideally, the keyboard should be used at elbow level. Your wrists are reasonably stress-free when extended in a straight line from your forearms. Some innovators think typing would be even more natural with your palms at angles to each other and some keyboards are designed to allow that.

Document holders placed next to or below your screen will spare your neck and head a lot of twisting and turning. Keeping the document holder in the same plane as the screen will cut down on eyestrain because you will not be continually refocusing as you look back and forth between the two.

Regardless of how your office is outfitted, if you do not take frequent breaks, it may not matter how good your furniture is. The most important part of ergonomics may require only a change in habits. A series of questions is contained in Exhibit 4.1 which facilitates the evaluation of the risk and degree of potential problems regarding your risk of repetitive strain injuries.

EXHIBIT 4.1
Checklist: Ergonomic Office

If you answer "No" to any question, you should rethink your office setup and correct situations that may increase your risk of developing repetitive strain injuries.

Posture

- ❑ Are your feet resting fully and firmly on the floor or footrest?
- ❑ Are your knees bent at approximately right angles and your thighs parallel to the floor, so the chair does not put pressure on the back of your thighs?
- ❑ Is your upper body straight, with your lower back firmly supported by the chair backrest?
- ❑ When you use the keyboard, are your upper arms hanging straight down at your sides, your elbows against your sides and bent at approximately right angles, and your forearms parallel to the floor?
- ❑ Are your wrists straight, neither bent up or down nor to the left or right?
- ❑ Is your head looking forward with only a slight downward tilt?

Chair

- ❑ Can you easily adjust the seat height?
- ❑ Does the backrest give firm support to your lower back? Can you adjust it?
- ❑ Is the front edge of the seat rounded to avoid putting pressure on the backs of your thighs?
- ❑ Does the chair swivel and have casters and a steady five-prong base?
- ❑ Do you have a footrest if you need one to rest your feet firmly on the floor?
- ❑ If you have arm rests, are they padded rather than hard?

Keyboard

- ❑ Is the keyboard on a surface that is adjustable for height?
- ❑ Is the keyboard thin and only slightly angled up?
- ❑ Is the keyboard placed on a foam pad to soften the impact of your fingers on the keys?
- ❑ Are the springs in the keyboard stiff enough to resist the weight of your fingers when relaxed?
- ❑ Do the keys give you tactile or audible feedback to prevent you from pressing them too hard?
- ❑ Are your fingers able to reach the Shift, Ctrl, Alt, and function keys without awkward straining?

Monitor

- ❑ Is the monitor on a surface that is adjustable for height?
- ❑ Is the center of the screen slightly below eye level?
- ❑ Is the monitor placed 1.5 to 2 feet from your eyes?
- ❑ Is the monitor directly in front of you, rather than off to one side?
- ❑ Is the monitor screen free of dust, grime, and glare?
- ❑ Do you use a copy stand, positioned about the same distance from your eyes and at the same height as the monitor, with equal lighting?

Work Habits

- ❑ Do you perform a variety of duties on and off the computer?
- ❑ Do you take adequate breaks from computer work? (At least 15 minutes after two hours or 10 minutes after every hour of intensive computer work.)
- ❑ Do you get up and move around whenever, or preferably before, you feel any symptoms?
- ❑ Are you allowing sufficient time during the workday to do relaxation exercises?

Exhibit 4.2 describes physical exercises that will assist you to reduce stress and feel better.

EXHIBIT 4.2
Checklist: Exercises for Computer Users

The following exercises are good for anyone, especially those engaged in sedentary types of work. While there is no prescribed number of repetitions, a good rule of thumb would be to do an exercise every time a break is needed. Especially do the exercises instead of reaching for a snack or a stimulant. Increase the number of exercises during tax season.

Eye Exercises

Visualization

1. Take off your glasses, if you wear them.
2. Lean your elbows on your desk and gently cover your eyes with your hands. Visualize a soothing, pleasant outdoor scene.
3. Look at different parts of the scene that you have visualized. Scan it slowly and peacefully.
4. Continue visualization for about 30 seconds longer.

Focus

1. Sit at your computer with a book in your lap.
2. Read a line of the book.
3. Read a line of your screen.
4. Look out a window or at a poster across the room. Blink, if necessary, to bring the distant object into focus.
5. Repeat steps 2 through 4 for approximately 30 seconds.

Stretching Exercises

This is one of many Chinese exercise sets known collectively as Qi Gong (Chee Kung):

1. Stand with your feet roughly shoulder-width apart, your knees slightly bent, and your stomach tucked in slightly. Relax. Touch your tongue to the roof of your mouth. Breathe deeply and slowly several times from your abdomen. Partially close your eyes.

2. Interlock your fingers and raise them straight over your head, palms toward the ceiling. Stretch. Feel your biceps close to your ears. Hold for about a minute, continuing to breathe deeply and slowly.
3. Inhale. Holding your stretch position from step 2, rotate your body slowly to the right, exhaling as you do so.
4. Inhale as you slowly return your body to a neutral position, then rotate your body to the left and exhale.
5. Rotate slowly to the right and left two more times.
6. Keeping your extension, bend and stretch slowly to the right and left. You should feel this under your arms and in your ribs and perhaps up to your fingers and down to your feet. Repeat two more times. Exhale as you bend, inhale as you straighten.
7. Bend forward very slowly from your hips, exhaling. Allow your head and hands to hang freely. Breathe as needed, but allow yourself to relax and bend lower every time you exhale. This stretches the hamstrings.
8. Stand slowly, then bend your knees. Squat down as far as you can while keeping your feet flat on the floor. Hold for three or four long breaths. This position stretches the muscles opposite the hamstrings.
9. Squat on your toes with your arms hanging down loosely. Hold for three or four long breaths.
10. Repeat steps 2 through 9 twice more. Return to the position of step 1, then open your eyes slowly.

What you do is less important than doing it consistently. Find a routine that works for you, and stick with it. Do not wait until you feel sore or tense. If you do not give your body a rest, you increase the risk of developing a repetitive stress injury.

INSTANT COMMUNICATION CAPABILITY

The key to an accounting practice's efficiency is instant communication ability. The basic necessary equipment is your computer system. This guide cannot give you the exact configurations for the ideal accounting office computer system. From the time that the manuscript of this book is written until the time of publication it is almost a certainty that the rapid rate of computer technology advancement will render obsolete the specifications for the computer system. Study your requirements carefully and match the solutions offered by the various vendors, which include Value-added resellers (VARs), conventional computer dealers, Internet vendors, and the build-to-order telemarketing and direct models, such as Dell and Gateway.

You will need at least one laser printer and fax machine unless you get multifunction equipment that faxes, prints, copies, and scans in one machine. The multifunction devices are suitable in a start-up accounting office in which the usage may be light, but faxing, printing, copying, and scanning are still necessary. With multifunction equipment, you get lots of capability without a big capital investment. Even if you have or later buy all those other machines, you may want to consider your multifunction device as back-up insurance should your front-line devices go down. A useful checklist of the common traits of small accounting business technology is shown in Exhibit 4.3.

EXHIBIT 4.3
Checklist: Common Traits of Small Accounting Business Technology

- ❑ Price sensitivity
- ❑ Limited resources
- ❑ No management information services support staff
- ❑ Piecemeal collection of office equipment
- ❑ Recognition of the importance of technology
- ❑ Reliance on friends and associates when selecting solutions

Small-Business Networks

Although accountants are value conscious, they are also aware of the growing and vital importance of technology. Computer communications and networking help accountants implement internal networks and tap into communications paradigms, such as the Internet. First and foremost, communications means networks.

Peer-to-Peer

Many accountants are ultra-small businesses, with fewer than 20 people, who rely on "sneaker net." Only about one third of these small businesses use a network. Those firms do not understand the benefits of sharing files, applications, and printers. For this segment, a return on investment (ROI) analysis of how much more efficiently associates and employees could work if they shared resources would be an eye-opener. That analysis should include hard savings in software licenses for multiuser versions versus individual licenses. For a comparatively small investment, even an accounting firm with as few as five people can see a big payoff from a network.

A peer-to-peer system, such as leveraging the networking capabilities in Windows 98 or NT Workstation 4.0, is one option for the smaller accounting firm. In addition to being able to share files and printers, Windows 98 will enable employees to connect to the Internet and use e-mail. NT Workstation supports peer-to-peer networking right out of the box. If the accountant must upgrade to newer, faster PCs capable of running Windows 98, the initial expense will be higher, but the efficiencies gained will be dramatic.

Client–Server Networks

It is possible that even a very small accounting firm may see a higher return if it installs a client–server network. This is especially true for firms with a great deal of computer consulting work and those who install and maintain client–server accounting solutions for clients. In addition to basic networking, accountants must have access to the Internet. They primarily use it as a research tool, but that is only a fraction of how an accounting firm can leverage its investment in this inexpensive, public network. Uses such as e-mail, electronic commerce, extranets, and pushed data can make even a small accounting firm as competitive as a large one.

The Internet is the "killer application." It empowers small businesses to market themselves like large organizations. Small accounting firms can communicate better with their clients, so they can retain them longer and with less effort.

Basic Authentication

The accounting firm is cautioned about slapping a marketing-aimed Web page up after it achieves basic connectivity. That may not be spending its Internet dollars wisely. It would be better served with projects that will allow it to communicate more efficiently with existing clients. This could be done with a simple Web page, secured with basic authentication so that it is accessible only to authorized clients. Most Web sites support basic authentication, but that is not an extremely strong method of security. It does not employ encryption, so someone who applied some effort could gain access. However, it will keep the casual surfer off pages meant for clients.

Database Integration

This application can customize information for the individual accounting firm. It is a Web/database integration that automates e-mailing a simple contact message to a client database or forwards a Hypertext Markup Language (HTML)-based newsletter to e-mail addresses. HTML is the standard dialect used by anyone who publishes to the Internet's World Wide Web. Imagination is the limit with the Internet, as long as the financial returns are clear and demonstrable.

Productive Software

Doing more with less is the byword with regard to software in the accounting business. The main reason an accounting firm is eager to get its computers networked is to boost productivity and get maximum performance from limited resources. Accountants generally agree that computer technology has helped them work more quickly and stay organized. The computer is not the key to increased productivity. It is the application that is really the primary reason the accountant invested in PCs.

Accounting, word processing, and tracking client and prospective-client revenue and prospecting information are the major uses of computer technology applications in accounting firms. In some cases, customized software provides more efficiencies and allows a firm to compete more effectively than the one-size-fits-all, shrink-wrapped products.

Teaming up with a VAR who offers custom software solutions for small-business customers in your target market niches is worth considering. It may be a way for you and the VAR to expand your portfolios to include systems integration products and services. The VAR can add incremental hardware revenue to its custom software sales, and you both can control hardware and software choices so that support of hardware-related problems does not erode support margins. Together, you can share revenues equitably in proportion to the value you each add, and you can offer services and get clients that you could not do separately.

VARs seek working relationships with accountants in their own quest to meet the needs of small businesses. An increasing number of top-tier vendors, such as IBM, Hewlett Packard, Microsoft, and Novell, are teaming with VARs and accountants. They offer a rich set of programs to target and pursue the small to medium-sized business market.

Some accounting firms have formed separate entities to perform VAR services and invested in or acquired VARs. Certain licensing restrictions compel the CPA to separate audit and attest functions from non-CPA activities and restrict the formal partnership/ownership of a CPA firm to licensed certified public accountants.

A useful general checklist summarizing the basics needed for setting up an accounting business is shown in Exhibit 4.4.

EXHIBIT 4.4
Checklist: Setting Up an Accounting Business

Obtain Permits and Licenses

❑ 1. Certificate and license from your State Board of Accountancy if you are a CPA.

❑ 2. Zoning and/or occupancy permits.

❑ 3. State, county, township, or city professional or occupational license, if required. Call the municipality for information.

❑ 4. Federal and state tax ID numbers for firm. For federal ID number, file Form SS-4 with the Internal Revenue Service Center for your state. For your state, call the district office of the state tax department.

❑ 5. Secure a resale tax number and permit if you will be reselling products for which you must collect and remit sales tax.

Establish Professional Relationships

❑ 1. Identify national, state, and local professional organizations. Apply for membership in every appropriate organization. Include all trade associations for your target market niches. If you cannot enroll in every group, at least subscribe to their trade publications.

❑ 2. Meet any other CPAs, accountants, and other professionals in your office building (potentially good referral sources).

- ❑ 3. Introduce yourself to the managers and loan officers of all banks in your office's neighborhood. Open business checking and/or savings accounts. Use at least two banks, and more if possible, for greater chances of referrals.
- ❑ 4. Find a knowledgeable insurance broker. Insure all contents adequately, and secure general liability insurance. Prospect diligently for this professional. They are one of the best referral sources and should be well cultivated.
- ❑ 5. Retain a business savvy and reputable attorney.
- ❑ 6. Identify computer VARs and systems integrators with whom to partner.

Business Details

- ❑ 1. Malpractice and errors-and-omissions insurance. Check with your state CPA society or other appropriate organization for details.
- ❑ 2. Order telephone service, a long distance carrier, white pages listings, and professional listings in the Yellow Pages. Get at least a separate minimum listing (low cost) for each market niche you have selected to target. Be careful about signing up for expensive Yellow Pages display ads. They are seldom productive.
- ❑ 3. Open all necessary utility accounts.
- ❑ 4. Request the forms to place your firm on the practitioners' mailing list from the Internal Revenue Service Center for your state.
- ❑ 5. Letterhead, business cards, and announcements. Find a graphic artist or good printer to design and produce effective professional image–building materials. The people you consult may also become clients or an excellent source of prospective clients.
- ❑ 6. Professional business magazine subscriptions. Get every appropriate periodical covering your target market niches. Most of the periodicals are controlled circulation, which means that there is no charge for qualified professionals.

5

CHARTING YOUR COURSE: THE BUSINESS PLAN

Two accountants went outside on a break from an AICPA convention, when it began to rain. "Quick," said one accountant, "open your umbrella."

"It won't help," responded the other accountant. "My umbrella is full of holes."

"Then why did you bring it in the first place?"

"I didn't think it would rain!"

YOUR BUSINESS PLAN IS A BLUEPRINT FOR MANAGING GROWTH, PROFITABILITY, AND SURVIVAL

Objectives

A good business plan will help you delineate objectives, directions, and strategies. It will be a useful way for you and your associates to reach a consensus about your firm's future. The business plan will bolster the confidence of clients. Affiliates, vendor partners, suppliers, and creditors will be influenced by the plan's demonstration of your business's ability to repay debt. Bankers, investors, and other sources of capital will see that you have planned for financial success. A well-crafted business plan can help you raise capital. Your business plan takes the unexpected into consideration—it directs your business in good times and stabilizes it during bad times. That is why a business plan is one of your most important tools: It assures business growth by providing a map to navigate the minefield toward a successful future. More important, it should be used as a *living document* to help you manage your business.

Accounting Business Components

Your business plan includes all the components of your business: the services and products you offer, the clients you target, and the ways you deliver one to the other. Your plan will help you determine how to meet your clients' needs. The ability to meet your clients' needs is the underlying value of your accounting business.

There is no substitute for thinking through your accounting business and taking the time to put your ideas down on paper. Having the right information to operate your business can make a significant difference where it counts—the bottom line.

Initial Business Plan

When you identify and analyze the present and potential "bugs" of your accounting business and work them out on paper, you will save yourself time and money. The initial business plan for a start-up accounting business should serve as a development tool for the firm's founders, a planning and evaluation tool for key associates, a mission statement for clients, and a sales document for raising capital.

The success of your accounting firm today is no guarantee that it will be as successful tomorrow. New technologies, changing client priorities, new competition, and a host of other external threats may arise. To prepare for tomorrow, you should know your business and your clients' businesses as well, or better than they do. Then you can anticipate what they are going to need and reengineer your business to fill these needs in a profitable way.

Preparing the Business Plan

Developing a business plan is widely considered to be the most important thing you do before going into business. The preparation of your business plan presents a unique opportunity for you to examine all phases of the existing or planned accounting practice. A business plan lets you refine differing strategies before testing them in the marketplace. But remember, for your plan to be a valuable living document, you must regularly assess your business's actual performance against the plan. Evaluate the results and revise your business plan accordingly. Weigh the consequences of differing marketing niches, promotion, production, and financing strategies. Determine the human and financial resources required to launch, develop, and grow the business. This simulation comes without the risk of trial-and-error operation.

Your plan should be as long as is needed to tell your accounting firm's story. An ideal length is about 25 pages; a start-up plan should not exceed 50 pages. A good plan should take at least six months to write.

Using the Business Plan

One successful professional accountant told of using her business plan to guide her initial activities; she then updated it as her practice developed. She found the plan invaluable as a guide to obtaining bank credit. She added that once her accounting business got going, she lacked the time to plan activities and examine alternative strategies that she had when first devising her business plan.

Business Plan Process

The process of putting the business plan together forces you to take an objective, critical look at your entire business proposal. For a start-up, the business plan is an assessment tool. As you work your way through the plan, you will have to continually reaffirm the viability of your business rationale. This can be very difficult. It is not easy to take your dreams and lay them bare in the stark reality of daylight. As your business grows, the plan and its revisions will help you chart the course of your accounting business through the myriad of details you can no longer keep solely in your head.

Information is one of your most important allies. Turn data into competitive intelligence. To get the most out of your business plan, present it in a format that is easily understood and that also provides the information you and your associates need to perform your jobs effectively. The plan's information must not only be timely and accurate, but must be communicated efficiently and intelligently.

GETTING STARTED

Following is a business plan outline to help you start writing.

Cover Page

Include your company name, address, telephone number, fax number, e-mail address, and the contact person's name.

Executive Summary

This part of the plan—appearing first, yet written last—is designed to entice readers. Summarize key points of each section. Write in a narrative fashion with no subheadings. Discuss the nature of the business, the location, and stage of operation. Clearly describe your services and specialties, service capabilities, clients, suppliers, and vendor affiliations. Identify your niche markets, and state any specific advantages you hold over your competition.

Delineate your primary goals and achievements. If you forecast a profit within a specific time frame, say so, and include financial projections to back it up. Describe milestones you have reached and their results. The summary should accentuate the positive and portray confidence that the accounting business will thrive.

If you are using your business plan to request financing, state how much money you need and for what purpose. Discuss the potential return on the investment and the payback period. Be concise but comprehensive, and remember, you get only one chance to make a first impression. Your one- to three-page executive summary should aggressively sell your business, enticing the reader to "read on."

Use plain English, not accounting jargon. Ask yourself questions. A meaningful business plan answers your questions, such as what do you need to make the business work? Ask yourself if it is realistic to expect that you will be able to provide everything the firm needs. Your business plan should point out areas (e.g., financing or technology) in which you will need help.

Profiling Your Firm's Strengths

Explain your business's nature and its major strengths. Remember, if you do not know what business you are in, you will not be in business very long. Itemize your capabilities. Categorize these capabilities as *primary, critical,* or *core.* Rank the capabilities in a hierarchy of ascending complexity, with primary capabilities on the bottom, critical capabilities in the middle, and the core competence at the top.

A plan is only as good as the people who implement it. Investors often put more credibility in the management of a business than in the services or products. Include biographies of yourself and other managers in the firm. Indicate each person's role and financial stake in the business. List all relevant skills, degrees, certifications, and prior experience. If you have not hired everyone yet, describe each open position and its required qualifications. One of the most common inadequacies of businesses is not developing in advance the plans for managing the business.

Market Analysis

Begin by sizing up your market. Include an industry overview for each market niche, trends, and any current or future governmental regulations. Identify your markets: Who are your clients and your prospective clients, and will they be attracted to your services and products? What is your pricing structure, and how did you arrive at it? A market overview should include the demographics of your target markets and the future outlook for those industries. Describe the competition and how your firm is positioned against those competitors.

After you have identified and analyzed the markets and demand for your services and products, define *marketing strategies*. Your plan must spell out the best ways to reach prospective clients.

Services and Products

Describe all the services and products your accounting firm offers, including vendor authorizations and certifications. Explain what makes your offerings better than the competition's. Include past and present results, as well as the potential of services and vendors represented. Identify your firm's intellectual property: patents, processes, industry, industry expertise, proprietary software, as well as any research and development of new products or processes.

Operations

In this section, explain how you create your end products and services and the service and support your firm provides.

Outline and schedule all business activities. How are you going to get the work out? Will you perform all work in-house or subcontract? What equipment, labor, and physical facilities will you need? Who is responsible for quality control, and how will it be maintained? Who are your equipment suppliers? What supplies and services are necessary for operations?

Marketing and Sales

Describe in detail your marketing strategy and how you promote and sell your services and products. Provide information about your sales personnel and marketing activities, with sales forecasts by category and time period. Nothing is more important than knowing your market and demonstrating that knowledge.

Your planning efforts should concentrate on a market study:

- To whom are you going to sell?
- Who is your competition?
- How will your accounting practice be unique?

Capitalize on your firm's core competencies by mixing and matching different clusters of your accounting business's critical capabilities, while weighing each combination's potential to satisfy the needs of your clients.

Management

Include an organization chart, management policies, and strategies. Owners, key personnel, and their experience should be listed. Define the legal structure: sole proprietorship, partnership, limited liability corporation, S corporation, and so forth.

Finance

Financial data and calculations are the make-or-break component of any business plan. Your goal is to show that the business will be profitable. Project for three to five years out, whether your firm is existing or a start-up. Annual financial statements must include a profit-and-loss statement and a balance sheet. Other basic elements of the financial section are the cash-flow forecast and break-even analysis. Analysis including liquidity, asset management, and debt ratios will lend credence to the financial projections. Too often, the entrepreneur will get caught up in wishful thinking. Realism is more convincing than naïve enthusiasm. After all, if we cannot get meaningful financial projections from an accounting firm . . . well!

As Andy Grove, Chairman of Intel Corporation is fond of saying, "Only the paranoid survive."

If seeking debt financing, propose the loan amount, interest rate, and repayment schedule. Describe how borrowed funds will be used, as well as any collateral that is to be offered. If seeking equity financing, describe the percentage of the business that will be given up, the proposed return on investment, and the anticipated methods of taking out the investor (e.g., buy back, public offering, sale).

Investor Considerations

If there is an intention to prepare for the sale of the accounting business to a consolidator or seek investment funds from other investors, where permitted by licensing regulations, additional information should be disclosed in the business plan.

There are five factors that are crucial to investors:

1. Appreciation of their goals and requirements
2. Evidence of focus on market niche(s)
3. Evidence of client acceptance, such as sales proposals booked or engagement letters
4. A proprietary or exclusive license, contract, authorization, patent, or copyright that gives you a competitive advantage
5. A top-notch, proven, and experienced management team

Appendices

Appendices should include resumes, references, market studies, patents, authorizations, certifications, contracts, engagement letters, and the like.

EVALUATING YOUR PLAN

The more you work with your business plan, the more you will realize how useful it is. An important factor to recognize is that you do not have to prepare a full-blown business plan to have an effective management tool. You can pick and choose the parts of the formal business plan that mean the most to you and omit the others. A detailed marketing plan may be the component you need the most, and that should be the one that gets your attention.

After you complete your plan, review the following:

- Is there a need, and is it large enough to support the business proposed?
- Is there a niche?
- Who are the clients?
- What is your assessment of present and potential competition?
- What is your competitive leverage?
- Are you the right person to realize the plan?
- Is the financing arrangement equitable?
- Are the odds at least 50–50 that projections will be met?
- Would you invest if it were someone else's plan?
- Remember to periodically revise your plan—a business plan is not set in stone.
- Most importantly, use your plan to gauge if you have accomplished your goals.

6

NICHE MARKET RESOURCES

INFORMATION FOCUS

If you are serious about selecting a market niche, you may already have collected a few facts in the face of incomplete information and the need to choose. You must make the best decision you can. Given constraints on time and resources, you need to focus on the information you can get. Do not feel guilty for not analyzing a problem exhaustively or become paralyzed by an avalanche of data.

Accounting business decisions are twofold:

1. Initial decision
2. Ongoing reviews to determine whether the decision should be reversed or fine-tuned

Each aspect requires different information. The more specifically each of them can be defined, the better the information you can get.

MARKETING IS NOT SELLING

The selling function in an accounting business is critical and must always be staffed by the best qualified and most effective people. A good salesperson does not necessarily have to be a good accountant. The two are rarely found in the same person. Having said this, an effective program of marketing activities will assist *any* salesperson(s) in being more productive. The role of marketing in an accounting business is to develop sufficient numbers of high-quality prospective clients for the salespeople to meet their revenue target. Prospective client quality and quantity are the key measures of marketing success.

Effective marketing complements skilled professional accounting salespeople. Salespeople who are backed by a strong marketing program have an easier time securing prospective clients. They experience shorter overall selling cycles and fewer sales situations that fall apart "for no apparent reason." Most important, salespeople who are properly backed up with effective marketing see greater success in transforming competitive situations into client relationships.

ESTABLISHING A MARKETING STRATEGY

Marketing is not selling. Marketing happens before and after the sale. An accounting business must:

- Be proactive in the marketplace and not solely reactive.
- Be clearly positioned in target markets/niches.
- Consolidate and strengthen market niche expertise, and communicate that expertise to the current clients and prospective clients.

Positioning

The concept of positioning has not been widely adopted or well executed in the accounting business. A potential client of an accounting firm does not always know the capabilities of the accounting firm. In an emerging or converging marketplace, confused positioning is not a big problem. However, when competition moves in, the professional accountant with a muddy position will rapidly lose market dominance and profitability.

Strategic and Market Focus

The need for clear positioning is critically linked to the need for strategic and market focus. At one time, accounting firms concentrated on traditional accounting services. When competitors entered the marketplace, they differentiated themselves from the entrenched, traditional accountants, and over time expanded to serve multiple market niches.

As niche markets are added to an accounting business, there is a natural tendency to generalize in order to manage the complexity of the business. However, the move to a generalist orientation is the kiss of death for the professional accounting firm. Accountants under market pressure need to increase the focus on each market niche and become "multispecialists," capable of dominating each market niche they are in. Market share is not the goal. Market domination must be the goal.

Consolidation and Strengthening of Market Niche Experience

The consolidation, constant strengthening, and continuous communication of niche expertise to the marketplace is a key requirement for the development and maintenance of dominance in vertical niche markets. Proactive, clearly positioned, focused, and knowledgeable accountants have nothing to fear when new competitors are unleashed in their geographic or market area.

MARKETING PROGRAMS FOR SUCCESSFUL ACCOUNTANTS

Successful accountants develop and deliver marketing programs at two different levels:

1. **Corporate marketing programs** are developed as a roof on the marketing program structure. The corporate programs are focused on proactively developing the position of the firm in the marketplace. Corporate programs transmit the message about what the accounting firm wishes to be known for. They are tools to assist with the positioning task.
2. **Strong niche market programs** are the pillars that support the corporate roof. Niche programs concentrate on communicating niche expertise to prospective clients so that the benefits will be clear to the client by the time the salesperson makes a call. Vertical niche programs deliver prospective clients to the salespeople. Niche market programs are also targeted at the current client base for referral or additional client engagements.

Marketing programs can be separated into offensive, defensive, and market support programs. **Offensive** programs create awareness of the accounting firm and its capabilities. The purpose of this type of program is to generate new leads and prospective clients.

Defensive programs increase selling opportunities to current clients and defend them from competitors. Defensive programs focus on the basics: inform the client base about the firm's full services, stay close to that client's business, and field any postsale problems before any negative word-of-mouth is generated.

Market support programs generate market data to allow the accounting firm's salespeople to increase the effectiveness of their selling activities.

An often overlooked variable is time. Experienced accountants know that by varying the marketing activities and the expenditure levels that they undertake, they can shift the elapsed time between the activity and the potential result. The accountant who never starves but is always hungry lacks focus on activities that are oriented toward the long term.

Marketing is a process that requires a large degree of creativity and, more important, a larger amount of consistency and discipline. The results of strengthening the marketing program may not appear for six months to a year. Be patient, but if you delay for long, it will be too late. New accounting competitors will have overrun your markets.

Segmentation and Differentiation

Segmentation and differentiation of accounting and consulting is one of the most pressing issues facing accountants today. As the marketplace becomes more competitive and the pressure on margins continues to mount, only those accounting firms that have selected a segment (or niche) and differentiated themselves from competitors will succeed.

Professional accountants differentiate themselves for both offensive and defensive reasons. Offensively, the needs of the marketplace are not homogeneous. There is money to be made offering different solutions to different niche markets.

Once in a niche, a reseller *must* continue to differentiate to succeed. Defensively, sameness breeds price competition. There are no winners in most price wars—unless you are a large-volume accounting firm and well enough capitalized to survive a price war, you must differentiate to survive, let alone succeed.

Ways to Differentiate Your Firm

There are numerous ways to differentiate yourself in the marketplace. Some are widely available to all accounting firms, whereas others are available only to a select few. The key to differentiation at the street level is superior execution of those things that matter to the accounting firm's current and target prospective clients. (See Exhibit 6.1.)

EXHIBIT 6.1
Sources of Differentiation

Source of Differentiation	Widely Available	Narrowly Available
Superior management		X
Superior capitalization		X
Superior efficiency		X
Superior technical capabilities		X
Superior market niche knowledge and experience		X
Superior marketing management and execution	X	
Superior sales management and execution	X	
Superior client work, service, and support	X	
Superior client satisfaction	X	

Source: The Accounting Guild.

NICHE MARKETING PLAN

Write a marketing plan to outline how your firm will be involved in targeted market niches. All other steps emanate from this specialized plan, which is separate and distinct from your business plan. You must decide the businesses that you will be in and how you will get there. Until you can commit your concepts to words on paper, you cannot execute those ideas. Writing down your overall objectives, the initial decisions to be made, and the ongoing operational decisions will help *clarify, refine,* and *focus* the objectives of your firm.

1. *How healthy is your business?* Are you starting up, growing, shrinking, or treading water? This information is key to developing your marketing plan in several ways:
   - Your financial health influences your strategic marketing choices. Do you need to bring in business quickly to pump up cash flow? If so, you will want to concentrate on activities that generate short-term fees and revenue, probably from established clients. If your business is relatively healthy, you can focus more attention on developing prospective clients, a process that sacrifices short-term profitability for long-term gain.
   - You need to establish financial milestones against which you can judge the success of your ongoing marketing efforts.
   - Marketing costs money, sometimes as obvious expense items (direct mail, transportation, and entertainment) and sometimes as hidden costs (your own time spent on marketing tasks). Before setting a marketing plan, you must have a handle on the availability of funds to implement strategies.
2. *Assess your skills and the skills of your associates and staff.* Do you have the skills to fulfill the program you have outlined? Can you hire additional talent, or can you and your staff get the necessary training for the new business roles?
3. *Inventory your technology infrastructure.* Do you have the required computer systems, hardware, and software to launch the new business activities? Do not attempt to do technology consulting for others if you cannot do it properly for yourself.
4. *Develop a technology budgeting plan.* How much will it cost to properly equip your firm, how will you finance it, and what is the timetable for purchase, installation, and training?
5. *Who are your current clients?* How can you categorize them? What are their similarities and differences? After you identify your loyal clients, the next step is to analyze your client database to look for patterns. What are the characteristics of the clients you are serving? What market niches do they represent?
6. *Survey your markets.* Who are your potential clients? Will they want the services you are preparing to provide? Who are your competitors and how formidable are they? You need to identify the accounting and consulting firms that offer the same or similar services or products as you.

7. *Develop a marketing plan for each market niche you are considering.* How will you reach prospective clients? Even if you plan only word of mouth (not a wise plan), you must consciously plan each component of the marketing plan.
8. *Create a failure plan.* You should have a contingency plan and make every effort to prevent its need. You should plan the actions you will take if marketing or operations are not yielding profitable results. Put a disaster plan in place in case you lose your data or a fire or storm destroys your office.
9. *Build consensus among the firm's decision makers.* The process takes time. Allow it to unfold, but do not let it paralyze your firm. A one- to two-hour discussion three or four times over two to three weeks should be sufficient. Schedule ample time to pass between each session so that people can digest what has been said.

Exhibit 6.2 is a checklist of marketing programs and the different approaches for differentiating between corporate and niche markets.

EXHIBIT 6.2
Checklist: Marketing Program

	Corporate Programs	Niche Market Programs
Offensive programs	❑ Advertising ❑ Brochures ❑ Receptions ❑ Corporate identification ❑ Direct mail ❑ Media relations	❑ Articles ❑ Direct mail ❑ Seminars ❑ Speeches
Defensive programs	❑ Client visitation ❑ Client service planning ❑ Client service review	❑ Industry research
Market support programs	❑ Market information ❑ Market intelligence ❑ Market training	❑ Competitor tracking ❑ Market training

Source: The Accounting Guild.

Information Trigger Points

Determine the **information trigger points** that lead you to make one decision instead of another. Ask yourself what factors will lead you to take one course of action over another. Information trigger points normally are not specific bits of data but a range of values.

Use the analogy of "traffic light" ranges. Values in the green mean that possibilities are positive if they work the way we expect them to. Values in the red mean that enough factors indicate change is required. Values in the yellow mean that close monitoring is needed. Set a green, red, and yellow range of values for each part of your market niche plan.

Shrewd Marketing

Shrewd marketing requires accountants to be skilled competitors. To compete, they must analyze how prospective clients value their own needs. Then the accountant should use the analysis to select specific niche markets. Evaluating prospective clients' needs begins with a market value analysis. This is a form of competitive intelligence that goes beyond the basic strength/weakness comparisons of service, price, promotion, and competition. It defines which benefits clients in a specific market category want and how they perceive the relative value of various competitive offerings. (See Exhibit 6.3.)

EXHIBIT 6.3
Checklist: Client Value Analysis

To conduct a client value analysis, follow these steps:

- ❑ 1. *Identify the major benefits clients value.* Ask your clients directly which benefits and performance levels they look for in selecting an accountant. You can gather this information through one-on-one interviews, questionnaires, or telephone surveys.
- ❑ 2. *Evaluate the quantitative importance of the different benefits.* Here, again, go to your clients and have them rank the importance of each benefit. (A simple 1-to-10 ranking works well.) Pay particular attention to any big variations in the ranking. This would suggest that you need to group clients by segment in order to make sense of the information.

- [ ] 3. *Evaluate your competitors' effectiveness in delivering benefits and price/performance values compared to their rated importance.* Also ask clients where they rank each competitor's performance on various benefits. Then find out how clients rank you on those same benefits. You might be surprised to find that benefits you emphasize are ones that clients undervalue, causing you, in turn, to pay insufficient attention to what your clients value most. You could be misdirecting your efforts.

- [ ] 4. *Monitor client values as an ongoing activity.* Technology breakthroughs, economic ups and downs, new software developments, aggressive challengers, and other powerful forces all feed changing client values, thereby justifying periodic reexamination.

SELECTING COMPETITORS

Determining which competitors to attack or avoid is vital to your marketing efforts. Otherwise, you needlessly waste your time and resources in attempting to tackle all opponents. Once you have completed your client value analysis, you are prepared to confront one of several categories of competitors.

Strong versus Weak Competitors

Experience indicates that it is best to choose a weak competitor who can be beaten rapidly with a minimum expenditure of resources and who is not likely to block your efforts. Be mindful, however, that all competitors, large and small, have both strong and weak points. Therefore, when planning your strategy, identify which of the competitor's strategies you can weaken to a point where there is minimal resistance against you. Determine which competitors are prepared (highly competitive) and ill-prepared (unable to match your strategies). Identify which competitors' plans and strategies you can duplicate before they turn them against you.

Select competitors by professional services type and market segment. Your aim is to go after a segment unprotected by a competitor. Also, be certain you are capable of holding on to clients despite the efforts of other competitors.

Similar versus Dissimilar Competitors

Typically, you would select competitors that most resemble you. The possible danger is that weakening a similar competitor may force that firm to join a larger competitor, creating a more formidable competitor than before. Therefore, try to assess the possible outcome of your strategy—it may come back to haunt you.

Favorable versus Harmful Competitors

Favorable competitors are those who play by the rules of the accounting industry. They favor a healthy growth industry in which clients are reliably served, avoid destructive price wars, and make honest efforts to address the special interests of clients. These firms also make investments aimed at achieving highly professional operations and make efforts to improve the quality and performance of their accounting services. Overall, competitors in this category are thinking of the long-term growth and health of the marketplace.

Harmful competitors look to buy client market share rather than earn it, take large risks, and tend to upset the equilibrium of the industry. Thus, it could be in your best interest to categorize your competitors and make your selection based on the long-term growth and prosperity of the marketplace.

Selecting a competitor to attack or avoid is an essential part of your planning strategy. The objective of a strategy is to reduce the level of resistance and secure a market position without experiencing price wars and other marketplace conflicts.

Winning numerous competitive battles is not the point. Rather, the aim is to create a competitive advantage without fighting at all or to create a situation in which competitors give up their efforts. If possible, determine the competitor's plans while concealing yours; you can then concentrate your efforts with greater efficiency.

Know your competitors and know yourself and you will never be at a disadvantage. When you are ignorant of the competitors but know yourself, your chances of winning or losing are equal. If ignorant of both of your competitors and yourself, you will be at a disadvantage in every competitive situation.

STRATEGIC ALLIANCES

Consider forming alliances with mutually supportive businesses. Certain businesses naturally cluster around markets and situations.

Analyze the situations that drive clients to call you and think about other businesses offering related goods or services. The computer systems networking specialist and other computer hardware and software retailers are excellent prospects with whom to strike a strategic alliance. You can mutually refer business to each other.

Investigate the potential alliances carefully to be sure of the quality and reliability of their services and products. Contact the owners or management and propose a mutual referral agreement. Share promotional opportunities, such as joint direct mailing, which will cut in half the postal charges and printing expenses. Give your marketing partner a supply of your business cards and any literature for passing along when recommending your accounting business. Be sure to get and hand out their cards as well.

Always keep your end of the bargain and send new business to your ally whenever possible.

A spotlight focused on accounting market niches is presented in Exhibit 6.4.

EXHIBIT 6.4
Accounting Market Niche Spotlight

Market Niche	Percentage*
Business valuations	82
Computer systems/Accounting software	73
Litigation support	68
Estate planning	65
Health care consulting	57
Industry specializations	55
Employee benefits	51
Mergers and acquisitions	50
Business management for wealthy individuals	46
Nonprofit organizations	45
Strategic planning/Business plans	42
Forensics/Fraud	42
Personal financial planning	40
International tax	39
Bankruptcy/Insolvency	36
Financing arrangements	36
Budgeting/Cash flow forecasting/Management	35
Compensation/Benefit planning	33
Medical practice management	33
Software development/Training	30
Business management for small businesses	24
Employee search	24
Lease vs. buy analysis	21

EXHIBIT 6.4 *(continued)*

Market Niche	Percentage*
Payroll services/Consulting	21
Other	18
Legal practice management	17
Receivables management	17
E-filing (tax)	15

*Ranked by percentage offered by top 100 firms in 1998.
Source: The Accounting Guild.

CLIENT (INDUSTRY) SEGMENTS

Manufacturing tops the list of most common client segments. Construction comes in second, with real estate close behind. The turmoil and consolidation in the medical profession has proven to be a mini-bonanza for some well-positioned accounting firms. Auto dealerships and nonprofit organizations are showing some signs of market saturation. (See Exhibit 6.5.) The Bureau of Labor Statistics projects that the 10-year period ending in 2006 will enjoy slower job growth than the 10-year period ended in 1996. Manufacturing could suffer the worst declines, even as professional specialty jobs increase.

EXHIBIT 6.5
Client (Industry) Segments

Client Industry	Percentage*
Manufacturing	70
Construction	60
Real estate	60
Pension plans	57
Professional services	55
Individuals	54
Health care facilities	54
Nonprofit organizations	54
Wholesale distributors	51
Retail trade	43
Hotels and restaurants	40
Small business	37
Banking and thrift companies	37
Auto dealerships	36
State/local government	29
Insurance agencies and brokers	27
Large businesses	25

Publishing/Broadcasting/Media	25
Brokers/Securities and commodities dealers	23
Entertainment	21
School districts	21
Finance companies/Mortgage banks	20
Franchising	19
Government contractors	19
Colleges and universities	18
Agriculture/Farming/Forestry/Fishing	17
Leasing companies	17
Other	17
Investment companies and mutual funds	14
Insurance carriers/Companies	12

*Ranked by percentage of top 100 firms.
Source: The Accounting Guild.

TECHNOLOGY CONSULTING

Technology consulting has evolved from just another value-added service offering to become *the* service that clients have come to expect from their accountants. This service is also generating engagements in other areas of the practice. Technology opens a lot more doors to other business for the accounting firm. Some accountants have been able to build a niche in a particular industry segment primarily due to their technological prowess. One accounting firm was able to build a construction client segment because it could provide construction firms with technological computer advice in addition to traditional accounting and tax services. The prospective clients for this service are entrepreneurial firms experiencing accelerated growth, from $2 million in revenues to 10 to 50 times that amount.

Technology can give you an edge that your competitors may not have. Accounting firms can easily build on their technology model, but it is a challenge to have the right people in place. This is an area that levels the playing field between CPA and non-CPA firms. The long- and short-term prospects for both CPAs and non-CPAs to expand into technology are excellent.

Networking groups through which accountants can build their technology practices are furthering the movement. The Accounting Guild, Las Vegas, Nevada, founded and managed by the author, Jack Fox (jfox1961@aol.com), is an Internet-based group that assists small to medium-sized firms in building their practices. At the same time, technology vendors, such as IBM, Microsoft, and accounting software developers, are offering numerous programs to make accounting firms viable, growing, and profitable sales channels.

A PLAN OF ACTION

At this point, you have investigated and brainstormed and probably lost a fair amount of sleep in the process. It is now time to evaluate your options and create an action plan for the future, defining the steps you intend to take in the next six months to a year, including dates and dollar amounts.

If your firm focuses on attracting clients in several market niches, be sure that you keep in mind that excellent training is a key component of a successful technology-oriented accounting firm.

Some firms will not focus on specific vertical markets until they have recruited the talent to serve such a niche market. Finding qualified technology personnel is not at all easy. The salaries of certified technology professionals can be higher than CPAs', which can cause rifts in firms in which accounting and tax partners are accustomed to feeling highly prized. There is a growing trend for tech people to earn more than their CPA counterparts, which does not sit well in many traditional CPA firms.

You should write down long-range goals to guide your ongoing business development. Prioritize your action plan. List the tasks/objectives in order of relative importance and which steps must be completed before other tasks can be tackled. This is the time to establish marketing requirements, crunch budget numbers, and commit to deadlines. With your marketing plan in hand and the path to your accounting firm's future clearly outlined, you can be assured that the future of your accounting business is literally in good hands.

ACCOUNTING NICHE MARKET COMPENDIUM

Accounting Outsourcing (Service Bureau Concept)

An increasing number of clients are choosing to outsource their accounting applications instead of buying software, hiring, training, supervising employees, and in many cases repeating the cycle. The question is whether smaller clients will understand the "pay more now to reduce costs later" argument.

The major focus of this service is to relieve the client of all of the burdens of operating an accounting department—a step beyond the "rent-a-controller" situation in which the client hires the accountant to perform the functions of a staff controller but on an independent contractor basis. With accounting outsourcing, the entire accounting function is managed by an independent accounting firm. Invoicing, accounts payable, accounts receivable, and all accounting activities are handled by the accounting firm.

Start-Up Resources

- **CCH,** Riverwoods, IL ProSystem, www.prosystemfx.com
- **RIA, GoSystem Remote Server,** www.gosystem.com
- **IBM Global Services,** www.ibm.com

Budgetary Processes Consulting

Accounting and consulting professionals can now market a complete line of industry-leading, personal computer (PC)-based budgetary processes and business planning management software. In the past, users required the resources of a mainframe or minicomputer and had to spend hundreds of thousands of dollars to achieve the results now provided by inexpensive software on a PC. Vendors provide the accountant with extensive expertise in terms of budgetary processes and business planning management software. Professionals are available to the participating accountant, ready to answer any questions either the accountant or the clients may have.

An eight-hour, eight-credit continuing professional education (CPE) course, *Accountants' Guide to Budgetary Automation,* published by The Accounting Guild, is the definitive reference course for professionals and end users. It is available to the professional accountant who may offer it for resale to clients, potential clients, and others once they have completed a certification training course. Prospective affiliates must attend the training course, but The Accounting Guild makes every effort to conduct seminars in strategic major market locations.

Start-Up Resources

- **The Accounting Guild,** 702-242-8725, 8713 Short Putt Drive, Las Vegas, NV 89134, www.accountingguild.com

Business Coaching

According to Coach University (www.coachu.com), business coaches are more than consultants, less than therapists, and often your friends. There are certification programs available, but many coaches substitute years of business experience.

Professional accountants who enjoy talking to their clients about future business plans and dreams can develop the knack for helping these clients set goals and help them stay on track to reach those goals. The concentration is on new businesses, start-up businesses, and fast-growing businesses. Lending a knowledgeable and yet impartial ear helps business clients who know how to run a business to run that business at a higher level.

Start-Up Resources

- **Coach University International,** www.coachuintl.com
- **International Coach Federation,** www.coachfederation.org
- **International Consortia of Business Coaches,** www.i-cbc. com

Business Valuation

A leading form of managerial advisory services that may be performed by the accountant is in the valuation area. Primary focus is on the management advisory and litigation support areas.

Management Advisory

- Business valuation
- Business planning
- Business financing
- Deal structuring
- Cash flow forecasting

Litigation Support

- Business valuation
- Lost profits tort damages
- Personal injury losses
- Divorce apportionment
- Other economic studies

Specific Assignments

The services you perform will depend largely on your specialty and market preference. A CPA license, if not a legal requirement, will usually be required by attorneys and banks for credibility and liability reasons.

Management Advisory Services

- Comparative reviews
- Business/Tax planning
- Business forecasting
- Benchmark valuations
- Debt or equity loan packaging
- Estate, gift, and trust planning

Business Valuation Services

- Estate and gift tax
- Marital dissolution
- Eminent domain
- Buy/Sell agreements
- Employee stock ownership plans
- Acquisition, sale, or merger
- Going public
- Dissenting minority stockholders
- Intangibles valuation
- Stock options

Litigation Support Cases

- Personal injury losses
- Contract disputes
- Divorce appraisal and allocation
- Stockholder disputes
- Patent/Trademark infringement
- Tort damages

Marketing/Client Base

- Current business clients

- Family law attorneys
- Corporate law attorneys
- Estate attorneys
- Other accountants
- Prospective business clients
- Court appointments
- Business brokers

Practice Start-Up Resources

1. Professional staff with a CPA
2. Accredited senior appraiser (ASA), granted by the American Society of Appraisers
3. Chartered financial analyst (CFC), granted by the Institute of Chartered Financial Analysts
4. Certified business counselor (CBC), granted by the Institute of Certified Business Counselors
5. Partner valuation experience in a variety of industries
6. Professional analysis and reporting tools
7. Liability insurance (errors and omissions)
8. Ancillary billable work while getting started
9. Marketing materials, sample reports, and budget
10. Marketing plan and administrator
11. **National Association of Certified Valuation Analysts,** 1245 East Brickyard Road, Suite 110, Salt Lake City, UT 84106; Tel: (801) 486-0600, Fax (801) 486-7500; www.nacva.com

Collection and Credit Tools and Services

Clients often ask the accountant to help with billing and statement systems and procedures. Sometimes, this service can become a regular profit center. The work is done either at the client's location or at the accounting firm's office.

Start-Up Resources

- **Axiom Systems,** 26212 Dimension Drive, Suite 260, Lake Forest, CA 92630; (800) 896-8960. Collection Manager interfaces with Accpac Plus from Computer Associates.
- **Dun & Bradstreet Small Business Advisor,** Three Sylvan Way, Parsippany, NJ 07054; (800) 552-3867
- **GetPaid Software,** 170 Changebridge Road, Suite D-6, Montville, NJ 07045; (800) 395-9996. GetPaid interfaces with accounts receivable packages from Great Plains, Macola, Open Systems, Platinum, SBT, and Solomon Software.

Electronic Data Interchange Consulting

Electronic data interchange (EDI) is the computer-to-computer exchange of routine business transactional data, such as orders, shipping notices, and invoices. Data are organized according to a standardized format that has been agreed upon by both parties. This information is sent across a network: It is essentially "hands-off" transmittal of business documents.

Your clients may eventually have to implement EDI in response to demands from their customers. In addition to providing information more quickly, EDI leaves a completely traceable audit trail for all data that pass between the trading partners. Methods like fax or e-mail can transmit as fast as EDI does, but cannot reliably track the origin or receipt of data. More and more companies ranging from manufacturing to retail are insisting that their suppliers use EDI. These suppliers will be seeking professional assistance in providing their EDI solution.

Start-Up Resources

- **EDS Electronic Business**, (800) 338-7767, www.eds.com
- **General Electric Information Services (GEIS),** (800) 560-4347, www.geis.com
- **Harbinger EDI Services, Inc.,** (404) 841-4334, www.harbinger.com
- **IBM Global Network,** (800) 588-5808, www.ibm.com/globalnetwork
- **Sterling Commerce, Inc.,** (800) 299-4031, (614) 793-7000, www.sterlingcommerce.com

Financial Planning

Turning tax clients into financial planning clients is a basic way to build a personal financial planning practice. It is a way to grow profits, add value to your services, and build client loyalty. Not pursuing this market niche could cost you clients if they look to another accountant or financial planner for these services. A major reason that accounting consolidators are acquiring accounting firms is that they want the firm as a conduit to their profitable financial planning practices.

Resources

- Internal marketing
- External marketing
- Use of tax season to transition existing clients

Training and Credentials

You must start at the beginning by getting the proper training and credentials. The worst thing you can do is to try to do financial planning if you are not qualified. Build a resume by joining planning organizations and committees and developing expertise in those areas in which you want to specialize.

Software Resources

- **BNA Software,** Washington, DC, (800) 372-1033; Income Tax Planner, Estate Planner, www.bna.com
- **Financial Profiles,** Carlsbad, CA, (760) 431-9400, www.profiles.com
- **Financial Navigator International,** Mountain View, CA, (650) 962-0300, www.finnav.com
- **First Financial Software Inc.,** Apopka, FL, (800) 719-8761, www.fplan.com
- **MasterPlan Financial Software,** Davis, CA, (800) 229-5080, www.masterplanner.com
- **Money Tree Software,** Philomath, OR, (541) 929-2140, www.moneytree.com
- **Morningstar,** Chicago, IL, (312) 696-6000; Principia for Mutual Funds, www. morningstar.com
- **RIA Group,** New York, NY, (800) 431-9025, www.gosystem.com

Broker/Dealers Who Cater to Accountants

- **Financial Services Corporation,** Atlanta, GA, (770) 916-6500
  FSC is one of the largest and most experienced providers of services to planners, with a broad range of quality nonproprietary investment and insurance products and services.
- **H. D. Vest,** Dallas, TX, (800) 821-8254
  Leads the category in financial planning products and services for accountants. Offers stocks, bonds, and mutual funds to accountants.
- **Hochman & Baker,** Chicago, IL, (847) 564-4244
  Formed by a CPA who serves accountants exclusively. Its stronghold is in the Chicago area, but it has also branched out to a number of states, including Florida, Ohio, and Pennsylvania. Products: stocks, bonds, mutual funds, insurance products.
- **Investment Management Research,** Atlanta, GA, (770) 393-3900
  IMR is a major broker/dealer with a Professional Partners Program for accountants. Through Raymond James & Associates, advisors receive research, trade execution, state-of-the-art technology, and fee-based asset-management services. Products: stocks, bonds, mutual funds, variable insurance products, and limited partnerships.
- **Linsco/Private Ledger Corporation,** San Diego, CA, (619) 450-9606
  LPL is one of the nation's leading independent broker/dealers, offering a full range of insurance and financial products. Products: stocks, bonds, mutual funds, and annuities.
- **Royal Alliance,** New York, NY, (212) 551-5335
  Royal Alliance is a big planner in the broker/dealer financial planning marketplace. The firm is owned by Sun America. It offers a wide range of mutual fund, insurance, and investment products; limited partnership; and fee-based programs.

Fixed Assets Accounting/Consulting

Accurate tracking and reporting of fixed assets is a growing requirement for clients. Most small to medium-sized clients are still preparing fixed-asset schedules manually or using a self-devised electronic spreadsheet program. The client needs this information for income tax filings, property taxes, capital budgeting, and depreciation calculations.

New software enables accountants to replace Excel and Lotus spreadsheets. Software is available that is network ready, has user-definable fields, projects depreciation into future years, and has custom report writer capability.

Start-Up Resources

- **Best Software,** Reston, VA, (800) 368-2405, www.bestsoftware.com
- **BNA Software,** Washington, DC, (202) 728-7962, www.bna.com/soft/
- **Creative Solutions Inc.,** Dexter, MI, (800) 968-8900, www.csi-solutions.com
- **MoneySoft,** Phoenix, AZ, (602) 266-7710, www.moneysoft.com
- **WorthIT Software,** Mississauga, Ont., (888) 967-8411, www.worthit-software.com

Forensics Accounting

You may not fit the hard-boiled Sam Spade image, but more and more clients are worried (with good reason) about fraud. Accounting firms that specialize in forensics are in growing demand. The forensics specialization also includes litigation support and can be very interesting and profitable. This niche is a combination of investigation and accounting.

Activities include gathering evidence, such as affidavits, and collecting physical clues, such as checks. The forensic accountant also compiles circumstantial evidence, such as who had access to the stolen money and who was in the area when the alarms were shut off. Circumstantial evidence is important when dealing with fraud because the cases usually lack a "smoking gun."

Clients may come from several sources. Banks may want an accounting firm to investigate a business it wants to work with. Accounting investigators may be called in to settle stockholder disputes and verify the books of a company. The forensic accountant may be contacted by an attorney to do a background check on an individual or work on a divorce case to find the value of the assets.

Getting Started

Developing your practice in this area primarily requires educating attorneys, company officers and directors, local law enforcement personnel, fidelity insurance adjusters, and others of the unique skills that make your firm most qualified to perform hidden asset searches. Attorneys generally are the most fruitful source of obtaining forensics accounting assignments. Getting started can be easier if you already have an established network from other forensic accounting projects in which you are involved.

Knowledge/Information Technology Management Consulting

Accounting professionals are working with clients to realize the promise of leveraging everything they "know" through the concept of knowledge management. Using groupware, databases, and other software tools, a growing number of accounting firms are trying to combine organizational data with the information in employees' heads to create a repository of intellectual capital. The clients' goals are to apply the collective intelligence of their employees—and the institutional memory of past experience—toward innovation and gaining a unique position in current and future markets.

At this time, no vendor offers an end-to-end knowledge management system, but several new products and technologies are designed to help companies get closer to capturing, sharing, and cultivating their intellectual assets.

Start-Up Resources

- **Autonomy's Knowledge Management Suite** places searches in context and conducts them in real time.
- **Cambridge Information Systems' Web Ensemble** lets users annotate documents, then stores them as objects.
- **Dataware Technologies' Dataware II Knowledge Query Server** aggregates search results from many sources.
- **Glyphica's InfoPortal** sends e-mail when new content is added to portal.
- **PC Docs/Fulcrum's PowerDocs and DocsFusion** let users search from within a Word document.

Paperless Office (Document Management) Consulting

Industry experts have been predicting the paperless office for years. To date, few companies have embraced any sort of document technology to any great degree. Document management itself defies a clear-cut definition. Yet, the industry-wide size of the market is estimated at over $5 billion, which means an incredible opportunity for professional accountants who choose to participate. In the past, some accounting firms have offered a limited document imaging solution as part of an overall accounting and work flow document management system.

The primary strategies to be successful in this niche market include:

- Committing the resources
- Intimately learning the technology, products, and applications
- Understanding client needs
- Effectively designing and implementing solutions

Start-Up Resources

- **Computer Language Research,** (877) 467-8483, www.clr.com
- **CPASoftware,** Visual Practice Management, (800) 272-7123, www.cpasoftware.com
- **Filenet,** Watermark, (800) Filenet, www.filenet.com/prods/watermark
- **IBM,** (888) 426-2992, www.businesscenter.ibm.com
- **Paperclip,** (201) 329-6300, www.paperclip.com
- **Research Institute of America,** (877) 467-8483, www.gosystem.com

Payroll Processing

Accounting firms can compete effectively with big service bureaus as the demand surges for payroll processing. Some accounting businesses use payroll preparation to strengthen ties to current clients, whereas others operate the service as part of the firm or a separate entity as a new or additional profit center.

Payroll services can give accountants a major presence in the client's business. Payroll clients often grow to depend on the accountant, who can often capture the rest of the client's accounting work. There is a lot of opportunity. A 1998 survey of payroll practices indicated that more than 42 percent of the companies that responded to the survey use a service bureau of some type. Forty-five percent of all organizations doing payroll in-house planned to outsource it within the year. Although large service providers, such as giant Automatic Data Processing (ADP) and Paychex, provide stiff competition to accounting firms, accountants are thriving as they provide payroll services to their clients.

ADP has changed its approach to the marketplace and increasingly involves accounting professionals in delivering services. ADP previously tried and did a very effective job of dominating the market for payroll services. Now, it views accountants as the gatekeepers to many businesses. ADP surveys indicate that companies turn first to their accountants for advice and service. ADP is now willing to share some of the revenue because of the flexibility and breadth accountants bring to the payroll scene.

ADP offers accountants several payroll processing options: outsourcing to ADP, EasyPay, AutoPay, and AccountantPay. It will also acquire an accounting firm's payroll clients when that accountant no longer wants to do payroll. Accountants who want to be successful at payroll processing must make sure they have service bureau–quality software and have the appropriate office flow controls in their business.

An accountant can make money at payroll because it is a repeat business; however, it is also a huge commitment on the professional accountant's part. Think of the consequences of having the computer go down at the end of the week and facing hundreds of people who are clamoring for their paychecks. Payroll can be a very important way to grow an accounting business. To build a clientele, accountants should begin with their own client base and add to it with direct mail and telemarketing. Network extensively with opinion leaders and other referral sources.

Some accountants find that doing payroll is less profitable than consulting with clients on their own systems. Working with a broad spectrum of businesses, these accountants help their clients integrate payroll and human resource functions and also train the clients' employees. However, the accountant who decides to offer payroll services has an edge in competing against service bureaus. Because of their intimate knowledge of their clients' businesses, accountants share a level of trust with their clients that service bureaus never achieve. Many accountants who perform payroll services believe that the primary reason to be in practice is to help clients succeed and will give whatever support is needed.

Start-Up Resources

- **ADP,** Roseland, NJ, (800) 225-5237; AccountantPay; www.adp. com
- **Creative Solutions,** Dexter, MI, (800) 968-8900; The Payroll Solution; www.csisolutions.com

- **Paychex,** Orange, CA, (714) 456-0100; RapidPay; www.paychex.com
- **Pay Choice,** (609) 231-4667, www.paychoice.com
- **UniLink,** Jackson Hole, WY, (800) 456-8321; PR*Plus; www. unilink-inc.com

Small Business

Small business has been recognized as the major creator of new jobs in America and is a driving force in new and innovative products and services. More and more accountants are recognizing small business as the major growth market niche that has needs beyond the traditional areas of tax compliance and financial reporting. The reported numbers of small businesses range from 11 million to 22 million, which include the figures from the Internal Revenue Service as to the number of Schedule C filings with Form 1040 to a census of business licenses.

Definition of Small Business

Small businesses are characterized by diversity in size, product/market niche, and stage of development. Without fail, these companies have limited resources. Usually, they are owner managed and thus closely associated with their owners' goals and objectives. These businesses are constantly changing in response to the environment, as they and their owner–managers grow and mature.

In most small businesses, especially in the early stages, the owner is the manager. The owner–manager is the main source of capital and other resources. A small business cannot go out and make opportunities, but must position itself to recognize and take advantage of opportunities when they appear. In the best sense of the word, small businesses are opportunity driven.

While small businesses need outside help, they frequently feel they do not receive what they need. The most common complaint from small business owners is that their advisors do not understand their businesses.

One factor is undoubtedly the varied nature of small businesses compounded by their rate of change. Another is the lack of internal staff to aid in diagnosing problems and translating technically oriented solutions into managerial programs. Thus, the burden of meeting small business needs falls to professional accountants willing to serve this neglected but promising market niche.

Small and medium-sized businesses are similar to larger businesses in that all seem to believe technology is the answer to their business problems. Technology, in and of itself, has never solved a single business problem. A recent study found that 85 percent of small businesses in the United States own at least one PC. Another study reported that 55 percent of the small businesses owning PCs have reported little or no value from the PC to their business operations.

One reason small businesses have failed to reap the benefits of technology is that the small business advisors did not perceive and then solve the problems facing small business. The tools are available, and the small business owner–managers must be trained to use those tools. Too often, business owner–managers have been given the proverbial fish instead of being taught how to fish for themselves.

Minority businesses offer special opportunities, particularly—but not exclusively—for minority accountants, most notably the special loan assistance and 8(a) procurement contracts with the federal government. The Small Business Administration (SBA) defines *minorities* as those who are socially and economically disadvantaged. The regulations governing the practical application of that definition are complicated and various criteria are used. Social disadvantage has to do with membership in one of several different racial or ethnic categories as defined by regulation.

Social disadvantage can also be determined on a case-by-case basis for those who feel they are socially disadvantaged (e.g., the physically or psychiatrically disabled). Economic disadvantage has to do with the barrier(s) that social disadvantage has placed in the way of an individual's participation in business and employment.

Start-Up Resources

- ***Accounting and Recordkeeping Made Easy for the Self-Employed*** by Jack Fox, MBA, John Wiley & Sons, New York, 1995
- **The Small Business Resource Guide,** Sources of Assistance for Small and Growing Companies, IBM Corporation, (888) IBM-5800, 411 E. Wisconsin Avenue, FL 18, Milwaukee, WI 53202; www.ibm.com/solutions/smbus
- **U.S. Small Business Administration,** (800) 827-5722, 409 Third Street, SW, Washington, DC 20416; www.sba.gov
- **Microsoft Corporation,** www.microsoft.com/smallbiz/, provides feature articles, resources and examples of how other small

businesses have successfully used the latest technologies to improve their operations and profits.

- **Federal Government Resources,** www.business.gov. This site, called "U.S. Business Advisor," is the federal government's one-stop resource for all types of business information and assistance. It contains links to search engines covering over 100,000 government databases.
- **Marketing on the Internet,** www.industry.net/guide
- **Direct Marketing Association,** www.the-dma.org
- **Small Business Toolkit,** www.toolkit.cch.com. This site contains numerous books for small-business planning and management, including sample documents, letters, and contracts, the mechanics of financing and marketing a business, and other practical information for the advisors of small and home-based businesses. Much of the material is offered at no charge, but there is a fee for some services.
- **The Accounting Guild,** www.accountingguild.com, offers an affiliation that recognizes that you are in business for yourself, but not necessarily by yourself. Membership in the Guild offers more than an accounting franchise could offer without the franchise fees and royalties.

Upon joining the Guild, you are given an effective marketing program designed to turbo-jump your accounting business by focusing on a neglected market—small to medium-sized businesses grossing from $500,000 to $10,000,000 annually. Your accounting business can offer a significant price advantage over traditional accounting services by using carefully researched and tested computer software. This software shifts the major part of the workload from the accounting professional to a para-professional and automation.

The Accounting Guild was founded by the author in response to numerous requests from readers of the first two editions of *Starting and Building Your Own Accounting Business.* The Guild encourages members to work together, using complementary skills, through a member-only Internet Web site. Cluster groups are formed on a geographic basis, and members in each cluster meet several times a year with professional support staff to discuss operating strategies, common problems, or the possibility of implementing group marketing programs, and participate in "road shows" featuring the latest in computers and software related to this market segment.

Technology Consulting

Across America, consultant practices and CPA firms are separating. Most remain linked through common ownership and many share a common roof. Some accountants have simply taken their CPA practice out of the public arena. The process may be called *Andersenization,* after Andersen Consulting, which years ago split from the operations of the Arthur Andersen accounting firm.

The most prominent group that is attempting to serve the accounting/technology consulting niche is the Information Technology Alliance (ITA). Until June 1997, the ITA was known as ACUTE (**A**ccountants **C**omputer **U**sers **T**echnical **E**xchange). The organization is serving not only consultants, but resellers and the computer reselling community in general—beyond accounting software.

Consultants are often not CPAs. Forming a separate niche unit enables the firm to provide the non-CPA consultant with a degree of equity ownership. Separating from an accounting firm also allows consultants to sell services to other accounting firms or to clients whose incumbent CPA feels threatened by a CPA consultant. For a consulting unit to succeed inside an accounting firm, the consulting operation must have someone with influence, preferably a partner, who is an advocate for the consulting unit. It requires a significant push by a "champion" in the organization to facilitate an effective pairing of CPAs and non-CPA consultants. When there is no champion, the consulting program can weaken or die.

Training Provider (Accounting Software Courses)

Small to medium-sized businesses are starved for accounting software knowledge for their employees. These employees have to perform much of the work previously done by accounting firms. However, in many areas, the competition in the generic—as opposed to the customized—training market is intense, and you must:

- **Understand** the local niche you serve.
- **Differentiate** your services, and leverage them with the rest of your accounting business.
- **Deliver** a custom accounting-related software training service in a manner that is cost-effective, timely, and convenient for the client.
- **Hire** real educators to staff your facility, not burned-out accountants looking for a cushy late-career job.

Differentiation

Differentiate your niche through client service in both public and custom training. Run very small public classes and charge more—up to $500 a day—for the extra attention. On the custom side, go the extra mile in customizing the package and integrating it into the client's accounting system. In generic training, you can achieve a degree of differentiation simply by being reputable and reliable.

Marketing

Marketing is typically the last issue to be addressed, which training providers insist is a mistake. On the custom side, word-of-mouth reputation may be paramount. In the training business, however, you need direct mail, seminars, and dedicated salespeople to fill the empty seats. Another option is to cultivate relationships with pure training firms. Infotec Commercial Systems Inc. (www.infotec-web.com), is a nationwide training company that specializes in Cisco Systems, Lotus Development, Microsoft, and Novell products, among others. Infotec frequently teams with accounting firms. You can also source Infotec training services through Tech Data Corporation, a national computer hardware, software, and services distributor. Another national distributor, Pinacor, Inc., also works with accounting training providers.

Cost Analysis

- *Trainer costs.* Instructors themselves are the largest expense for a training operation.
- *Salary.* Trainers' median salaries range from $36,000 (applications instructor) to $59,000 (certified technical instructor).
- *Bonuses/commissions.* Bonus, commissions, and other non-base salary components are estimated at $3,400 to $9,700 a year.
- *Overhead.* Direct costs, such as travel expenses, training expenses, and benefits, and indirect costs, such as allocated office space and computer/fax/phone services associated with each trainer.
- *Utilization.* The average number of billable teaching days per trainer is 12.2 a month, or about 146 a year.
- *Class size.* Based on the above analysis, if an accounting firm charges $300 a day per student, it needs at least three paying students in class to make money.

7

ACCOUNTING SOFTWARE

ACCOUNTING SOFTWARE SEGMENTATION

Accounting software ranges from packages costing under a $100 to about as much as you can justify spending. The software covers a wide range of functionality from basic bookkeeping to enterprise-wide systems. The market is segmented into three different groups of PC Accounting Software:

1. Low-cost
2. Mid-range
3. High-end

The division primarily reflects pricing, which in turn reflects functionality. No grouping will meet with universal acceptance.

Software publishers use a variety of different terms to describe their software. Many describe the market by the revenue of target clients, but even here vendors use revenue ranges that vary dramatically, and the terms *mid-range* and *middle market* are sometimes interchangeable and sometimes not.

Low-cost accounting software (which includes checkbook and bookkeeping packages) has packages that generally cost less than $300, many of which are sold in retail stores. The software is sold in a single, shrink-wrapped package and is generally designed for SOHO (small office–home office) users with limited or no accounting staff.

Mid-range accounting software includes modules such as general ledger, accounts receivable, and accounts payable. These are sold as separate components of the accounting software system. The market ranges from $300 for all-inclusive packages to components selling up to $1,200 to $2,000 per module. Software in this category is sold almost exclusively by professional accountants as well as value-added resellers (VARs) for software vendors. Their partner programs may also include consultants who implement the packages. The accounting software products in this category are much more flexible than the low-cost packages and are designed for larger clients with ample budgets.

High-end PC accounting software embraces two separate areas:

1. Traditional personal computer–local area network (PC-LAN) accounting packages
2. PC-based client–server software

These software lines are generally sold through professional accountants and VARs. At the higher end, some vendors use direct sales forces to reach clients. While this category may start at $800 a module, the client–server entries cost much more and often reach into the hundreds of thousands of dollars for large enterprise installations. High-end products have many more modules available than the mid-range lines and often serve more specialized markets, such as construction, distribution, and manufacturing.

ACCOUNTING SOFTWARE FEATURES

Accounting software programs are Windows-based and all have very different interfaces. The menu bar is the only visual element they have in common. Also, the interfaces do not have colorful icons and graphical charts that are usually found in entry-level programs. Reporting capabilities vary between programs. Most programs allow for a selection of sorting criteria, and some let the user redesign the layout.

Data entry and retrieval are critical features. If it is a fight to enter data in entry fields, and even more difficult to cut through the information to find crucial numbers, then the software becomes a hindrance rather than a tool for growth. The daily functionality of the software and its intuitiveness, including ease of use for repetitive tasks, must meet the user's requirements.

QUEST FOR AN EDGE

Most accounting professionals consider technical expertise their main value-added benefit, but a lot more than technical knowledge goes into running a successful accounting business. In fact, as technology grows more complex, it demands a greater investment in management skills. The sales cycle with prospective clients grows longer, and supporting clients gets more complex and costly. Of course, the potential for profits is greater as well.

These exciting but stressful conditions put an accountant's management ability to the test. Among the skilled staff you will find at an accounting firm are top-notch accounting software people. Their talents are paying off more for accounting firms that concentrate on software than for traditional firms with conventional tax compliance and financial statement services.

Experienced accountants indicate that technology consulting calls for a strong ability to identify clients' desires. This is not so easy to accomplish. The number one skill that is needed is the ability to listen to the clients. What keeps the accountant successful is understanding what the clients are saying and reacting to what they want.

DETERMINING CLIENT NEEDS

The accountant must be careful when trying to identify client needs. It can become a sticky situation when the client insists on the implementation of changes to proprietary software, especially if the clients have strict processes in place that they do not want restructured.

You do not want to overstep any boundaries when presenting changes. Present the changes as improvements and not as a new way for your clients to work. Clients who know their business do not want to be taught about their business. They want advice on how to do things better, but they are not looking for an entirely new process.

SELECTING AN ACCOUNTING SOFTWARE VENDOR

Many firms seeking to align themselves with an accounting software vendor make the mistake of starting with product comparison. Look first at your accounting firm and determine your area of expertise. Then, match it with the potential vendor partner.

If your strengths are in particular market niches, then search out vendors who specialize in marketing to those industries. Also, look at the size of your clients and prospective clients. If you are concentrating on small to medium-sized businesses with revenues from $2 million to $30 million, you need to partner with a vendor whose products are appropriate for businesses of the same size.

Identify the leading software vendors within your target markets. The accounting software industry is constantly changing, and the strengths and advantages of a vendor's products can change with every new release. Select a vendor who is consistently rated among the top five accounting software publishers. Once you have identified the top vendors, examine each vendor's strengths and weaknesses. (See Exhibit 7.1.)

EXHIBIT 7.1
Checklist: Vendor Attributes/Characteristics

These are some of the major characteristics that must be addressed before making a decision to align with an accounting software vendor. Focus on the attributes and do not get sidetracked as to whether the vendor has programs running under client–server or Windows. Clients buy benefits first and features and technology second or third. If the benefits are there, they will not care about the operating environment.

❑ ***Marketing***

It does not matter how good your services or the vendor's products are if the vendor does not do a good job marketing and generating leads. Find out if the vendor's advertising program offers co-op funds for marketing. See if the vendor has an internal marketing support department to assist you in advertising, direct mail, and trade shows.

❑ ***Vendor Partner Requirements***

Vendor partner requirements is an area which shows how committed a vendor is to the accountant. What does it take to get into the different partnership programs both from a monetary and training standpoint? Some vendors have a significant fee and training requirements. Others will sign you up if you are breathing. The vendors that you want to work with and who are serious about you are usually the ones that require an up-front investment in both time and money.

The Accounting Guild will, on request, share its research on the vendor and refer you to other accountants and resellers who have personal experience with the vendor and the particular software programs you are investigating. In this way, you can gain valuable insights as to how a vendor treats its partners. Is there strong competition in your specific geographic and target market niches, or does the vendor restrict the number of partners within each market area? Does the vendor have annual reseller and consultants' conferences?

Is there an accountant–reseller council in which top consultants and accountants can exchange ideas with the vendor's executive team? You want to be treated as an active partner and not a silent partner.

❑ *Support and Upgrades*

Satisfaction with support and upgrades is difficult to measure. What you are looking for here is the vendor's continuing commitment to support. Is the vendor constantly trying to improve the level of support? Support satisfaction comes up in every sales cycle one way or another. If clients are not happy with the level of support they receive, your job is going to be that much tougher. How does the vendor handle upgrades and updates? How often do they come out? Is there a controlled early release program? Does the vendor charge for upgrades and early releases?

❑ *Margins*

Margins are critical for a professional accountant–reseller. Most vendors have margins that typically range from 30 percent to 60 percent. Your level of margin is usually dictated by the volume of product that you resell. However, you can leverage on the buying/reselling volume of the members of The Accounting Guild. The Guild has negotiated margin levels with a large number of vendors based on the combined purchases/sales of all members of the Guild.

❑ *Lead Distribution*

Lead distribution is another factor that you should learn about before selecting a vendor. Most vendors distribute leads based on the reseller's business volume. Some vendors match leads with a reseller's expertise. If the lead is for a manufacturing company, then the vendor should try and pass it on to an accountant who has experience in manufacturing in that specific industry. Again, affiliation with The Accounting Guild brings enhanced lead participation.

❑ *Product Features*

Product features are not as important as product benefits. Accounts payable is accounts payable and general ledger is general ledger. You cannot do much with these packages from a features standpoint. What really does separate the vendors' offerings is how they handle order entry, purchasing, inventory control, budgeting, and bill of materials. You really have to analyze the software packages. Make sure that the vendors you choose have the strongest programs that deliver the benefits your clients require and that fit within your niche market(s).

Determining the criteria and components regarding the purchase and resale of accounting and business productivity software is outlined in checklist form in Exhibit 7.2.

❑ *Third-Party Products*

Third-party products are often an overlooked topic when choosing a partner. Third-party software programs or add-on packages can make or break a potential sale.

If your target market is wholesale distribution companies, two common requirements are return material authorization (RMAs) and multicurrency. If your vendor's core programs do not have these features, you must ensure that you can satisfy the needs through third-party products or add-ons.

EXHIBIT 7.2
Checklist: Purchasing/Selling Accounting Software

❑ 1. *Do your homework.* Read product reviews and comparisons for background only. Familiarizing yourself with the current uses of technology in accounting software for the particular applications being considered, as well as the current range of functions and features, will give you a strong background to begin a requirements definition.

❑ 2. *Do NOT purchase or sell a product based on the latest and greatest hot review.* Reviews are only as good as the reviewer. Even a great reviewer has biases that may have nothing to do with your client's business and its specialized requirements. So read the reviews, but draw your own conclusions based on your expertise and the requirements of your client.

❑ 3. *Determine your client's requirements BEFORE you meet with specific software vendors.* Otherwise, you are likely to be impressed with the software based on sales skills or marketing materials, rather than product fit. Besides, identifying areas of poor fit for the product you ultimately select will greatly help during the implementation phase.

❑ 4. *Do not recreate the client's same weak system.* As you define the client's requirements, capture the underlying business needs rather than just how a process is currently performed.

New software will not handle everything in the identical way as the client's current system—but you would not want it to, or else why replace the present system in the first place?

- ❑ 5. *Evaluate the need for a formal needs analysis.* While documenting system requirements is critical, it may not be worth the effort to prepare and distribute a formal Request for Proposals (RFP). Unless you plan to recommend a very expensive system (e.g., Oracle, SAP, PeopleSoft) or one that involves significant customization, many software publishers or resellers will not respond to a lengthy RFP. Ironically, those who do fully respond may have time on their hands. Some vendors are much better at writing proposals than writing effective software. Is this the profile you want for your software vendor?
- ❑ 6. *Get feedback and buy-in from the client at regular intervals.* Involve the users of the information, not just users of the system itself, in the selection process. This will not only ensure a stronger system but will also foster more cooperation during the implementation.
- ❑ 7. *Prepare a realistic budget.* Research should help you determine a reasonable budget. The budget should include software, new or upgraded hardware, consulting, training, maintenance, data conversion, customization, and support. Be prepared, also, for "invisible" expenses like custom forms, temporary help, software escrow fees, and overtime pay. An unrealistic budget sets the stage for disappointment and failure.
- ❑ 8. *Prepare reasonable target dates for selection and implementation.* Do not assume that, just because a software product runs on a PC, selection and implementation should be minimal. Ultimately, the time required will depend upon the availability, ability, and effort of you and your team.
- ❑ 9. *Consider adding another consultant to your team.* Using another resource can minimize disruption to your accounting business and provide important product knowledge and other project skills. Internal project team members each have a full-time job and may not have the skills, experience, or focus to be fully effective.
- ❑ 10. *Take responsibility.* Responsibility for a successful selection rests with you and your accounting software team. External

resources, regardless of the strength of their skills and product knowledge, cannot know your business the way you do.

KEEPING GOOD FAITH

Keeping in good standing with all current clients can be the difference between feast or famine. Happy clients can be worth many times the revenue that their single projects bring in; continually servicing those clients should earn many more future projects down the line. Adding new clients takes more than just word of mouth. Accountants have to constantly update their skills and products to keep up with the niche markets. Attending trade shows and enlisting current clients to help with the changes can ease the burden of staying up-to-date. Studying support call records and sending out client satisfaction surveys also should keep your products and services in line with the needs of the marketplace.

OVERCOMING HURDLES TO SELLING NEW TECHNOLOGY ACCOUNTING SOFTWARE

The mandate for professional accountants may very well be "acquire or expire." You cannot thrive or, for that matter, survive without taking on new technology in the accounting business. You must continue to take on new accounting software products, operating systems, computer hardware systems, and practice management technology. It is a matter of discerning what will work and what your clients will buy.

Whether they run a high-tech network practice or cozy niche clientele, it is easy for accountants to fall into the trap of complacently doing what they do best. It may appear that the work will just keep rolling in. Accountants who have been there caution against the slow, painful penalty such a short-term outlook brings. Too much time gets eaten up responding to low-profile matters. Although the projects may feel good, there is not much profit in them. Many accountants fall into the rut of doing a lot of single low-tech systems. There is not much initial profit in these commodity types of accounting systems, and the lack of complexity does not produce much follow-up implementation and consulting work.

Taking on new technologies is not easy, and it is not without risk. Some technologies are leading edge and low margin at the same time. These can be better termed *bleeding edge*. Herein lies the dilemma. If you do not invest, you risk becoming obsolete. If you do, you have to leverage already marginal business in order to keep up, without being sure of the payoff. In the final analysis, technology remains a double-edged sword for accounting professionals—creating great new opportunities, but also inflicting its share of pain. Technology is both increasing customer expectations and improving accountants' capabilities to meet those expectations.

The leading technology issues facing accountants in 1999, as determined in a survey conducted by The Accounting Guild, are reported in Exhibit 7.3.

EXHIBIT 7.3
Top Technology Issues

- Increases client expectations
- Expands professional account capabilities
- Speeds services delivery
- Reduces time to think, evaluate, and analyze
- Undermines value of information
- Places premium on value of knowledge and wisdom
- The complex must be simplified for clients
- Knowledge avalanche threatens to crush accountants and consultants
- Internet equalizes Big 5, sole practitioners
- Never out of touch with the office
- Never "off duty"
- New security, privacy, and confidentiality concerns

Source: The Accounting Guild

The technology related hurdles facing the accountant are enumerated in checklist fashion in Exhibit 7.4.

EXHIBIT 7.4
Checklist: Technology Hurdles

❑ 1. **Cost** is the number one obstacle to investing in new technologies and selling them to clients. There are soft costs and hard costs. Soft costs include lost productivity, marketing campaigns, and lost opportunities to get engagements in existing markets. Other soft costs are training and travel fees, overtime for staff covering for those in training, market research, training marketing people, and developing or acquiring the software required to integrate the technology with existing systems. Accountants should strive to acquire and implement, not acquire and invent. Hard costs are typically more visible, but no less expensive. They include the purchase of new equipment and software required to adequately evaluate and deploy a new technology. There are also costs associated with finding out that the costs are going to be too high. Before reaching the point of no return the accountant may realize that the firm would not be able to support the technology.

Several techniques can be used to overcome the cost hurdle. Surveying clients and calculating the return on investment are good safeguards. Most professional accountants make sure there is enough interest among existing clients, then look to the new technology to expand that market. The timetable for recouping such investments varies from six to 18 months. One way of managing cost is to know what income stream to measure against it. Do not calculate profit margins on specific components, such as the hardware or software package. Your profit comes on service. Deliver all the services to clients that they will ever need. While the goal is to make a profit, that profit comes because successful implementations bring continuing business from those clients. You have to offer value not generally available in-house or down the street. You have to offer service. Clients may value those services more if they are not bundled on estimates and invoices with hardware.

❑ 2. **Clients' lack of understanding of technology** leads the professional accountant to take on only those technologies offering a clear business benefit to clients. The client does not have to understand the technology, but they must understand the problem the technology can resolve. Another way to overcome client resistance is to leverage the built-in acceptance of the professional accountant's expertise. The clients will buy because they believe it will help their businesses.

❑ 3. **Lack of standards** is a major obstacle to investing in and selling new technology. Low reliability of new technologies is cited by many accountants and consultants as a major pitfall. Every plan has to consider the unexpected.

Accounting software deployment is always different from what you thought it would be. A good rule of thumb is to calculate the time a project should take and multiply it by a factor of two or three, depending on how many unknowns you think you might encounter during the project. Overestimating the time required for a project greatly increases your chance of encountering pleasant, as opposed to unpleasant, surprises.

❑ 4. **Lack of information** is difficult to overcome and discourages many accountants from investing in new technology. It seems they are so busy creating new technology that no one has time to write the manuals anymore. Reading, attending trade shows, talking with others, and technology reports and manuals from The Accounting Guild keep professional accountants and consultants cognizant of new technologies in general. The best reason to focus your attention on a technology is that your clients want it. It is easy to get caught up in the hype of a new technology, but do not mistake excitement for opportunity. There are no sure formulas for success. Even with the best research, choosing which new technologies to go with is still very much by gut feeling.

Exhibit 7.5 provides a checklist for successfully using and selling new technology in your accounting business.

EXHIBIT 7.5
Checklist: Selling New Technology

❑ *Consider new technology a plum.* Be aware that new technologies keep technicians interested and current. If a new technology demands the addition of staff, train new hires on the existing services and let current staff take on the new services. At the same time, do not go too far afield of a staff member's area of expertise.

❑ *Pick the right vendors.* Make certain you are selecting not only appropriate technologies, but vendors with whom you will be happy working. This is a particular concern when you will be relying on the vendor for a great deal of support. Also, be alert for vendors that overdistribute or have overly ambitious sales expectations. A significant number of professional accountants and consultants surveyed named vendor distribution policies as an impediment to technology investment. They reported that this greatly affected their ability to sell new technology.

- ❑ *Make sure it really interests you.* Some accountants have related that they went against their better judgment when they took on what a particular important client requested. The product may be fine, but if you are not really interested in doing more things with the technology, you will not make much money on it.
- ❑ *Look to vendors and reliable resources for market research.* If you cannot get good research, that is a sign that you should not work with that vendor. Networking with clients and industry contacts, such as The Accounting Guild, can help you gauge the technology's acceptance.
- ❑ *Do not take on what you do not have time to service properly.* If there is no room in your accounting business for a new technology, leave it alone. If you are already overwhelmed, taking on a new technology will only make matters worse.
- ❑ *Figure out how you will recoup your investment.* The marketplace is not always willing to pay for your investment in new technology. If you cannot explain to yourself how you are going to make money with a new technology, you will not.
- ❑ *Plan finances carefully.* Budget to spend some money researching where to spend more money—or, just as important, where not to spend any more.
- ❑ *Ride the wave.* One sure way to avoid having money swept away by a new technology is to set up 90- and 180-day checkpoints. If your plans for the new technology appear to be losing momentum, it is time to critically reevaluate your commitment.
- ❑ *Be patient.* If a technology is brand new, wait. Worthwhile technologies do not go away that quickly, and they need time to have the bugs worked out and to catch fire in the marketplace. Timing, as they say, is everything.

The implementation stage of installing a computerized accounting system is the most critical step in the entire process. A checklist to assist the accountant in meeting the client's needs and expectations is offered in Exhibit 7.6.

EXHIBIT 7.6
Checklist: Successful Accounting Software Implementation

- ❑ 1. *Due diligence.* Ensure that the client's goals are understood and the accounting system being installed more than meets the client's needs and expectations.
- ❑ 2. *Implementation planning.* Identify all the steps in the software installation and create a realistic timeline for the project.
- ❑ 3. *Environment preparation.* Evaluate the computing environment, scrutinizing the existing hardware and software and the operating system components.
- ❑ 4. *Implementation and training.* Hold an entrance conference in which you address communication and training issues. Create detailed manuals of 80 to 100 pages, customizing each step for the client. Implement the system. At an exit conference, review the success of the implementation and address any outstanding issues.
- ❑ 5. *Ongoing support.* Give short- and long-term support. Review annually the client's setup, and address additional technology needs.

Source: The Accounting Guild

KEEPING CLIENTS SATISFIED

Have you ever thought about why you do business with the clients and vendors you do? In many cases, you probably commit to business relationships out of necessity. You need widget 123 and the Acme Company has it, so a deal is struck. The same may be true for your clients. But at some point, don't you evaluate each of your business relationships based on how you and your affairs are handled? If you are like the average customer, you do. You can be sure that your clients evaluate you on the basis of how you treat them.

You may already have noticed that client satisfaction is directly related to your firm's profitability. Think about it—dissatisfied clients do not stay dissatisfied for long. If you do not make earnest attempts to hear and resolve their problems, they will take their business to a competitor that will take better care of them.

When you see an accounting business with a high client turnover rate, you can be sure that client satisfaction is low and so are profits. Losing clients is expensive. When current clients leave, new clients have to be brought in. The process of soliciting prospective clients takes far more time and money than keeping existing clients satisfied.

Happy clients become long-term, loyal clients. That means if you have shown them the respect and attention they deserve, they will keep their business with you and refer others. Keeping your clients satisfied is no easy task. The unfortunate truth is you will not be able to please all your clients all the time. Your aim should be to try to please as many of them as you can, not because it is the noble thing to do, but because it is the smart thing to do.

The Accounting Guild prepared a checklist on a client's perception of whether you are a vendor or a consultant. The perception of being a consultant in the client's mind will go a long way in your quest to achieve your goal of building a successful business. The Accounting Guild's checklist is presented as Exhibit 7.7.

EXHIBIT 7.7
Are You a Vendor or a Consultant? (Client Perceptions)

Vendors

- ❑ Primary focus is selling
- ❑ Look out for their own needs
- ❑ Avoid difficult questions
- ❑ Minimize costs
- ❑ Are committed for the short term
- ❑ Lack integrity
- ❑ Are motivated to close the sale

Consultants

- ❑ Primary focus is to give valuable advice
- ❑ Look out for client's needs
- ❑ Raise difficult questions
- ❑ Identify total costs
- ❑ Are committed for the long term
- ❑ Demonstrate integrity
- ❑ Want a successful/satisfied client

Source: The Accounting Guild.

ACCOUNTING SOFTWARE VENDOR COMPENDIUM

Low-Cost Software

Best!Ware, Rockaway, NJ, (800) 851-1812, www.bestware.com

M.Y.O.B. (as in Mind Your Own Business) Accounting Plus is the third most popular off-the-shelf accounting software in the United States, behind Peachtree and Intuit. Intuit is far and away number one (four times the combined sales of all the other vendors).

To survive in this market, Best!Ware has developed partner programs specifically for professional accountants and consultants. Their vendor's certified consultant program trains and supports resellers who specialize in recommending, providing, and implementing single and multiuser accounting solutions.

Intuit, Inc., Mountain View, CA, (800) 446-8848

Intuit's QuickBooks Pro is designed for a small business that most likely has a nonaccountant at the keyboard. The "EasyStep Interview" is a great step-by-step setup utility. QuickBooks Pro is a very good product that offers important accounting functionality and proves that the price of the software does not dictate its usability.

With an 80 percent market share, little is left to other low-cost vendors. Intuit is the largest maker of personal finance software, has a product line that includes Quicken (personal finance), QuickBooks and QuickBooks Pro (small business), TurboTax for Business (corporate tax returns for PC users), MacInTax, (for Macintosh users), and Turbo Tax Pro Series (for tax professionals). In 1998, Intuit acquired Lacerte, a high-end tax software vendor with more than 30,000 professional user clients. Intuit sponsors the QuickBooks Professional Advisors Program, which offers professional accountants and consultants a one-year membership for $199. The membership includes the latest version of QuickBooks Pro for Windows, a dedicated toll-free technical support number, client referrals from the Web, customer list rentals, discounts on Intuit products, and free QuickBooks trial versions for clients.

Working in the low-cost segment with Intuit or the other low-cost vendors has low-income potential. The only way to make money with these products is to provide training and consultation. The user of low-cost accounting software will be loath to pay consulting fees of $125 to $175 an hour for a product that cost less than $100 and was purchased primarily to avoid retaining a professional accountant.

When Willie Sutton, a notorious bank robber in the 1950s was asked why he robbed banks, Willie replied, "Because that's where the money is." By no means is the robbery analogy to be projected onto accounting software, but the low-cost market is *not* where the money is.

Peachtree Software, Inc., Norcross, GA, (800) 228-0068, www.peachtree.com

Peachtree Software Inc., which was sold to Sage Software in 1999, is a leading developer of low-cost accounting software. In an attempt to boost the quality and sales of its Peachtree Office Accounting package, Peachtree introduced a new developer program centered around the product. The developer program gives developers and professional accountants and consultants the opportunity to customize and extend a $99 product that is a high-volume seller.

Peachtree Office Accounting is an easy accounting software package that integrates with Microsoft Office. As with all Peachtree products, it is aimed at the very small business and single-owner, home-office market. A major asset for Sage is Peachtree's one million plus registered users and the potential to blend its product line with Sage Software. Another possibility is that Peachtree could learn about developing a reseller channel from Sage. For the most part, the Peachtree Partner program offers the professional accountant and consultant little more than a discount price on the suite of Peachtree products.

Mid-Range Software

AccountMate Software Corp., Mill Valley, CA, (800) 877-8896, www.accountmate.com

AccountMate provides Visual AccountMate SQL/Database Limited accounting software. The product serves up to 16 users and was developed in response to reseller support for the SQL Server platform and user interest in a more affordable option. It is modeled after its enterprise version. Accountants can make money from consulting on selling and customizing the modules in SQL/DBL. Professional accountants and consultants find that it gives small business clients the power of SQL Server and complete integration with Microsoft BackOffice.

Accpac International, Santa Clara, CA, (800) 773-5445, www.accpac.com

Accpac International is a spin-off of its parent company, Computer Associates International. It often introduces reseller and qualified installer programs for its Accpac for Windows and Accpac Plus accounting software lines. A recurring theme in the programs is multilevel tiers with different levels of training and technical support.

Personal experience with the programs demonstrated the lack of follow-through and a constant revolving door of Accpac personnel. To be fair, that experience was during the time that Accpac was a product line of Computer Associates. The programs may now be operating at a much higher professional level.

Best Software, Reston, VA, (800) 368-2405

Best Software has a specialized line of accounting software limited to payroll, fixed assets, and human resources solutions for accountants to sell to clients. The company offers several levels of participation: Partners can resell Best's Human Resource Information Systems (HRIS), which includes its Abra payroll, human resources, and recruiting products, and its Fixed Asset System (FAS) line of depreciation and fixed asset management software. They can also become consultants and qualified installers for both HRIS and FAS, and referral partners for FAS only.

Both Best and its Business Partners generate sales leads through marketing activities. Best spends upwards of $1 million annually generating leads. It employs several marketing representatives who call prospects to make sure they are genuinely interested in having a Business Partner contact them. The company uses an automated contact management system to match leads with the appropriate Business Partners, based on the reseller's geographic territory, specialty, and qualifications. Best also tracks whether a reseller has followed up a lead and the outcome and requires each reseller to provide feedback and forecasts.

As an alternative to becoming a reseller, Best offers accountants a referral program that allows the accountant to get a discount for clients when recommending Best products and to attain preferred pricing for in-house use. Some of Best's resellers often earn money when selling the software in combination with other vendors' software. Several accounting software vendors, such as Platinum, Sage, and Solomon integrate their systems with Best's.

Cyma Systems, Inc., Tempe, AZ, (800) 292-2962, www.cyma-systems.com

Cyma seems to suffer from an identity crisis. Several years ago the vendor dropped its per module price by more than 60 percent. It claimed that the effort was intended to eliminate any price barrier. That is something akin to stating that scuba divers would no longer require oxygen tanks since that could remove the barrier that someone might have about being incapable of breathing underwater without air.

The vendor has several reseller programs and says that the profit is generated on services: training, consulting, and support. That supports the findings that the consulting revenue stream is the charm in the business. The money is in the services.

Great Plains Software, Fargo, ND, (800) 456-0025, www.greatplains.com

Great Plains is a public company and is one of the fastest growing and most profitable company in its class. From a philosophical point of view, Great Plains sees accountants and consultants as an integral part of its distribution strategy and the right fit for its market. Great Plains spends about 35 percent of its total revenue on sales and marketing. A fundamental belief of the company is that a partner channel that includes accountants and consultants is no less expensive than direct sales forces. It believes that the partners, the accountants, consultants, and VARs have to have a profitable business model or they cannot reinvest in the training, the knowledge, and the skills they need to keep up with all the technology changes that the vendors are throwing at them.

A recent development is the Certified Account Executive program, which is an effort to increase reseller support. Getting a Certified Account Executive designation requires several steps; the most onerous is the eligibility restriction requiring the reseller to limit sales exclusively to Great Plains' products. A firm may resell software from other vendors, but the candidate may not. Next, the candidate must attend two one-week sales training sessions. The two-week tuition is $3,500. The candidate must attend three Great Plains' internal sales meetings a year. Each meeting lasts from two to four days. Finally, the candidate must attend the annual conference as well as a business-building conference held each winter.

Macola, Marion, OH, (800) 468-0834, www.macola.com

Macola is a major accounting software vendor and certainly worth a close look. The company espouses consultive selling and has a strong professional accountant and consultant reseller base. It is innovative, and its "Business Partner Implementation Guidebook" is an excellent partner resource.

Navision Software U.S., Inc., Norcross, GA, (800) 552-8478, www.navision-us.com

This Denmark-headquartered vendor has been making major inroads in the United States by marketing Navision Financials system as a versatile package that can be well suited for the middle market. Its United States efforts, conducted by affiliate Navision Software U.S., Inc., in Norcross, Georgia, features a channel strategy that emphasizes accounting industry expertise among its resellers. The company typically recruits resellers who are technologically savvy, have CPAs on staff, and the capacity for lead generation in the middle market. Their success depends equally on the software and the service from their resellers. Navision resellers agree that the vendor sets high standards. They are selective in choosing resellers and insist that the accountant or VAR have a good technical staff, be capable of making a commitment to extensive training, and give up a percentage of revenues.

Navision Financials is an integrated, customizable, 32-bit, multiuser accounting and business management software. Based on NT client–server architecture, it is Microsoft-certified and has a UNIX version. C/SIDE, its relational database manager, is designed for high-volume transaction processing. It also features built-in OLAP tools allowing for data analysis, which can be interfaced with other multidimensional databases.

RealWorld, Manchester, NH, (800) 678-6336, www.realworld.com

The company is again repositioning its accounting software. The line features RealWorld Expertise.SQL and RealWorld Enterprise. ENT software. RealWorld Classic Accounting is a character-based accounting software.

RealWorld had been a pioneer in DOS-based accounting software and was very late in adapting to Windows. The vendor remains a "stealth" player in the marketplace.

Red Wing Business Systems, Red Wing, MN, (800) 732-9464, www.redwingsoftware.com

Red Wing has approximately 275 resellers and is working at building a national awareness of the company's accounting software. Its focus is on professional accountants and consultants. Its programs have been favorably reviewed, although it has some drawbacks, such as reports that are not customizable and the lack of user-defined fields. Many of the reports do offer several sorting options that help view the data from several different perspectives, such as sorting and subtotaling by salesperson instead of by customer.

The major drawback for the professional accountant and consultant evaluating Red Wing as an accounting systems vendor/partner is the relative anonymity of the company.

Sage Software, Irvine, CA, (800) 854-3415, www.sage.com

Sage Software is the new name of State of the Art Software following its purchase by the United Kingdom–based Sage Group. The vendor will continue to market its Acuity, MAS 90, and BusinessWorks accounting software.

Sage has initiated a communications and training program designed to help resellers enhance their overall business operations rather than just helping them sell more products. This noble effort, named "Strategic Advantage," relies extensively on Internet-based communications to provide reseller access to information used directly in product sales. Also, assistance in business operations including marketing and practice building are given.

This vendor's new approach coincides with the current intense competition among vendors for high-quality resellers. The competition is most evident in the middle market, where some high-end vendors are trying to recruit professional accountants and consultants, and established players are trying to guard against the encroachment. The marketplace is consolidating, and the stronger vendors are taking advantage of their positions by expanding their links to partners.

SBT Accounting Systems, Sausalito, CA, (415) 331-9900, www.sbt.com

SBT is a developer of modifiable database accounting systems with several suites of accounting software. Its software features seamless integration into the database requirements of firms in the $5 million to $200 million range.

Solomon Software, Findlay, OH, (419) 424-0422, www.solomon.com

Solomon Software has enjoyed phenomenal growth in recent years. Their market share is expected to expand even further with the release of a new version of Solomon IV. The new version is said to be a more robust, sophisticated solution with the most advanced technology available for client–server software. Built on Microsoft's Back Office and the SQL database platforms, the software will give users access to powerful financial and management suites that were once available only to larger enterprises.

Usually, Solomon IV, right out of the box, will meet 70 to 80 percent of a given business's needs. That other 20 to 30 percent, however, is the part that makes the package so valuable to users and such a generator of revenues for accountants. The software was created with a flexibility that allows it to be tailored to the needs of a specific client. This enables Solomon IV to provide a nearly 100 percent solution. The main reason that medium-sized clients opt for customized client–server software is the add-ons that accountants create to help clients manage businesses better.

Solomon has been a true marketing innovator when it introduced "boot camps" to maximize the efficiency and capability of its accounting software resellers and consultants. The training program teaches resellers what they need to know to keep up with not only technology but the growth they can expect once they begin marketing the product. They learn how to select prospective clients and redirect those they cannot help. Training is offered in transitioning into project management and how to manage their own business and deal with growth.

High-End Software

The firms engaged in consulting and reselling enterprise-class software systems are large integrators and Big 25–type accounting firms. The systems for large enterprises are priced in the millions of dollars and require several years for specification, installation, implementation, consulting, and training.

The top ten enterprise application vendors, as ranked by The Accounting Guild according to enterprise specific software sales in 1998, are shown below in Exhibit 7.8.

EXHIBIT 7.8
Top 10 Enterprise Application Vendors

1. SAP AG, www.sap.com/usa
2. PeopleSoft, www.peoplesoft.com
3. Oracle, www.oracle.com

4. Computer Associates, www.cai.com
5. Baan, www.baan.com
6. J.D. Edwards, www.jdedwards.com
7. System Software Associates, www.ssax.com
8. Geac, www.smartenterprise.geac.com
9. IBM, www.ibm.com
10. JBA, www.jbaworld.com

Source: The Accounting Group

8

DEVELOPING THE MARKETING PLAN

WHAT IS MARKETING, ANYWAY?

For many accountants, "marketing" has uncomfortable and unprofessional connotations. It conjures up stereotypes of high-pressure time-share salespeople and annoying mealtime telephone solicitations. Those are merely annoying *sales* techniques. Real marketing is the art of making your existing and prospective clients aware of what *you* can do to serve their needs.

Marketing encompasses selling. Think of marketing as every activity that is performed to induce prospective clients to inquire about the services of your firm or respond to the overtures designed to induce a discussion of your products and services. **Selling** is everything done thereafter to persuade a specific client or prospective client to take advantage of your products and services.

There are several distinct aspects of marketing and selling: **strategic positioning, pricing, advertising, handling inquiries, qualifying prospects, dealing with objections,** and **closing sales.** We will devote special attention to the post-sale aspects of an accounting business, such as training, installation, and ongoing support, because they are so important to your marketing efforts. Many accountants practice some or most of these marketing techniques intuitively with some success. By consciously knowing, planning, and practicing them, you will find that you can dramatically improve your success rate.

MARKETING PROGRAM

The marketing program is crucial to establishing a successful accounting business. If the ability to gain a clientele is lacking, the rest is futile. An accountant is not required or expected to be a seasoned salesperson but must be sufficiently knowledgeable in accountancy and general business services to introduce that accounting firm as one offering a unique set of services. Ted Bates, a legendary advertising genius, first introduced the concept of the **unique selling proposition** (USP). The accounting firm must establish its own unique selling proposition. Nothing can be left to chance. The accountants who follow this unique selling proposition cannot help but succeed. When presented expertly, the concept works. It has been tested on small to medium-sized businesses and has succeeded.

The concepts and techniques of marketing give you direction in developing services that are in demand as well as methods of pricing and promoting those services. Neither technical competency nor a CPA certificate is automatically rewarded by a retinue of clients. The world does not beat a path to the door of the person with the "better mousetrap." The marketplace needs to be informed and persuaded before making most purchasing decisions.

Development from a Marketing Standpoint

- What services should and can be offered?
- Who needs these services?
- Who should perform the services?
- When, where, and how should the services be offered and performed? At what price?
- How can the value and availability of these services be communicated to those who need them?

The development of your marketing professionalism is an evolving process. The following pointers will go a long way toward your professional maturation.

Developing Marketing Professionalism

1. **Be dependable.** Always do what you say you will.
2. **Stay motivated.** Keep moving toward your goals.
3. **Be technologically competent.** Keep up with what is new to maintain productivity and stay current.
4. **Be honest.** No sale is worth risking your reputation.
5. **Be diplomatic.** Form long-term relationships with your clients.

MARKETING PROGRAM

Function of Marketing

Marketing's major function is to present the accounting firm's range of services in a manner that will enable clients to recognize their value. Value recognition comes when clients appreciate the benefits that result from the services. Clients do not hire accountants; they hire the accountant's ability to increase cash flow, reduce inventory costs, secure financing, decrease or defer taxes, and construct statements. The client's basic motivation is to make money, reduce operating costs, or satisfy a legal or social obligation. Clients may not be the best judge of technical competency, but they do recognize the person who can solve their organization's problems.

Systematic Marketing Approach

Indeed, clients have a number of problems to be solved and a variety of benefits to be sought that offer unending opportunities for the aspiring accountant. To realize fully this opportunity, the accountant must use a systematic marketing approach. This involves each staff member. A thorough analysis must be made of the services the firm can offer and deliver at a sufficient profit. The analysis answers several questions that bear on marketing planning and strategy:

- What are the capabilities that define the charter of the firm and set it apart from other firms? (What is the firm's unique selling proposition?)
- Who are the firm's target clients?
- How are these clients being served presently, and how can the services be improved?

These questions create an equation that requires simultaneous solution, for an answer to one question interrelates with those of the other. For example, the means by which clients may be better served defines the firm's future identity.

The challenge lies in exploring, identifying, and defining the many ways in which accounting and related services can be utilized. The depth of a firm's services is defined by matching its resources with the potential recognized in its niche markets. A smaller firm chooses a segment it can serve well and for which it can create a productive program. A larger firm may serve several market segments and perhaps tailor a different marketing program for each. For the smaller or larger firms, marketing programs must include appropriate personnel reward systems to encourage them to attract and serve their target markets.

Once it has been decided which prospective clients should be approached and which services are appropriate for them, a marketing program can be planned. A marketing program consists of developing promotion and pricing elements to match the services to be offered. The effort expended in implementing it determines the effectiveness with which the firm will achieve its objectives. These objectives, among other things, state the dollar revenue figure sought, how many and what profit target is desired. There are major differences in which elements of a marketing program are to be emphasized. These depend on the particular attributes of the accounting firm. For example, the burden placed on advertising to create awareness and provide information may vary from none at all to a substantial amount.

Promotion

Promotion is an essential component of the marketing program. It communicates with prospective clients to inform, persuade, and remind them of the benefits of doing business with your firm. Promotion can increase a firm's practice with marketing tools such as direct mail, publicity, and advertising.

Personal selling is an essential part of the marketing program, although not technically grouped in the promotion category. Accounting and related services must be sold personally by accounting or marketing professionals skilled in conveying the benefits of accounting and related services. Recently, accountants have taken to marketing services on the Internet with some success. Some resellers of accounting software have used the Internet to sell software programs at discounted prices, albeit without installation and support services. Upon learning of the Internet sales without support, the software publishers de-authorized the offending resellers. Perhaps there will come a time when interactive selling will replace or augment personal selling, but that time has not yet arrived.

Successful selling begins when the opportunity is found to translate a firm's capabilities into client benefits. The professional must be positioned in appropriate situations to initiate sales. This **"face time"** is the amount of time the accounting or marketing professional spends in face-to-face meetings with clients or prospective clients. Its importance becomes clear when the professional realizes that the firm prospers when incremental business is brought in, which occurs when the professional educates and inspires clients to take action. That happens because of their sales calls. Less face time equates to fewer opportunities for this to happen. Face time is an important measure of the marketing people's effectiveness.

Prospective clients rarely purchase accounting services on impulse. The purchase of accounting and related services is not an act but a process, a "creeping commitment" that occurs over a period of time. A bold attempt to close the sale at the beginning of a relationship usually does more harm than good. Some clients may be obtained in this manner, but those can subsequently be lost just as quickly. It is important to note that selling does not cease when a commitment has been made. Incremental business from existing clients is a major source of growth in services and revenues.

Publicity

Publicity is a nonpaid form of communication that can have a significant impact on maintaining "word-of-mouth" recognition. Even though the sponsor does not pay for publicity (the article in the publication or spot on television or radio is written and accepted for its newsworthiness), time and effort are required to prepare press releases, write articles, and make speeches. Because of the time involved, you should direct these activities at selected audiences. It is important to remember that you should transmit information to persons in one's own profession and community as well as to target prospective clients.

Advertising

Advertising delivers a message to a large number of people. It also gives visibility through selected media and can increase the client awareness of an accounting firm. To some degree, these clients may be presold by an effective advertising campaign. Advertising can also transmit a firm's image to a preselected audience of readers, viewers, and listeners.

It is vital to identify target clients clearly so that the firm can plan and implement each aspect of the promotional program. A promotional program is a mode of communication. Accountants must be mindful of professional ethics and customs, because they are held to a higher standard, when communicating to clients and prospective clients.

UNDERSTANDING WHY ACCOUNTING SERVICES ARE PURCHASED

Clients and prospective clients are not usually "accounting experts" and must be fitted with a pair of "spectacles" that will assist them to see and ascertain value. Basically, clients buy benefits, not features. Clients do not automatically recognize that the benefits received are greater than the fees paid. They should be educated and guided by the establishment of a climate of trust. Unfortunately, some attempts to educate clients are limited because clients normally have little time to devote to purchasing decisions and the subsequent use of the accounting products and services. This is true whether it is related to the acquisition of a new computer system or the engagement of an accounting firm.

Therefore, the client's decision to engage an accounting firm or to expand the use of a firm's services depends largely on faith in the professional accountant's ability to supply solutions to the client's problems. This faith derives from the reputation of the firm and from a rapport developed in areas of mutual understanding and interest, such as golf, the stock market, or charitable endeavors. It is important that the professional be mindful that civic, recreational, and other activities make a significant contribution to the firm's marketing program. A client who is given the opportunity to establish a relationship with a professional can sense much more than is made apparent about the professional's ability.

With this understanding, the accountant has most of the basic knowledge to sell. There is another concept that the accountant must grasp to forge and manage a partnership with a client. That concept is that benefits are linked to a deeper reason to buy: *needs*. Needs drive the specific benefits sought by the buyer. The accountant satisfies these needs with services. In many cases, especially with small to medium-sized businesses, the business needs and the personal needs of the owner are intertwined. Furthermore, the accountant must look at needs through the clients' eyes.

There are certain key words that prospective clients and current clients use when they are expressing a need. The astute accountant will quickly pick up these words and begin to address those needs. Whenever a client says something like the following, he or she is expressing a need:

- "I wish I could figure out how to . . ."
- "What we need now is . . ."

- "For the last six months, I have been looking for . . ."
- "I want to improve my cash flow, but I don't know how."

Business Needs

When we think of satisfying needs, we probably think first of business needs: audited financial statements, business plans, budgets, financing, strategic planning, profit improvement studies, systems reviews, and so on. These are all important, but even in the larger enterprises, there is some personal need behind the business need. When working with the owner–manager, that personal need often cannot be separated from the business need.

Personal Needs

Accountants must always be aware that they are dealing with people whose perception of their business needs is based on their personal needs. These needs have a basis in both their fundamental personality type and in their professional status as members of a business organization. Even though they are buying something for the business, as an individual they have a personal stake in the purchase and its outcome. We have all heard someone say, for example, that the client's ego was involved in selecting a prestigious firm to audit the company. Such a statement reveals that the buyer is satisfying a personal need. In addition to wanting a competent audit, the client may feel it fits his or her image as an executive to be associated with a prestigious firm. It is simply impossible to make a business decision without one's personal needs coming into play.

For today's business decision maker, *survival* is often the name of the game. As the pressures of competition and downsizing become universal, many decisions will be driven by the need to get the lowest price. That decision can make the difference between profit and loss. The need not to make a costly mistake with severe professional or business consequences may drive other decisions.

When Alice in Wonderland asked the Cheshire Cat which road to take, he asked Alice where she was going. Alice replied that she really didn't know, which prompted the Mad Hatter to reply that if you don't know where you're going, it doesn't matter which road you take. A good part of knowing where one is going is the goal-setting process. Part of being successful in the accounting business is having a clear vision of what you want to accomplish. The other part is the constant reinforcement of positive statements, such as the following that one is a successful and worthwhile individual:

- **"I am a successful partner in a quality CPA firm that helps its clients become more successful."**
- **"I enjoy showing others in my firm how to bring in new business."**
- **"I am proud of the new business I can bring into my firm."**

A quiz is presented in Exhibit 8.1 to assist you in a self-assessment of your goal-setting status.

EXHIBIT 8.1
Goal-Setting Self-Assessment Quiz

1. I know the number of new clients, their initial billings, and any additional business from current clients on a weekly basis. **True or False?**
2. All of the professional staff in my firm have individual, written business development plans that include new business goals. **True or False?**
3. All of our professionals complete an annual, written goal-setting plan. **True or False?**
4. The professional staff of our firm meets on a monthly basis to review our marketing and selling success and activity. **True or False?**

(Answers: You should have answered each question "true.")

MARKETING EFFORT

Your marketing program delineates how much marketing effort you must exert to convert identified opportunities into clients and achieve the firm's revenue objectives. Marketing planning enables a firm to design a program that, when effectively implemented, will minimize wasted effort and project a consistent image. For example, it will orchestrate personal selling to avoid unnecessary duplication. It will plan advertising and publicity to convey messages in a manner that does not create conflicting impressions. If accounting services can be sold only by professionals, the use of those professionals' time for selling is a resource that requires planning.

Once a marketing program has been set in motion, the firm has more control over its destiny in terms of growth and the nature of the business. The development and maintenance of an accounting business by implementing a marketing program, allows the firm to take a proactive initiative rather than merely reacting to whatever business happens to come through the door.

Setting and achieving effective and measurable goals for both firm and individual marketing will be a major determinant of the firm's success. It is important to consistently maintain a client orientation. Marketing is a philosophy of business that holds that the underlying purpose of any firm is to deliver client benefits and develop client satisfaction and loyalty. These must be created while also meeting the objectives of the firm. The key to good marketing and quality management is to remain focused on client needs throughout the relationship. This concept establishes a point of reference that, by education, persuasion, and reorientation, permeates the thinking of each partner, associate, and staff person in the firm.

Exhibit 8.2 presents an aid to assist your evaluation of business related goals. SMART is derived from using the first letter of each goal criteria.

EXHIBIT 8.2
SMART Goals

1. *Specific.* The goal is targeted and has an understandable and clearly defined objective.
2. *Measurable.* The goal has a specific deadline, and results can be quantified.
3. *Attainable.* Confined to events and forces that are within you or your firm. You must have or be able to get the resources to achieve the goal.
4. *Realistic.* Recognizes and accounts for the aspects that are outside of you and your firm. Within your environment, make certain that you can accomplish that goal. There are no known external forces that will stop you or your firm.
5. *Tangible.* The goal can be easily visualized by the person who is to accomplish it. If you cannot visualize it or dream it, you surely will not be able to accomplish it.

OBJECTIVES

Your short-term efforts to persuade clients to use existing and additional services should not obscure the long-range objective of identifying and creating new services to satisfy and serve tomorrow's clients. Marketing encourages strategic thinking. Like the tournament chess player who makes room for the move instead of moving where there is room, the professional makes room for the strategic moves. A future-oriented strategy requires planning for tomorrow's clients, recognition of the future impact of present decisions, and anticipation of change.

Your emphasis is on marketing, not selling. It is a healthier emphasis for all concerned, because marketing's focus is on the client's needs, whereas selling's focus is on the provider's needs. Moreover, an overemphasis on volume and growth can eventually lower quality and long-term profitability. A sales-oriented strategy would start with an evaluation of existing services and determine the volume necessary to achieve predetermined income results. The emphasis, more properly, should not be on today's revenue but on long-term profitability. A marketing-oriented approach is initiated by examining current and prospective clients in relation to their needs; it plans the services to be offered and the effort required to meet these needs and generate revenue by delivering client satisfaction. It is not marketing that is placed at the firm's core. It is not a winner versus loser situation for the firm and its clients. The clients receive more value from services rendered than fees paid, and the professional receives more in fees than it cost to provide them.

The question becomes "How do we apply this concept to developing smart marketing goals?" Exhibit 8.3 illustrates the SMART process.

EXHIBIT 8.3
SMART Illustration

Let's assume that your firm is planning to target small to medium-sized businesses that need consulting expertise to establish enterprise-wide budgetary processes. You might define a smart goal as the following: From now until December 31, 20XX, we want to develop $350,000 in new business from providing budgetary processes services. Unfortunately, this statement is far from developing a true smart goal.

To develop a smart goal—an ultimately effective goal—you must ask the following questions:

- How many new clients will it take to reach the $350,000 goal?
- Do we have a target for realization of or profitability in achieving that goal?

- Will this volume goal come from new clients or expansion of service to existing clients?
- Will we allocate the necessary resources to achieve this goal and budget the appropriate marketing time and dollars toward advertising, promotion, practice development, and so on?
- Do we possess the necessary talent, whether it be in the form of technical or marketing abilities, to either create the lead or participate in closing the sale?

ACTION PLAN

At this point, the real work is only beginning. We call this the **action plan**. If we know that we need $350,000 of business and that the average client fee for budgeting work is $14,000, this tells us that we need 25 clients. It takes 10 proposals for every new client landed. So, to obtain 25 clients, we need to get in front of 250 prospective clients. How do you get to see 250 qualified prospects? By appointment. Appointments are scheduled by telephone. But 250 calls will not get you 250 appointments.

Response rates range from as low as 1 percent to as much as 10 percent. Let's use a conservative response rate of 2 percent, which means that 12,500 contacts will be necessary in order to schedule 250 qualified appointments.

We have now reached an interesting and somewhat controversial point in the process. At this juncture, there are two options. The first is to develop a telemarketing program that is supported by a direct mail campaign. The second choice is to forgo direct mail.

In marketing professional accounting services, there are no direct mail campaigns. What you have is a telemarketing program, which may or may not be supported by a mailing piece that precedes the telemarketing call. Either way works effectively. But direct mail without phone calls is like a lonely voice in the wilderness, not to mention a complete waste of money.

Now is the time to choose your firm's message and, of course, the list. This is an important moment because this is what niche marketing is all about—setting your sights on the targets by choosing the list and then designing the collateral materials (specialized brochures, newsletters, etc.).

Your goal at this point is to choose a combined mail piece and telemarketing approach that will produce a high lead-generation ratio for the widest possible target audience. This will lower the net cost of new client acquisition as well as accelerate the pace of incoming clients.

Pause and think for a moment: 12,500 mail pieces, telemarketing fees (use an outside firm, it is more efficient), list codes, administrative costs. When the rubber meets the road, what about the time to go out and meet with 250 people?

Marketing is expensive. It costs money to make money. Many people still carry a hope of wanting to get something for nothing. Accountants too often ask, "What should we expect from our marketing program? How will this dollar investment translate into increased revenue?" Although these questions seem appropriate, they are the wrong ones when it comes to marketing. The job of an accounting firm's marketing program is not to increase revenues. The goal of marketing is to create an environment in which the client appreciates the benefits of doing business with your firm and in which your firm discovers how it can contribute to the client's success. The sale will follow.

MARKETING PROGRAM GOALS

Here are eight tangible, measurable goals your marketing program should achieve:

1. *Clearly differentiate your firm from its competition.* From the client's viewpoint, there is often no way to pinpoint why it is beneficial to do business with one accounting firm rather than another. If this happens, the final decision will, more often than not, be based on price—and price alone.

   In far too many instances, accounting firms steal ideas from each other when it comes to their marketing efforts. Many of the brochures look alike, with the same illustrations, the same words, the same cover designs and often done by the same suppliers. How many times have you heard someone say, "In our industry, this is how it's done"? Maybe it is, but looking like everyone else can be a killer today.
2. *Create a continuing flow of quality leads.* Accountants tend to focus on how marketing will increase sales. In reality, the proper test is to measure the number of appropriate leads—both currently and over an extended period of time. Although it may seem obvious, it is necessary to remind ourselves that leads *precede* sales. If the marketing professionals are busy following up on qualified leads, sales will naturally increase. However, if the accountants must spend their time trying to get through doors and locate prospective clients, then their time will be used prospecting—and not making sales.

3. *Keep the firm in the minds of clients and prospective clients.* Although we want to think that even our best customers think of us first, they may be considering buying products or services from others, even if we can handle the engagement. A key role of marketing is to stay in the client's mind at all times. Developing programs that reinforce awareness is an essential element of good marketing.

4. *Give your firm a stronghold in the marketplace.* Too many firms hold the view that "doing a good job" is all that is necessary to get business. If this is true, then why are so many incompetent, second-class competitors still getting business—and in some cases, taking business away from firms that can do better, more reliable work? Being recognized as a serious player and a leader in your field is essential to attracting clients today. To be perceived accurately by clients, you must make the effort to plan and foster a consistent image.

5. *Communicate your firm's expertise and knowledge.* Today, perhaps more than any other time, what should be communicated are your firm's capabilities. The best way to differentiate an accounting firm is through its level of knowledge. That is what sets you apart from everyone else in the field. You have to be able to say, "This is what I can do for you that no one else can."

6. *Give the firm a long-term orientation.* American business seems to be suffering from the fast-food syndrome. "The quicker the better" has become the dominant business philosophy. We think only in terms of a week, a month, a quarter—at the most, a year. We are so preoccupied by *today's* performance that we do not have time to implement strategies for making certain we have clients three, four, or five or more years from now. One of the functions of a marketing program is to keep our eyes focused on making certain we are in business for many, many years.

7. *Be client-oriented.* As a marketing services group, The Accounting Guild was recently asked to review and then comment on an accounting firm's brochure. The brochure was to be the centerpiece of the firm's marketing activities. In a report to the managing partner, the Guild pointed out that the brochure contained just three headings: *Our* goals. *Our* approach. *Our* experience. Could this brochure be used? Absolutely. In fact, it would make an effective orientation document

for new employees of that accounting firm. It tells the firm's story from its own viewpoint, but it fails to communicate the message that it understands its clients and *their* needs. A marketing brochure must direct attention to clients.

8. *Be a vital force in client retention.* Firms sometimes get so concerned about getting new clients that they tend to forget about maintaining and expanding existing business. It is a mistake to think marketing has to do only with picking the low-hanging fruit. It has just as much to do with caring for the fruit that has already been picked to make sure it does not spoil. Clients often leave when they feel ignored, insignificant or forgotten. The eyes of the professional accountant should always be on current clients in an effort to strengthen the relationship between them.

"I just want one new client per month with a monthly fee of $1,000!" exclaimed the frustrated accountant. "I don't want to get involved with all these marketing expenses. I just want the clients. When can I get them?"

There is no easy way of dealing with these frustrations. This accountant eventually gave up and purchased an expensive off-the-shelf law firm marketing package. (The accountant could not find an off-the-shelf accounting marketing package.) The last I heard, this accountant was spending an inordinate amount of time taking lawyers out to lunch, spending lots of money, and waiting for new referral clients to result from these activities.

You, as a more aggressive firm, might decide to go ahead. You already know the mechanics of list selection, designing a mail piece, and printing considerations. It should be fairly easy to map out a timetable, with contingencies, and accomplish this phase of a marketing program. But it would be suicide to drop all 12,500 pieces in the mail all at once. You cannot possibly call all of those people in a week. Start by determining the number of leads (appointments) per day that you would prefer to generate from the program. Let's assume that your firm employs two marketing professionals, each of whom can handle three appointments per day.

Campaign Results

Six appointments per day means mailing (and calling) approximately 300 listings daily. This translates into 15 to 20 dialing hours per day at 20 dials per hour. These figures will hold only for the first week or two of dialing. After a week and a half, you must decrease the mailings and dialing hours because the lead-ratio per dialing hour will increase as the telemarketing firm builds up an "inventory" of prospective clients that need to be called back at a later date.

The marketing professionals will need time to return and see some prospective clients on more than one occasion before they consent to see a partner of the firm. The office staff will need to block out time for the proposal and follow-up. All of this will affect the timing and pace of mailing and telemarketing efforts for your program, as the marketing professionals will have complex scheduling and coordination issues that require a great deal of attention. (The GoldMine contact management software program can be extremely useful for the entire staff.)

When will you get new clients? Studies have shown that the sales cycle is about 60 days, starting from the first phone call to landing the client. By the time you have acquired the first client, you should have a rather substantial investment in "prospect inventory," which will yield new clients on a fairly continuous basis throughout the year. (See Exhibit 8.4.)

EXHIBIT 8.4
To Get 25 New Clients, Call 12,500 Prospects

How It Works:

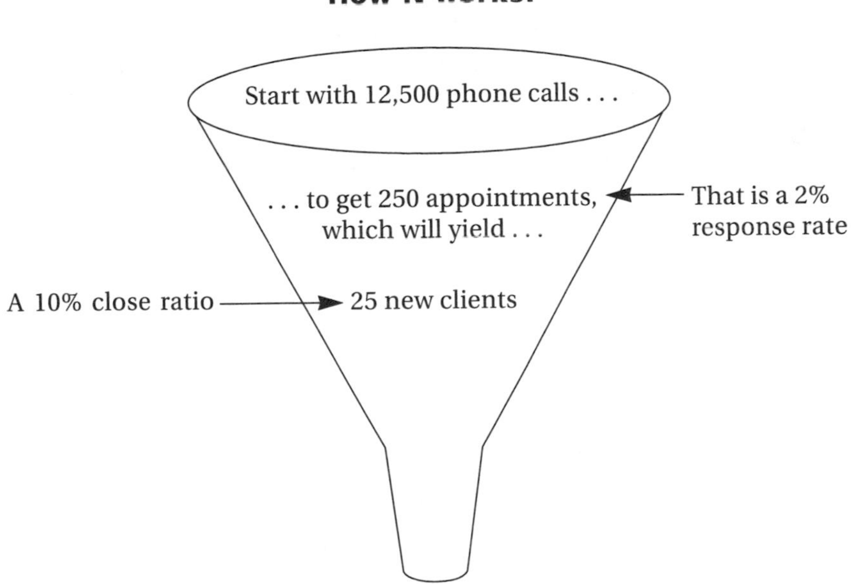

STRATEGIC POSITIONING

Strategic positioning refers to the long-term impression you hope to create in the minds of clients. For example, when you think of a Mercedes automobile or Cartier jewelry, you probably think to yourself "expensive, well-made, high-class, status" products. Such impressions are the result of carefully crafted, long-term positioning efforts by the manufacturers of those products. This book contains advice to assist you to position your firm, relative to the competition. Because pricing plays such an important role in your positioning efforts, it is discussed in detail in Chapter 16.

Without even consciously striving for a particular kind of positioning, you will create implicit positioning, that is, if the prospective client remembers you at all. What kind of impression would you like to make? Are you a "high-end" firm hoping to attract financially sophisticated clients? Or, are you hoping to expand your services among certain market niches? Are you the kind of firm that wants to project a progressive, high-tech image? Do you want to expand and capitalize on the high demand for accounting and financial software and related consulting?

Handling Inquiries

A critical factor contributing to the success of the marketing process is the way you handle the inquiries that result from your advertising and prospecting efforts. The probability for success will increase if this aspect is not left to chance. Client questionnaires, printed case studies, white papers, list of recommended computer configurations, and engagement letters are best prepared in advance. With those materials in hand, the professionals will conserve precious time by making sales efforts more efficient. The impression of an organized firm will be conveyed to the prospective clients, communicating an overall image of competence and experience.

Do not forget to instruct the telephone receptionist about where to route telephone inquiries. Few things cause clients to lose confidence quicker than the perception that your firm's right hand does not know what its left hand is doing. Make sure the person or persons designated to handle follow-up know their responsibilities in this regard.

Follow-up is a crucial component of the sales process and will increase the chance for success when prepared well in advance. When handling initial inquiries, the goal should be to qualify the prospective client, provide any necessary information, and obtain a commitment for the next stage in the marketing process.

Advance Work

Before the first response comes in, have pricing, installation, and training policies firmly in hand and down on paper. It impresses clients when they are handed an information packet with a prepared pro forma engagement letter. Such responsiveness tangibly illustrates the commitment the firm is prepared to make on their behalf, namely, that the firm will always be there to help them if they get into trouble. With a plan and sales materials in hand, your sales efforts are also more efficient and your precious time is conserved.

Qualifying Prospects

Obviously, some products and services will be better suited to some of your clients than others. It is especially important to qualify prospective clients if you plan to advertise outside your existing client base.

Here are key qualifying questions to ask:

- When people inquire, what is their potential as a client?
- What is the nature of their accounting system?
- Are they using another type of accounting software?
- If so, are they satisfied with it? What are its shortcomings?
- What kind of volume are they presently handling (checks, deposits, invoices, etc.)?
- How much setup work is required?
- If we could help them [restate problem here], would it be of interest?
- Are they already using another accounting firm?

Obviously, the questions could go on. There are going to be additional questions related to the prospective client's needs and expectations. The important thing at this stage is to make sure there is a genuine understanding of the prospect's needs. The goal of these questions is to determine the fit between what the firm can offer and what a prospective client needs.

Make sure that your entire staff that plays a marketing role in the firm (which should be everyone) knows how to qualify prospective clients. The easiest way to do this is to give them a written list of qualifying questions they can use with clients. Periodically, you may want to remind the staff so they do not forget to bring up the subject with clients or prospective clients.

Dealing with Objections

You need not cringe when clients or prospective clients raise objections. Those experienced in sales will tell you that objections are crucial to the selling process. The person with no objections seldom buys. Instead, he or she walks away. Objections are opportunities to explain how your services are different from other accountants' services. It is helpful to think through potential objections in advance and prepare checklists for your own use listing possible objections and your responses.

Closing Sales

Successful sales cannot happen without successful closings. A closing is the point at which you ask for the sale and/or your prospective client says, "I'll do it." One accounting firm managing partner relates an interesting anecdote about one of the firm's clients. Speaking with a client three months after the client attended a seminar conducted by the firm, the client asked why he had not yet called to schedule a new accounting system installation. The CPA replied, "I didn't know you wanted it." Answered the client, "I've been waiting three months for you to ask!" It always pays to ask for the order.

Love Your Products and Services

If you are in business to sell products and services, you must love and believe in your products and services. This is especially true when engaged in selling accounting services, software, consulting, or other services in selected market niches. If you do not personally believe that your firm's products and services are going to make the clients' business lives easier and more profitable, you will have a difficult time persuading clients that it will make their business lives easier. You will also face some internal tensions when "pushing" a product or service in which you have insufficient confidence.

Accounting firms that have seen extraordinary success universally took the time to use their products and services themselves. By installing and using the software and productivity products they market in their own offices, they learned what the various products and services could and could not do and how they worked. Firsthand experience with the programs will build the expertise you and your staff need to support clients and answer their questions confidently during the sales process. Firsthand experience will vastly improve confidence and marketing efforts.

Nothing Sells Itself

Your clients expect you to understand their business and look out for their best interests. This includes finding ways to help them solve their accounting-related problems as well as virtually every other business-related problem they encounter. Studies have shown that business owners turn to their accountant with the majority of their business problems. They will go to their accountant before consulting with their attorney or specialized consultant. Time and again, the business owner will seek advice on the type of new computer equipment to purchase before contacting the computer reseller.

All successful installations of accounting products and services start with an accountant who understands the client's needs and can translate those needs into a solution and language the client understands. Then, the accountant must demonstrate the benefits of the program to the client. As useful as any product or service is, it will not sell itself, run itself, or yield benefits by itself.

VIRTUAL MARKETING

The survival and growth of an accounting business depends on the intelligent use of information technology. In your marketing plan, you must examine the way the firm markets and the way clients and prospective clients like to buy. Then, factor in how computers and software programs can help you serve the clients more effectively. As difficult as it is to have to invest time, effort, and money to determine what equipment and programs to buy and how to use them, there really is not much choice. The old adage about the shoemaker's children going barefoot was not an idle figment of someone's imagination. There is no way of building a successful accounting business that provides expert advice and assistance without practicing efficient and effective mastery of state-of-the-art business technology.

Knowledge Is Power

With an intimate knowledge of how to sell and how and why your clients buy, you hold the keys to using technology effectively. Asking the right questions is where good accounting practice automation begins. The first step is thinking or rethinking how you market your products and service from the ground up. Why go to all that trouble? Because virtually every part of your business affects every other part. (See Exhibit 8.5.)

EXHIBIT 8.5
Ten Steps Toward Virtual Marketing Automation

1. Do a structured analysis of how you work.
2. Automate only what can be improved by automation. Computers are no cure for poor management, ineffective sales techniques, weak strategy, or inadequate planning.
3. Get support from all management people in the firm. Your business-wide computing costs will probably go up in the first year, but so will quantifiable benefits, such as revenue and the amount of time the staff spends with clients rather than paperwork.
4. Buy and deploy your technology carefully. If you use a consultant or a systems integrator, do not let that person dazzle you with technology.
5. Get the users of the system on board. Make sure the system works the way they really need it to.
6. Do rapid rounds of prototyping. Develop each version of new applications with the users looking over your shoulders. If your users want to turn into computer gurus, make sure they know what they are doing. Those users-turned-gurus may turn out to be the core of your firm's computer software consultant staff.
7. Train, train, train—both in the technology and in new work methods. Training in new work methodology can cost one and a half to two times as much as the technology does.

8. Motivate the staff. Keep reinforcing the reasons the system is good for everyone.
9. Administer the system. Make sure the data in the system are accurate and relevant to your accounting business. A technology-savvy user might become a part-time database administrator.
10. Keep measuring the impact the system is having on your firm, and keep communicating that impact to all members of the firm so they will stay committed.

A checklist is provided in Exhibit 8.6 to facilitate the completion of steps necessary to manage your practice development plan. This process should be an ongoing exercise. Remember, what you can measure . . . you can manage.

EXHIBIT 8.6
Checklist: Practice Development Plan

Goal

- ❑ Increase size of small and medium-sized business practice.

Objective

- ❑ Maintain a 20 percent compounded annual increase in billed hours to small and medium-sized clients.

Strategies

- ❑ Educate staff by training them in marketing ideas, professional selling, and client relation skills.
- ❑ Develop a client-centered perspective.
- ❑ Inform referral sources, such as bankers and lawyers, about the type of new business the accounting firm is seeking.
- ❑ Develop promotional and publicity programs directed toward the market niches the firm serves.

Monitor and Measure

- ❑ Monthly review (by originator) of new clients acquired and expanded services provided to existing clients.

- ❑ Review increase in inventory of tangible resources (brochures, newsletters, business aids, surveys, etc.) developed for small and medium-sized business and other niche markets served by the firm.
- ❑ Compare budget to actual practice development expenditures.

Rewards

- ❑ Provides a basis for additional compensation (and recognition) for members of the firm responsible for practice development success.
- ❑ Development of partners and staff who understand the small and medium-sized business and niche markets the firm seeks to serve.
- ❑ Overall strength of the firm improves because partners and staff are pulling together toward agreed-on market objectives, thus increasing the probability of long-range success.
- ❑ Focusing on the future will orient the firm toward dealing more effectively with subsequent changes in the environment for serving small and medium-sized and other niche market clients.

9

PROSPECTING MEANS BUSINESS

WHAT IS PROSPECTING?

Pros-pekt-ing: the act of surveying or examining; the search for a potential customer.

Prospecting is not selling. Prospecting is the beginning of the sales process. It is the systematic and effective identification and contact of every qualified prospective client in your market. Because business comes by way of people, a *prospect* is a potential client for your accounting business. Not everyone is a prospect. To be a prospect, a person must be qualified to become a client or directly influence a qualified decision to buy.

The criteria for a qualified prospect include:

- **Openness** or willingness to communicate
- **Potential** needs or wants to satisfy
- **Authority** to decide or to influence a buying decision
- **Resources**—the ability to buy and pay for your services.

AIDS TO PROSPECTING SUCCESS

Prospecting strikes fear in the hearts of most accountants. It is an activity that probably ranks right up there between the fear of public speaking and the fear of death. The following aids to prospecting, and your perception of this valuable activity, are presented in short steps that will assist you in becoming a business winning prospector.

1. *Make an appointment with yourself.* Prospecting requires discipline. Schedule yourself to prospect for a set amount of time every day.

2. *Make as many calls as possible.* Research your target market niches to be sure of reaching the best qualified prospective clients.

3. *Make your calls brief.* The objective is to introduce your firm's services and products and to get an appointment. It should take only two or three minutes to do so. Then, find out about the prospective client's needs, and give the prospect a good reason to meet with you.

4. *Be prepared with a list of names.* Do not waste prospecting time trying to find the names to call.

5. *Work without interruption.* As with any repetitive task, the more one prospects, the better he or she becomes.

6. *Call during off-peak hours.* Conventional wisdom says call between 9:00 A.M. and 5:00 P.M. But that does not always work. Try calling between 8:00 and 9:00 A.M., or between 5:00 and 6:30 P.M.

7. *Vary your call times.* If a prospect cannot be reached at a certain time, call at some other time of the day.

8. *Be organized.* Keep a record of who is called, when, and what was discussed. This information will be helpful when an appointment is finally set. It will also help to keep track of who needs a follow-up. The GoldMine software system is excellent for prospecting purposes as well as other organizational requirements.

9. *Visualize the end before the start.* Establish the goals, and then develop a plan to get there. If the goal is to get the appointment, your plan—your cold-call script—should be designed and redesigned to achieve your goal.

10. *Don't quit.* Persistence is one of the key skills every successful professional accountant shares.

As long as you are in business, you can never have too many prospects. Success depends on your willingness and ability to find and develop meaningful relationships with prospective clients, *persistently* every day.

To be effective at this activity you must know the following:

- Where to find potential clients (prospects)
- How to contact them

- How to differentiate between potential prospects and qualified prospects
- Which situations are worth developing

For many accountants, prospecting is one of the most time-consuming and least popular aspects of selling. In practice, it is only part of the job because half of selling is making contacts. The other half is getting decisions from those contacts. Why is prospecting so unpopular? Most potential clients are unfamiliar, unqualified, and initially unwilling to pursue a business relationship because they have other priorities at the time you call. Attempting to "sell" them anyway only causes disappointment when they say "No."

The reality is that the professional accountant must contact a lot of potential clients in order to find some who are qualified prospective clients with a willingness to discuss business now. Even among those qualified, some are not closeable in the near future (today or this month). So prospecting is a searching, sorting, sifting, and cultivating process for getting into high-potential business situations.

WORKING THE SALES DATABASE

As long as there are qualified prospective clients, you have an excellent probability of securing profitable business. Find your prospective clients—one at a time—and build a database.

Your prospective client database can be built from many sources, and it must be kept full. Any shortcuts that are taken concerning what goes in at the top (the funnel) usually result in your getting short-changed by what comes out at the bottom (the active client). There is even more to it than that. There are **referrals** from satisfied clients. These referrals make it possible to spend less time and effort prospecting in the future. Your ultimate goal is to do *all* business by referrals.

Steps for Getting the Most from a Sales and Marketing Database

Achieve the maximum benefits from your sales and marketing database by taking the following steps:

1. *Recapture prospective clients.* Use the database to locate prospective clients who have not been contacted for a time. Requalify the prospects and begin marketing activities.

2. *Turn empty inquiries into clients.* Review the database for prospective clients who made one or more inquiries, but never became clients. Statistics show that most inquiries turn into business—maybe it is with your competition.
3. *Monitor competitor activity.* Your competitors' clients should be your prospective clients. Track the focus of competitor campaigns. Then, use that knowledge to help your marketing forces penetrate that market.
4. *Spread territory success.* The database will reveal not only what services and products the firm is selling, but also who is doing the selling. Which marketing person consistently closes more business than others? Find out their strategies for leveraging leads, and communicate them to the entire marketing staff.
5. *Eliminate contact overlap.* Your database will indicate if more than one salesperson is calling on the same prospective client or if there are duplicate addressees for mailings. When this overlap is identified and stopped, the result is reduced costs and no embarrassment.
6. *Isolate incoming call activity.* Look for patterns in incoming prospective client and client calls. Isolate your busiest and slowest periods, and schedule staffing and promotions accordingly.
7. *Cater to historic habits.* Both management and salespeople should use the database to scrutinize what, how much, and how often each client purchases. Use that information to cater to client preferences and to help cross-sell.
8. *Capitalize on competitor advantages.* Your database should reference each competing product's specifications, pricing, and knockoff points. Give the sales staff access to that information, and they will have fighting knowledge to help them close more sales.
9. *Slice and dice your marketing mix.* Identify which combinations of marketing tools—phone calls, faxes, e-mail, direct mail, trade shows, seminars, and advertising—your current clients responded to. When appropriate, have your salespeople try a repeat performance on new prospective clients or niche markets.
10. *Target decision makers.* When the decision maker is identified at each prospective client, the salespeople can go directly to the source and close the next sale faster.

Exhibit 9.1 is a basic list of sources for entries into your prospective client base. Your database should not be a repository for prospective client contacts but should be worked with regularly. Add entries when you first learn of them and eliminate entries that are no longer prospects. Be certain to update the classifications and categories. A new client may question your firm's capabilities if they receive prospective client offerings and mail solicitation.

EXHIBIT 9.1
Sources for Prospective Client Database

- Referrals
- Seminars
- Surveys
- Current clients
- Telephone prospecting
- Direct mail
- Affiliate referral exchanges
- Service organizations (Lions Club, Kiwanis, Rotary, Jaycees, etc.)
- Trade organizations
- Business journals
- Newspapers
- Niche market trade journals
- Inactive clients
- Leads
- Vendor-supplied leads
- Advertising
- Public relations
- Publicity
- Media appearances (local radio and television)
- Your imagination
- Cold calling
- Bank officers
- Stockbrokers
- Personal financial planners
- Attorneys
- Commercial real estate brokers
- Insurance agents/brokers

- "Tip clubs"
- Dun & Bradstreet reports
- Standard & Poor's Register of Corporations
- MacMillan Directory of Leading Private Companies
- Social activities
- Church/Synagogue
- Friends and relatives

Source: The Accounting Guild

Your prospective client database:
EQUALS Positive Encounters
EQUALS Qualified Prospective Clients
EQUALS Eligible Prospective Clients
EQUALS CLIENTS
EQUALS REFERRALS

Just some of the types of prospective clients you can incorporate into your marketing plan are listed in Exhibit 9.2. The list does not imply any sales or profitability potential but is designed to get you to think of the various types of clients, which will define the character of your business.

EXHIBIT 9.2
Types of Prospective Clients

- Advertising agencies
- Apartment rental companies
- Appraisers
- Architectural firms
- Auctioneers
- Auto dealerships
- Building contractors
- Cemeteries
- Charitable foundations
- Chiropractors
- Churches
- Condominium associations
- Construction firms
- Dentists

- Distribution companies
- Electrical contractors
- Engineering firms
- Exporters
- Fast-food chains
- Financial services companies
- Freight carriers
- Funeral homes
- Hotels
- Insurance agencies
- Law firms
- Manufacturers
- Nonprofit associations
- Nursing homes
- Physicians
- Property management companies
- Real estate developers
- Realtors
- Retail operations
- Synagogues
- Townships
- Trucking firms
- Unions
- Veterinarians
- Wholesalers

Source: The Accounting Guild

PROSPECTING CALLS ARE NOT SALES CALLS

Prospecting is not selling over the telephone, Internet, or direct mail. If you do start selling over those media, it is a little like a good friend of mine describes dinner theatre, "It's not really dinner and it's not really theatre." Moreover, you are likely to get poor results by attempting to sell in a prospecting situation. The purpose of a **prospecting call** is to obtain qualifying information and qualified appointments. The purpose of a **sales call** is to obtain a buying decision, including a decision that may advance the sales process.

Structure of a Prospecting Call

1. *Pre-call preparation:* Research (the higher you reach in an organization, the more important pre-call research will be)
2. *Opening* statement to explain the purpose of call
3. *Ask* questions to qualify/analyze needs
4. *Offer* to help meet needs in general
5. *Invite* to talk, meet, discuss (do not offer solutions).

Exhibit 9.3 presents the results of an original marketing research study by The Accounting Guild in 1999. This study utilized focus interviews with accountants in order to learn more about the subject of sales prospecting in the accounting business. Highlights of the results are included in the exhibit. The high interest in prospecting has led the Guild to consider hosting an Internet forum on prospecting.

EXHIBIT 9.3
Prospecting Tactics

The ranking of these lists was determined from original survey data gathered during focus interviews conducted with a cross-section of accountants representing diverse geographic locations.

By Usage

1. Customer referrals
2. Accounting software vendor–supplied leads
3. Trade shows
4. Seminars
5. Direct mail
6. Telemarketing
7. Advertising
8. Public relations

By Effectiveness

1. Customer referrals
2. Seminars

3. Trade shows
4. Direct mail
5. Telemarketing
6. Advertising
7. Public relations
8. Accounting software vendor–supplied leads

Source: The Accounting Guild.

Structure of a Sales Call

1. *Pre-call preparation:* Set objective.
2. *Open:* Establish meeting objectives.
3. *Ask* questions to qualify/analyze needs.
4. *Present* targeted solutions.
5. *Provide* additional support/benefits to inspire engagement or change.
6. *Close:* Request buying decision today.

Let's look at Exhibit 9.4 to see how prospecting precedes the sales process.

EXHIBIT 9.4
Prospecting Process Chart

- **Conduct research and develop prospect list**
- **Phone contact** (opening statement of purpose)
- **Questions to qualify** (establish personal credibility and ask business questions)
- **Positive encounter** (qualified prospect)
- **Recommend appointment** (in-person meeting continues the sales process)

Prospecting starts the sales process. It gets you talking to a qualified prospective client instead of wasting time talking to people who cannot or will not consider your services. Its goal is to identify opportunities for business, not to sell by telephone, mail, or Internet. When you find a good opportunity, the goal is to obtain an appointment.

IDENTIFYING AND QUALIFYING TARGET PROSPECTIVE CLIENTS

Determine the profile of your prospective clients. These are the businesses or individuals most likely to be clients for your services and products. Concentrate on the market niches you have decided to cultivate or you run the risk of pursuing more leads that do not fit your firm or are unlikely to become clients. That will waste precious time and money. Develop a target profile of those businesses or individuals in your market niches that merit the time, effort, and expense you will invest in the selling effort. It is important to separate the wheat from the chaff in pursuing your marketing and sale processes. Questions that must be answered to correctly segment and qualify your prospective clients are posed in Exhibit 9.5.

EXHIBIT 9.5
Checklist: Prospective Client Qualification

- ❑ **Identify prospective clients (suspects).**
- ❑ **Find leads (prospecting).**
- ❑ **Qualify leads.**
- ❑ **Convert leads into qualified prospective clients (turning lead into gold).**

Businesses

❑ 1. *What industries are represented in my niche market plan?* Segment your current clients and prospective clients into specific industries. Assign a Standard Industrial Classification (SIC) code to each of your current clients and every prospective client in your database. The SIC is far more important than the code for filing with the IRS. Identifying prospective clients by SIC will enable you to literally find the location, address, phone number, and key contact person of every business in your market area with that SIC.

❑ 2. *Geographic location?* Location is not a primary factor in targeting prospective clients. What is important is knowing whether the prospective client is a headquarters or merely a branch office. There is little likelihood of obtaining accounting work from a branch office.

❑ 3. *Size ($ volume, number of employees)*. An excellent criterion to further identify your prospective clients is by determining their sales volume and number of employees. For example, if you know that your ideal client is an automobile dealer with a sales volume between $35 million and $60 million, has fewer than 50 employees, and is headquartered in your market area, you can locate a list of all automobile dealers that fit this description.

Individuals

- ☐ 1. *Net worth?* If you are building a market niche of individual tax and consulting clients, you want to segment your clients by their net worth. Individual clients who have a high net worth are excellent leads for estate planning, other types of tax planning, and investment-type consulting.
- ☐ 2. *Geographic location?* Is there any pattern to where your individual clients live? Do they belong to the same country club, church, or synagogue? Try to find any patterns among your clients and extrapolate those patterns in prospecting for clients.
- ☐ 3. *Income level?* This information is readily available through the tax returns of your current clients. It may come as no surprise to find out that 20 percent of your tax return clients may be producing 60 to 80 percent of your tax preparation and consulting revenues.
- ☐ 4. *Occupation?* It is important to segment your current clients by occupation. For example, you may find that a significant segment (15 percent or more) of your individual clients are engineers or software programmers. This may suggest new niches for you to develop.

Each prospective client must be analyzed to determine if they fit with your firm's profile targeted client. The questions presented in the analysis checklist (Exhibit 9.6) provide a framework for determining prospective client qualification.

EXHIBIT 9.6
Checklist: Prospective Client Qualification Analysis

The following analysis checklist will assist you in qualifying leads:

- ☐ 1. Does my prospective client have a real need?
- ☐ 2. Does this prospective client recognize his or her need, or can I show the prospective client that he or she has a need?

- ❑ **3.** Is my prospective client committed to fulfilling his or her need?
- ❑ **4.** Does the lead fit the market niche where I have decided to concentrate my experience and expertise?
- ❑ **5.** Do I present a viable solution to the prospective client's need?
- ❑ **6.** Have sufficient funds been allocated, or are funds available, for my solution?
- ❑ **7.** If required, can I provide a sound cost justification for any solution?
- ❑ **8.** Have I identified the decision maker and key recommender?
- ❑ **9.** Can I reach the decision maker?
- ❑ **10.** Can I secure the concurrence of the key recommender?
- ❑ **11.** Do I know the decision criteria?
- ❑ **12.** Can I get the prospective client to commit the time, resources, and money to examine and implement my suggested solution?
- ❑ **13.** Do I know who the competitors are?
- ❑ **14.** Do I know if the prospective client is tied into an existing accounting firm and what the lead likes or dislikes about that relationship?
- ❑ **15.** Can I communicate my firm's strategies effectively?
- ❑ **16.** Do I have a specific plan for turning this prospective client into an active client?

Spinning Lead(s) into Gold

Recognize and define the qualification level for each prospective client in your database. This will allow for effectively managing your time, making accurate forecasts of productivity, and fully realizing the potential for your accounting business. The preliminary element for this process is structuring a formal **prospective accounting client evaluation** (PACE).

PACE

The PACE approach is highly proactive, based on categorizing every prospective client according to clearly defined profiles. PACE is not a one-time function or an initial approach to prospecting. It is a continual process in developing your accounting and consulting business. The purpose of the system is to introduce into your marketing database qualification information that is clearly identified and sorted as to priority and probability for success.

MARKETING DATABASE EXPLOITATION

Database exploitation is the strategy of marketing your services to segments of the marketing database on a consistent basis. You must carefully and consistently note every contact, the steps taken, and the result. In effect, a complete history is created and maintained, making possible the individual evaluation of each prospective client. With such a prospective client marketing database, a body of valuable information is available to work with in various ways. Everything from specific significant contacts to e-mails to newsletter mailings to proposal preparation to presentations and engagement letters serves as the basis for developing additional tactics for each prospect.

CONTINUAL DATABASE MONITORING

The regular review and analysis of your information is essential for transforming prospective clients into active clients. Moving a prospective client from one category to another at the opportune time is essential to the successful implementation of the system.

At the time of publication of the second edition of this book, it would have been wishful thinking to even suggest the tasks just outlined. However, now all of the above tasks and much more are possible with the GoldMine software program, which is justifiably cited as "the ultimate management system for today's professional." GoldMine 4.0 client and prospective client marketing management can be a major contributing element to your business's success. With the emergence of the Internet, intranets, effective prospecting, and management activities, vast amounts of data are relatively easy to gather. It is difficult to organize and share this information without an effective contact management software program. GoldMine offers a technology-enabled selling solution that transforms data into meaningful information. This information will increase efficiency and profitability. While the software is extremely valuable to the sole practitioner, with multiple users, everyone has access to the database and everyone works to turn each contact into a client and each client into a loyal, lifetime client.

In addition to instant access to important information on all your prospective, active, and former clients, you have advanced project and opportunity management. With real-time response to opportunities, every qualified lead can become a client. Repetitive tasks are eliminated, streamlining services and marketing. Many accountants and consultants have made GoldMine such an integral part of their business that in addition to using it internally, they offer the sale, installation, and training of the software to their clients. More about GoldMine Software Corporation is included in Chapter 6.

Prioritizing your marketing activities is vital to maximizing your sales potential. The qualification level you must assign to each prospective client is defined in Exhibit 9.7. This level will change with time and activity. Always ask yourself, "Is this the best use of my selling time?" Only you know the answer.

EXHIBIT 9.7
Defining Qualification Levels of Prospective Clients

- *Potential prospective client.* Someone likely to have a need (sometimes referred to as a suspect)
- *Positive encounter.* A potential prospective client with an identified need, available funds, and the authority to make a commitment
- *Qualified prospective client.* A positive encounter with a decision maker who has expressed an openness or willingness to talk with you
- *Closeable prospective client.* A qualified prospective client who can make a decision within a month

EXHIBIT 9.8
Category Designations

Designation	Type of Prospect	Closeability
A	Best closeable prospect	30 days
B	Qualified prospect	31–60 days
C	Positive encounter	Next 61–90 days
D	Potential prospective client	Over 90 days

Decide to distinguish between about four different levels of prospects in your accounting business. However many you choose, be sure to define your terms when you put together a sales forecast or marketing strategy, so that everyone in your organization knows what they mean. Your designation ranking generally includes criteria such as the potential fee, potential profitability, and your initial estimate of the likelihood of converting a prospect into a client. The important thing is to concentrate your initial energies toward the **A** prospects.

SOURCES OF PROSPECTIVE CLIENTS

There are a number of sources and ways to identify and find prospects:

1. *Current clients.* In the accounting business, existing clients are the best prospects for new services, new products, or leads to other departments within the client company where new business could be developed, especially in the management advisory services area.

2. *Referrals.* Ask your friends, clients, and others for names of prospects. This is generally the leading source of new business contacts. Say hello to people. Be friendly. Smile. Have a goal of meeting two new people a week. Network. Become active in trade or professional associations.

3. *Your own marketing efforts.* Your marketing activities may have identified many prospects, industry profiles, client profiles, and data banks of prospect sources. Work with your local business reference or nearby college or university librarian for assistance in developing this area of your prospecting.

4. *Leads.* Telephone-ins, responses to advertising, references from local trade shows, and vendor provided leads are good sources of prospects.

5. *Trade associations and local business clubs.* Networking groups of noncompeting sales representatives are flourishing in many cities and metropolitan areas. Organizations like Jaycees and speakers' groups (e.g., Toastmasters), Kiwanis, Rotary, Lions, and booster clubs are good social as well as business contacts. One of the best sources for finding associations that

match your target market niches is *The Encyclopedia of Associations,*[1] published by Gale Research.

6. *Billing and work-paper records.* Your own billing records may indicate new opportunities. The work papers may have lists of prospects to contact for additional engagements.

7. *Business directories,* such as Standard & Poor's, Moody's, Dun & Bradstreet, Million Dollar Directory, Polk's Directory, and others relevant to your specific market niches, can tell you a company's name, address, names and titles of principals and officers, type of business, size, number of employees, affiliates, and subsidiaries, as well as other information. If your office does not have them, the library does.

8. *Local trade organizations and journals:*
   - Chamber of Commerce
   - Local trade journals, business journals
   - Business section and other news sections of local newspapers
   - Classified ads

9. *Telephone directories.* The Yellow Pages of your local telephone directory lists professionals and the many businesses that comprise your selected market niches. A reverse telephone directory lists subscribers by street, making it invaluable in locating businesses in your market area. Many of your competitors use the directories for cold calling on prospects. When you work a telephone directory, begin in the back of the book. Every salesperson has good intentions when beginning a prospecting program. They enthusiastically start with the AA Manufacturing Company or with Ms. Alice Aaron, believing that someday in the future they will get to the Zzyx Company or Mr. Zzor. It just never happens. Cold calling is not forever. The professional will soon be working on referred leads, and the amateur, if he or she has not found a way to get out of the Yellow Pages, will be gone. It is very likely the Zzyx Company and Mr. Zzor have never received a prospecting call.

10. *Special events.* Accounting firms are finding this "soft marketing" is not difficult to do and often produces good results.

---

[1] Encyclopedia of Associations: National Organizations of the U.S., Parts 1, 2, and 3 (34th ed.). Gale Research.

Special events include exhibiting at trade shows, sponsoring events with charities, or even teaching an adult education program or MBA program at the local college. Each one of these requires special skills. Trade shows are great opportunities to talk with decision makers. If you decide to sponsor an event with a charity (e.g., golf tournament), you should expect a lot of name recognition but not much business. Teaching at the local college or university helps to establish name recognition, is a good source for recruiting, and, depending on the course, will also provide you with leads.

11. *Seminars.* The prospecting seminar is a key relationship marketing tool that gets the accountant closer to the client before issues arise and puts the professional accountant in the role of consultant instead of salesperson.

12. *The Accounting Guild.* The Accounting Guild is a national, Internet-based organization providing effective marketing programs to accountants and consultants. These include professional direct mail programs, advertising, promotional material, seminar-in-a box production for various market niches, and ongoing consultation. The Guild encourages its affiliates to work together whenever possible. This allows all to benefit from the input provided by each member of its growing network. Affiliates working together also conduct seminars for clients and prospective clients, appear as panelists on cable and/or public access television programs, and staff booths at professional conferences, county fairs, business expositions, and other heavily attended business events. You will also be able to purchase computer software and hardware for your business and for resale to your clients at discount pricing available only to members of the Guild through the leading national distributors.

13. *Professional relationships.* Many referral sources are not necessary if each of your sources can refer three to five new prospective clients. With five good sources (lawyer, banker, financial planner, real estate agent, and stockbroker) you should be generating 18 to 30 clients per year from them. This will take much work and relationship building.

In turn, make sure to feed referrals to your sources. The key is to identify your main referral sources and then track what they give you. See these referral contacts at least once a month.

DECISION-MAKING AUTHORITY

One of the criteria for a good prospective client is having the authority to decide or influence a buying decision. Talking to the wrong person is one of the biggest time wasters in business. Knowing who to contact is very important. In your defined market niches, there are probably specific job titles, authority levels, and buying motives that will clue you in to who can make a buy decision.

Who has the authority to make the decision? Use the following checklist to identify:

- ❑ Who generally makes buying decisions in a particular market niche?
- ❑ Who influences decisions in your prospective client's organization?
- ❑ What is their authority level? Who influences them?
- ❑ What are their respective job titles?
- ❑ What are their general motives for buying?
- ❑ Who knows the decision makers and influencers in your prospective client's organization?

Exhibit 9.9 assists in determining the name and title of the person who has the actual authority to make the decision of contracting for your firm's services.

EXHIBIT 9.9
Who Has the Authority to Make the Decision?

Contact/Title	Authority/Influence	General Buying Motive

OPENING STATEMENTS

Start a prospecting conversation with an opening statement that includes a legitimate business reason for calling and shows respect.

Which opening statement do you think would be most successful in prospecting?

- **Statement #1:** "Good morning, Ms. Smith. How are you today? I'm with Hartly Effective, CPAs, and I'd like to talk to you about the benefits of our auditing and taxation services."
- **Statement #2:** "Good morning, Ms. Smith. My name is Carole Olafson and I'm with the XYZ Company. We recently became an authorized partner for a budgetary software that offers many benefits to small companies like yours in the area of budgeting, business planning, and cash requirements forecasting. If we could talk for a few minutes, you can decide if our services might benefit your company."

A good opening statement meets the following criteria:

1. *States a legitimate business reason.* There are many legitimate business reasons that can be used in an opening statement. They include:
   - Referral from another business or department
   - The ability to solve a common business problem
   - The benefit of an important product or service
   - A recent news event
   - Availability of a new product or idea

   (*Note:* Use only benefits that are highly likely to be accepted throughout your prospect's industry. Generic benefits seldom have much impact.)

2. *Invites the prospect to listen with an open mind.* The only request made during an opening statement is to ask if the prospect is willing to talk with you (now) for a few minutes. By your voice inflection and words, you should sound open-minded yourself. That is far better than sounding like you are under the pressure of selling.

3. *Acknowledge the prospect's right to decide.* Show that you respect the prospect's right to *decide* if they would like to pursue a meeting. This builds confidence and goodwill. (Trying to "sell" an appointment causes pressure.)

PROSPECTIVE CLIENT QUALIFICATION

A *potential* prospect is someone whom you suspect might be a possible client. A *qualified* prospect is someone who meets the following criteria:

- The prospect is **open-minded** (i.e., willing to talk with you).
- The prospect has **potential** (i.e., has a potential need for your kind of products/services).
- The prospect has the **authority** (i.e., can make or influence a buying decision).
- The prospect has the **resources** (i.e., has the resources to implement your kind of solutions if he or she does decide to buy). "Resources" could include more than money. It might also include time, space, expertise, personnel—whatever is needed to implement your solution.

A smart accountant invests time and money only in those opportunities that have a good potential for a profitable payoff. Because time is money, invest time only in situations that meet the above criteria and have potential for a mutually beneficial outcome. To determine a good situation, ask qualifying questions that fall into these general categories:

- Can we have this telephone conversation? **(open to discussion)**
- Is there a need? **(potential)**
- How are decisions made? **(authority)**
- Are resources available? **(resources)**

Qualifying questions save a lot of time. You will do less talking to the wrong people, investing time in poor situations, and getting stuck behind people who have no authority to make a decision and no motive to advance the process.

Uncovering Potential

Good fact-finding questions are phrased slightly differently depending on whether products, services, or ideas are being sold. Some examples might be:

Services:

- "What type of methods/procedures do you use for your budgeting process now?"
- "How long have you been using them?"
- "Are there any specific (or unusual) applications you are exploring?"
- "What kind of result are you trying to achieve?"

Products:

- "Which software are you using for general ledger applications?"
- "How long have you had it?"
- "What other applications are you using it for? How is it being used primarily?"

From these starting questions, further information can be obtained by asking additional "open-ended" or "closed" questions.

Open-Ended (the prospective client can answer with freedom to expand or express opinions at length):

- "What kind of feedback do you get from your users?"
- "What is your opinion of . . . ?"

Closed (the prospect must respond with a definite answer—yes or no, or one way versus another):

- "Are your trucks owned, leased, or rented?"
- "Do you have any need for changes?"

Uncovering Authority

When formulating fact-finding questions to uncover decision-making authority, you basically want to know:

- What is the decision-making process for this type of commitment?
- How does the person to whom you are speaking fit into the decision-making process?

To avoid wasting time, you should ask qualifying questions like:

- "If your company were to make a change in accounting firms, are you the person who would authorize such a change?"
- "Would this be part of your budget?"

Uncovering Resources

Be sure to ask qualifying questions to uncover resources.

Open-Ended:

- "What are your thoughts on the costs of upgrading your computerized accounting system?"

Closed:

- "If you were to decide to add a new software system, would it come out of your budget? Are funds available?"

Obtaining enough information to know if a prospective client is a good business opportunity requires more knowledge and skill than you might imagine! Asking good business questions is not tough. Getting the prospective client engaged in wanting to answer the questions is the hardest part. That is what takes skill. In particular, it takes:

- Good opening statements: what you say and how you say it
- Sensitive listening: reading the head and the heart
- Credibility and rapport skills: keeping the person willing to talk further, even if objections or concerns are raised

PROSPECTING BY TELEPHONE

Prospecting by telephone has several advantages:

- It saves money compared with knocking on doors.
- It saves time compared with driving time.
- It is easier to structure and make routine.
- There is no face-to-face indifference from unqualified suspects.

Specifically, contacting prospective clients by telephone is more effective and cost efficient than a letter or unscheduled visit (cold call), especially when your purpose is to:

- Qualify needs
- Survey the situation
- Get the decision maker's name
- Obtain appointments

However, you may want to contact prospective clients by mail or e-mail in addition to calling them on the telephone. Why? There are direct benefits to your prospecting efforts when you combine methods. The percentage of contacts making next-action commitments increases when you use a combination of mail, e-mail, and telephone. You can send customized letters, brochures, or appropriate literature to each prospective client in advance of calling by telephone.

Setting Your Expectations

To be effective at telephone prospecting, you must set realistic expectations, in line with typical prospecting outcomes. Here are numbers that are typical for an untrained amateur:

- Typically, an amateur averages better than three contacts per hour. Sometimes, it may take 10 to 20 calls (dials) to make one contact (i.e., talk to the right person).
- Ten percent of these contacts will make next-action commitments, such as attending a meeting, demonstration, or seminar. If you combine direct mail and telephone, then you can increase next-action commitments to 15%.
- Twenty percent of next-action commitments will become "hot" or closable prospective clients. Thirty percent will continue the sales process (e.g., by arranging more meetings).
- You will hear 80% of all prospect reactions in the first 50 contacts.

Consider each of the previous items in detail. Accounting marketers must become skillful enough to perform better than an untrained amateur. The numbers indicate that for an amateur, it takes two hours of prospecting to get one good qualified appointment. You will want to do better than that.

Structuring Your Prospecting

It is important to define the purpose of your call before you make it! This establishes what should be accomplished with the telephone call. Is the purpose of the call to survey companies and obtain valuable information? Is it to generate appointments? Have a clear picture of the purpose of the call before picking up the telephone.

Key Prospecting Skills

There are key communication skills required to do telephone prospecting well. They are:

- Making opening statements that promote openness, interest, and dialogue
- Listening for both facts and positive/negative inclinations (the person's willingness level)
- Demonstrating personal credibility and rapport skills
- Asking clear, simple qualifying questions that get straight to the point

You may feel that you have the knowledge to know what to do in each of these key areas. However, keep in mind that there is a profound difference between knowing what to do and being skillful at actually doing it. By skillful, we mean competent to the degree that people feel like they want to explore or do business with you.

Identifying Telephone Screens (Gatekeepers)

More often than not, you will find yourself needing to get past the decision maker's secretary who is screening calls. If this is the case, then what can you do about it?

- *Do your homework.* Do pre-call research so you know something about a prospective client's business before contacting the executive. Learn about the company from social contacts, other companies in the industry, and public reports.
- *Anticipate a gatekeeper.* Remember that this person has to decide if you are going to waste the executive's time or if you have a valid business solution that could help.

Treat the person screening the call as a *decision maker.* Use your people skills and pre-call research to briefly explain how you may be able to help the executive meet his or her goals.

Do not quit if this professional approach does not work at first. *Persist.* Develop a relationship with the screening person, and in most cases you will eventually get through (often with at least an implied recommendation). Do not expect to get past every single screening person. No one can—not every time.

PREPARATION FOR PROSPECTING

Pre-Call Preparation

- Where do you obtain names of prospective clients?
- Whom do you want to contact directly?
- Can these people make or influence the decision to buy?
- What do you already know about the prospective client's business or situation?
- What information is available from public records, industry publications, or business directories?
- What applications and needs is this prospective client likely to have? What is required to be considered "qualified"?
- What idea or benefit is likely to focus his or her attention and generate some interest?
- What will you actually say to begin a telephone contact? How will you state your reason for calling?
- Is your calendar clear for qualified appointments?

Initial Contact—To Qualify the Prospective Client

- What benefit, reference, or value to the prospect will you state to start the conversation? (Opening statements/purpose for calling.)
- Do you have the ability to read and address the prospective client's point of view at the moment?
- Do you have the ability to establish credibility and open-mindedness at that moment?
- Do you have the ability to obtain cooperation even if you encounter initial objections?

Assessing Potential

- What is the prospective client's situation?
- Is he or she satisfied with the present situation?
- What potential problems exist that you might be able to solve? How aware is the prospective client of these problems?
- What are the prospective client's main needs for your kind of services?
- Is he or she currently looking for a new accounting firm?
- Does a budget exist for new management advisory services?
- What is the prospective client's procurement procedure?
- Who makes and who influences buying decisions?
- What service or products do you want to show the prospective client? Can that even be determined at this point?
- Does he or she have the necessary funds, space, time, talents, tools, personnel, and so forth to implement your kind of solutions?
- If an appointment is appropriate, who should attend in addition to the prospective client who is now on the telephone with you?

Additional Qualifying/Probing

- What specific problems or needs exist?
- How critical are they?
- How often are these problems occurring?
- What is the cost in dollars, time, productivity, and so forth?
- How are these problems or needs impacting the organization?
- What if these problems or needs are *not* fixed? What would be the ongoing consequences?
- What kind of solution is needed?
- Is the prospective client open to looking at your ideas?

THE FIRST FIFTEEN SECONDS OF A COLD CALL

Attitude is one of the most important elements of a successful telephone prospecting cold call. When your prospective client says, "I'm not interested," it sounds like an objection. But is it a valid objection? Always notice where the objection occurs during the cold call. If your prospective client is saying, "I'm not interested" in the beginning, the prospect is probably trying to get you off the phone. The prospective client simply does not know enough about you or your firm to say "no" so quickly. The chances are the prospect is not objecting to your services, products, or firm, but to your approach.

Because of nervousness, we may have a tendency to say too much too fast. Use the checklist that follows as a guide to build key phrases. This will help you get started writing effective dialogue for your accounting business. You want to ease yourself and your prospective client into a conversation. In the first fifteen seconds, simply answer the questions that probably come into your prospect's mind when he or she hears a stranger on the other end of the phone:

- ❑ **Who is this person?**
- ❑ **Why is he or she calling me?**
- ❑ **What does he or she want?**
- ❑ **How long is this going to take?**

During the first 15 seconds of your telephone cold call, *do not* do the following:

- *Do not ask, "How are you?"* You may be saying this because you feel a little uncomfortable. In a cold call, you want to be genuinely helpful and direct. Asking "how are you" is canned conversation that does not carry much meaning.
- *Do not make outrageous claims.* This approach immediately gives the prospective client a point to argue, and it puts you on the defensive. That is pretty shaky groundwork to lay in the first 15 seconds. Use a smart-sell versus hard-sell routine. Rather than saying "I know I can . . ." try saying, "There's a possibility I can help . . . " Rather than saying, "If I could save you $10,000 this month, would you be interested?", try saying, "There's a good possibility I could save you a lot of money—that's why I'm calling." Remember, this first call is the first step in building trust and rapport.
- *Do not launch into a monologue or script.* Chances are, your prospective client will not hear every word you are saying in the first 15 seconds. Start with a broad statement and get the prospect interested in hearing more. This gives the prospect time to catch up with you for a two-way conversation. You want

to say, "This is who I am, this is who I think you are, let's explore the possibility of working together." Here is a sample:

> **"This is __________ with ______________. I've enjoyed reading about your business recently. I understand that you're the person to talk to about the ________________________. I'd like to explore the possibility of working together. I may be able to help. This should take only five minutes. Is this a good time?"**

Engage in useful dialogue. By being genuinely helpful, you set yourself apart from the other cold callers from whom your prospect has heard. Just slow down and relax. Before you know it, you have just begun a great conversation and the beginning of a beautiful relationship.

Army drill instructors have an adage, "Prior planning prevents poor performance." Although the expletive has been omitted, the accuracy of the message is in no way diminished. The degree to which you plan and prepare for your sales calls will directly affect the results you achieve. Exhibit 9.10 outlines your approach plan in checklist form.

EXHIBIT 9.10
Checklist: Plan Your Approach

❑ **1.** Did I introduce myself first?

- "My name is ______ with __________. We have an office in ______________."

❑ **2.** Does the prospective client sound distracted, rushed, or annoyed?

- "You sound very busy."

❑ **3.** What do I know about the prospect that I can use to start off the conversation?

- "I hear that you are . . ."
- "I noticed that your company . . ."
- "I was reading about your company in the newspaper . . ."

❑ **4.** What do we have in common?

- "I came across your name (business card) and it occurred to me . . ."
- "You may recall reading about . . ."

- "It's been a long time since we talked. I remember that you mentioned . . ."

❑ 5. What do I know about this contact?

- "I understand that you are the person that I should talk to about . . ."

❑ 6. What does this prospect have in common with my clients?

- "We are working with . . ."
- "We are helping our clients cut back on their . . ."

❑ 7. Why am I calling?

- "We have a seminar planned for next week that you . . ."
- "We just moved into the neighborhood and I want to personally invite you . . ."

❑ 8. Is there a possibility we can help the prospective client?

- "There's a good possibility that we can help you, too."
- "We have something that you may want to seriously consider."

❑ 9. Are there other contacts to mention?

- "Your name came up in conversation recently."
- "__________ asked me to call you. He/she thinks we may be able to . . ."
- "I am working with ___________ in Operations. I would like to discuss some of our ideas with you."

❑ 10. Is the prospect interested in talking a little?

- "This should only take about five minutes. Is this a good time?"

PLAY IT STRAIGHT AND YOU WILL GET TO THE BUYERS

Avoid the following phone tactics when you deal with telephone screeners or voice mail so that your approach will not clearly identify you or your marketing aide as a time-wasting, self-interested salesperson:

- *Leaving only a name and number for a call back.* Not identifying your company suggests you have something to hide. Granted, the tactic almost forces the prospective client to return the call, because they might think the call is a prospect or customer. They might even get their expectations up. But the bubble bursts when they realize it is a salesperson trying to sell something. That is certainly not the frame of mind in which you want potential customers when speaking with them.

- *Making a statement, then a demand.* As in, "I need to speak with Troy Brand. Please connect me." Sure, let's try to intimidate the telephone screener into putting the call through. What are the people who use this tactic thinking—that the telephone screeners are bumbling idiots who can be bullied?
- *Following this misguided advice: "Never give the telephone screener any information because they cannot buy from you."* Maybe most of them cannot make the final buying decision, but they can make the decision that no one will buy from you. In some scenarios, a screener might indeed be the person you would work with if a business relationship is established.
- *Do not sound and act like a stereotypical salesperson.* You will get through more often and have more calls returned, giving you a chance to sell your appointment.
- *Ask for help.* This is the simplest, yet one of the most effective techniques. You appeal to a person's innate sense of feeling needed, wanted, and important.
- *Ask for information.* Gather as much qualifying information as you can before speaking with your decision makers. They expect it. Their job is not to waste time educating you with information you should already know by the time you reach them. Preface your questions to telephone screeners or assistants with, "I want to be sure that what I have to say will be of interest to Barbara. There's probably some information you could give me . . ." Or, "I want to be certain that what I discuss with him or her would be of interest. Please tell me . . . ." This also positions you apart from typical salespeople who do not respect the buyer's time.
- *Have something of value.* This is the not-so-secret "secret" to getting people to return your calls or at least having them in a positive frame of mind when you call back. You must have something of interest for them. Why would they take your call otherwise? Your value should answer a question: What will you help them gain or avoid? They do not care about your services or products. They will let you through or return your message if they suspect you might be able to help solve their problems or avoid something they do not want to have. The more customized and relevant your value item, the better.

10

SELLING SKILLS FOR ACCOUNTING PROFESSIONALS

Professionalism (pro-fesh'on-o-liz'om). n. 1. Professional status, methods, character, or standards. 2. Having great skill or experience in a particular field or activity.

One of the most misused words in the language of business. An ideal to which many aspire, but few achieve. An elusive trait, a welcome adjective, a noble goal.

Can a single word be all these things? In the accounting business, it is all these things—and more. For those engaged in marketing accounting services, it is the difference between survival and the alternative. *And nothing else!*

THE WINNING ATTITUDE

The willingness to confront and risk failure is the single most essential trait of the successful accounting marketer. Most people rationalize that if they never come to bat, they will never strike out. Others understand that if they never come up, they will never hit a home run.

Regardless of how technically proficient and expert people are, or how adept at marketing their services, they cannot succeed without the ability to risk failure. If the prospect of failure and rejection were not a part of business, successful accounting professionals would be far less special individuals and would be compensated accordingly.

Part of the winning attitude of successful accountants is based on the confidence that is built on the failures they have experienced over time. Instead of taking failure and rejection personally, successful accountants take them as learning experiences. They understand that failure is not the opposite of success, but rather its companion and forerunner. With such an invaluable insight, they do not give up. Instead, they learn, adjust, and try again.

ACCOUNTING AND PRODUCT KNOWLEDGE

These are the most basic and obvious of the accountant's qualifications. They can be used only when prospective clients are ready to buy and need to decide on the specific service they want. You do not reach this point every day, not even any day. Most of our work takes place on the prospects' "turf" and many times on their terms as well. Once accountants can amass the fortitude to enter the arena, they had better be prepared with something more substantial than just the desire to succeed.

The author recalls an incident during his fledgling sales period when he circled a retail store prospect many times before getting the courage to overcome his fear of cold-call selling. When he finally entered the store and introduced himself as a salesman to the shop owner, the owner was nearly overcome with relief. "Ah, you're a salesman. I thought you were casing the store so you could come in and rob me."

Successful accountants must fully understand the features and benefits of accounting services, software and other accounting products, and any specific market niches they are cultivating. Further, accountants had better possess a thorough knowledge of the competition's services and products. In an environment that is as constantly changing as the accounting services industry, the maintenance of knowledge is almost a full-time job in itself. Accountants who will not or cannot make the commitment to keep their expertise at the top of the industry are sorely disadvantaged. And isn't the competition already bad enough?

The manufacturers, publishers, and other vendors of the products you market offer a variety of in-depth knowledge. Seminars, videoconferences, training tapes, road shows, meetings, and other educational services are provided for your mutual benefit. You must find the time to attend the events and study the materials afterward. Product knowledge and skills, along with market familiarity, are unquestionably among your most powerful tools for success. It is impossible to become a professional in the eyes of your clients without them.

THE ART AND SCIENCE OF SELLING

Contrary to many widely held beliefs, there is a great deal more to selling accounting services and products than a glad hand, a round of golf, and a fast close. There is an art to it and a science as well.

There is *art* because of professional selling's dependence on feelings and self-expression. Professional accountants give of themselves; they do not simply take orders. And there is *science.* When people are the major component of your profession, you must learn about them to succeed. Remember, markets never buy anything—people do.

An analogy for the sales process is the bicycle. The rear wheel drives the machine. It provides the power and the speed and requires the most energy to operate. It is virtually useless without the front wheel under the control of a capable rider.

The same is true of the relationship between product and professional knowledge and people knowledge. Professional and product expertise drives the sale and powers the process, like the rear wheel of our bicycle. But people knowledge, the art and science of selling, provides the guidance and direction our bicycle needs to get us there.

Selling through Sales Myths

Every industry and profession has myths that affect the way business is conducted, and accounting is no exception. The sales field is rife with its own myths. They are particularly interesting because each one is crafted to rationalize the problems and foibles of the selling profession. The myths apply to accounting. If one accepts the myths uncritically, it is probable that they will impede improvement. By analyzing them carefully, it is possible to achieve breakthroughs in selling accounting and consulting services. Here are 10 accounting sales myths with a twist to improve your selling techniques:

1. *It's not who you know that counts, it's who knows you.* There may have been a time when knowing all the right people led to success, but today the tables are turned. Now it is *who knows you* that gets you the business. Making a name for yourself is the key. If you are known as the leader or expert in the field, two things will happen: (1) you will get in the door, and (2) business will come to you.

2. *It's not high price that kills sales, it's low credibility.* If you run into the objection that your prices are too high, zero in on the true issue. More often than not, price objections are the result of inadequate marketplace credibility. Low prices become the deciding factor when firms fail to communicate to clients other, more significant reasons for doing business with them. Drive up your firm's credibility, and the price problem will diminish.

3. *It's not a lack of leads that causes a decline in sales, it's a lack of clients.* Having more leads is not the answer to boosting sales. Calling on free advice seekers wastes time. What every professional accountant needs are clients who want to do business with them. If a firm is not producing qualified leads, it is shortchanging its salespeople.

4. *It's not that prospective clients refuse to buy, it's that they buy from someone else.* What is worse than outright rejection? Indifference. It is far worse. Most prospective clients do not reject doing business with a firm; they simply have a reason—ranging from minor to significant—to buy from someone else. Arming prospective clients with valid reasons for doing business with you is the basis for winning clients.

5. *It's not a poor location that keeps clients away, it's lack of excitement.* Of course, location is important, but it is not as essential as some would have you believe. A less-than-desirable office site need not be a negative. If there is excitement, flair, and enthusiasm in the marketing and presentation, clients will find you.

6. *It's not the prospective client's objections, it's following the salesperson's agenda that eliminates prospects.* Some salespeople kill sales before they get started with a prospective client. In an attempt to qualify a lead, they say, "When do you think you'll be ready?" or "Where are you in the decision-making process?" Instead of tuning in to the prospective client, they press forward with their own agenda. If they do not hear the right words, they dismiss the prospect.

7. *It's not that our client bought services from a competitor that's distressing, it's that they didn't know we offer the same service.* Whether the firm's offerings are narrow or broad, it makes no difference. Whether your services are few or many, clients think about what they want, not what you sell. A consistent

effort to keep your services or array of products in front of them will get you the business when that specific need arises.

8. *It's not competitors who create a sales problem, it's a firm's lack of a unique identity.* Blaming competition for taking away business is like blaming a health insurance company for being sick. The problem is not what the competition is doing but what you have not done to present yourself as a resource for clients and potential clients. Does anyone ask you, "And what is it that you do?" If so, your firm has a bland, unexciting image. It is time to change it.

9. *It's not the decline in sales that's the source of difficulty, it's failing to take prospective clients seriously.* Some call it skimming the cream off the top. Whatever the label, it's a process of screening leads to get the "hot" ones, those believed to be instant clients. Once the "ready-to-buy-now" prospects have been culled, there is still plenty of business—and someone will get it. The key is to evaluate the prospective clients and create ongoing plans to stay in contact with them until they become the cream. They will become clients at some point. The goal is to be there at the right time.

10. *It's not that they don't need what you offer, it's that they aren't convinced they need you.* Just because prospective clients may have a need for the services you offer does not mean that they will give your firm the business, even if you perform better than others. In fact, there are times they may want what you offer, but they do not want it from you. Spending time developing solid answers to the question "Why does the client need us?" is a major step in building revenues. When price, deliverables, quality, and performance are virtually the same, why should the prospective client want to do business with? If you cannot come up with reasons, neither will the client.

Believing in myths keeps professional accountants from maximizing sales effectiveness. Dispensing with the myths frees the mind to gain new insights to break through the barriers.

Relationship Selling

The accounting business is far different from most others. We cannot close once and consider the sale complete. If we are to see a constant flow of business from our clients, we must be prepared to provide a constant flow of services and attention. We must build a relationship based on respect and trust. While this is simple in concept, it is not easy in practice. There are four essential, relationship-building steps, each requiring continuing development and reinforcement. Think of them as your four steps to success:

1. *Building trust.* Accounting is a very personal business. The accountant usually invests a great deal of time with the client, looking at procedures, analyzing alternatives, installing systems, training the client's staff, and being an all-around business confidant. The last thing clients need is an accounting professional whom they do not feel they can trust. What they do need is an accounting professional on whom they can depend—someone who always has the answers and is interested in the long-term business relationship. This trust relationship is not easily developed. It takes time, attention to detail, personal care, and commitment. It has to be earned.

2. *Interviewing.* This step is the one most commonly omitted by novice accountants. They rush to the close without first determining what the needs are. No one appreciates that their time has been wasted, especially by an unprofessional accountant. Before you can fill the client's need, you must determine what it is. So simple, yet so frequently forgotten.

3. *Consulting.* As you learn more about the customer's needs from the interview process, you can address them logically, cogently, and effectively. In essence, you become the client's consultant even before a formal agreement is reached. You respect the prospective client's time and intelligence. You become in his or her eyes a true professional, especially when that prospect recalls visits from rookie nonprofessionals.

   After all, isn't that really what selling our services is all about—determining the client's needs and then meeting them? When the client has needs in the future, he or she will think of the knowledgeable, trusted professional who previously assisted them. That is relationship selling.

4. *Getting the commitment.* This step is often the most difficult for many people. It consists of establishing the agreement between the accounting firm and the client. A hard close, complete with signing on the dotted line in blood, is not necessary. What is needed is an understanding that your contributions will be recognized and you will be rewarded with the business. Again, this is the nature of the relationship sale.

Your follow-through with the four-step relational selling process will empower you as a professional accountant. Keep the process natural and orderly. A confident and consistent performance will give you a real edge on the competition.

SELLING SKILLS EMPOWERMENT

The material in Exhibits 10.1 through 10.5 is designed for self-study so that you can proceed at a pace that makes sense for you. To help you understand where you are in relation to the area of your selling skills, we ask you to answer some subjective, self-analysis questions. The sole purpose of these questions is to identify the specific subject areas where special attention should be directed. It is important to understand and always keep in mind that the emphasis of this work is on you. For this material to be truly effective, you must be absolutely and sometimes brutally honest with yourself. Your responses are for you to keep. They are not intended to be graded. To get the most out of this book, you must be completely candid with yourself. It is the only way to ensure that the time you invest in yourself will produce the rewards that you deserve.

Your assignment is to complete the questionnaire on the following pages. Use separate pieces of paper for your responses. Remember—be honest.

If you are new to the accounting services industry and have not had any field sales experience as yet, call on your experience from any previous sales job. If you have not had any sales experience, respond to the questions that apply to your personal situation. Do not feel at all disadvantaged if you lack sales experience. You may have avoided negative attitudes that would have to be overcome. You are now entering the most exciting area in business without preconceptions that could serve to slow you down.

EXHIBIT 10.1
Sales Skills Empowerment Questionnaire

Record your responses on a separate sheet of paper and file in a three-ring binder, which should be kept in a safe place for later review. Your responses will not be graded and are solely for your use. All exercises in this book are intended to be personal and confidential.

Your three-ring binder will become the basis for your personal accounting business owner's manual. Date each response sheet and note the title of the specific questionnaires. Similar questionnaires appear throughout the book and are intended for comparison purposes by you. Together, they should tell you much, not only about yourself but also about your progress.

Above all, be honest and frank with yourself when completing the exercises.

EXHIBIT 10.2
Self-Concept Analysis

Self-Concept

One personal trait or special quality I possess that makes me feel confident and that I use extensively with clients is: ______________

____

Fears

My biggest fears in making sales calls and selling our products and services are: ______________________________

____

What would happen if my fears came true?

____

EXHIBIT 10.3
Sales Skills Empowerment Exercise

RATE YOURSELF ON THE FOLLOWING SUBJECTS:

(Answer *Usually, Often, Sometimes, Seldom,* or *Never* for each question on a separate sheet of paper)

1. I am able to present my ideas comfortably and confidently on a sales call.
2. I can give prospective clients at least three reasons why our services and products are superior to our competitors'.
3. My first impression on prospective clients is very professional.
4. I listen on sales calls more than I talk.
5. Prospective clients know that I am sincerely interested in solving their problems.

6. I am able to quickly determine my prospective client's needs.
7. I am successful in building trust with my clients.
8. I am able to sell myself as an advantage to dealing with my firm.
9. I never have any problems getting commitments from my clients.
10. I am organized effectively every day for sales calls, follow-up, telephone calls, and billable activities.
11. Before I offer a specific benefit to a prospective client, I make sure I understand the prospective client's needs.
12. I am constantly refining my understanding of accounting services and products in general and our services and products in particular.
13. I am able to handle client and prospective client objections easily and professionally.
14. I am very goal oriented, even to the point of putting my goals in writing.
15. I am always seeking ways to improve my performance in my professional life and in my personal life as well.

Knowing your personal strengths and weaknesses regarding the specific skills you need in building your business will contribute greatly to your success. Deficiencies in certain areas may indicate the need to complement your skills with others to build a viable business. In Exhibit 10.4, check the skills in which you feel you need improvement.

EXHIBIT 10.4
Selling Skills Inventory

I need greater skills in:

- ❑ Product knowledge
- ❑ Time management
- ❑ Sales call planning
- ❑ Overcoming call reluctance
- ❑ Closing statements
- ❑ Sales call follow-up
- ❑ Effective telephone techniques
- ❑ People knowledge
- ❑ Prospecting
- ❑ Effective listening
- ❑ Feature and benefit statements
- ❑ Handling client objections
- ❑ Asking the right questions
- ❑ Speaking before groups

EXHIBIT 10.5
Agreement with Myself for Learning

In order to maximize the benefits of this sales skills learning opportunity, I, ________________________, sincerely commit to improving my knowledge and expertise in the following areas:

1. ____

2. ____

3. ____

4. ____

Date: ______________ ______________________________
(Signed)

You have now identified some strong points and some areas that need improvement. You have found some areas that could be problematic to your success. Most important, you have confronted your fears.

Do not be concerned if you focused on your fears. Any successful businessperson who claims never to have experienced them is either untruthful or unintelligent, or both. Fear is normal for the accounting professional—the test is in overcoming it. That takes brains and truth. Remember, FEAR could also mean: False Evidence Appearing Real.

You have also analyzed the specific skills you need to deal effectively with your fears. This paved the way for completion of your agreement with yourself. Once you signed the agreement, you participated in a very dynamic exercise in goal setting—even if you did not realize it at the time. You wrote down your goals for the book.

What is the significance of writing down your goals? The significance is that they are concrete. You have made a conscious commitment to take action to achieve an end: a goal. You must not fail to understand commitment. A goal that is written down is a commitment.

Writing goals down is effective in one's personal life as well. Whether the goal is to take five strokes off your golf game, to spend an extra measure of quality time with your family, to take that long-delayed trip, or to be the top accounting professional in your area, committing goals to paper and looking at them frequently is a powerful first step.

The primary point to remember is that the goals must be challenging but not impossible. If the goal is not achieved, failure does not necessarily result as long as your best effort has been put forth. If the effort is not there, however, failure most certainly will result. That makes for much poorer company than the bumps and bruises of a good honest try.

THE THREE TYPES OF SELLING

There is very little out there that is really "new." Things are packaged differently, called by different names and heralded as breakthrough discoveries, but they are nonetheless pretty much the same as that which has gone before.

Trade, business, and accounting were part of human life long before mankind's earliest records. In the truest sense, the world's oldest profession is undoubtedly sales related. The three basic types of selling have been with us all that time.

The Drummers

Drummers are the stereotypical salespeople. They are the ones with loud suits, the backslapping manners, the ready jokes, and the hard closes, "shotgunning" the message to the greatest possible audience in the fervent hope that some of it might stick. Drummers were on center stage with the traveling medicine show and are with us today in the form of mass media advertising.

Virtually all forms of advertising are designed to broadcast a message that can realistically be picked up and acted upon by only a small percentage of the marketplace. Much of it is designed to be subliminal in nature. Such messages sell us on the natural simplicity of a particular deodorant and the inescapable allure of a specific perfume.

What is the problem with this hard, compliance-type technique? It tells, it does not ask. This approach may work if you have the time and the money. But in the accounting business, we can get only so much out of advertising and very little in personal sales out of the Drummer approach. What you *could* get is thrown out of prospective clients' offices—counterproductive and painful.

Drummer Sales–Type Translation Dictionary

When they say this:	They really mean this:
• Completely open	There is a 50 percent chance that it will work with your existing system.
• Installed at over 250 sites	Actively used at 125 sites, uninstalled at 125 sites.
• Twenty-four hour support	It will take at least 24 hours to get back to you.
• Our services have scalability	Watch as we try to sell you more and more.
• Full heterogeneous operation	If our products will not work, we can blame the others.

The Entertainers

Entertainers are usually more successful than Drummers. They are socializers, the good ol' boys or girls who get the business in two ways: because they are liked or as a payback for the entertainment. There is nothing wrong in developing a strong rapport with the clients. It is encouraged, to be sure. Likewise, there is nothing wrong with entertaining good clients, within the bounds of propriety. These types of activity can help build trust and confidence between you and the client. They are not, however, sufficient to promise you success.

What is wrong with this approach? There is always someone who will out-buy, out-smile, or out-entertain you, and *they* will get the business. It is that simple. Moreover, a client cannot make a commitment to give such a salesperson his or her business without being made to feel "bought." Thus, Entertainers may spend their careers giving clients basketball tickets and never see any commitment, much less *meaningful* payback. This is probably because our next type is beating the Entertainer's action.

The Professionals

Real pros sell by finding the need, then acting to fill it. That does not mean that they are "strictly business," or overly severe in style, behavior, or dress. Rather, it means that pros will not waste the client's time, energy, or money. When the small talk is over, they get down to business. Professionals do not stop working when sales calls are over. There are always other actions to take, questions to get answered, and details to follow up. The other salespeople often forget. The professionals do not.

STEPS TO SUCCESSFUL SALES

Everyone can close a sale. However, replicating that success daily, weekly, and yearly requires a level of personal investment that is defined by your ability to plan your work and work your plan. A basic schedule for closing more accounting services sales includes the following steps.

Step 1: Motivation

Answer two questions for yourself: Why am I in accounting? Why am I selling these particular services for this particular firm? Accept your positive response as rationale for deserving success.

Step 2: Know Your Services and Products

Complete product and services knowledge means either having the knowledge yourself or knowing where to access the correct information. This combination will ensure your credibility during the sales process.

Step 3: Sales Flow

In one form or another, the accounting business sales process will include the following:

- Opening
- General accounting/Consulting questions
- General client needs
- Specific services questions
- Specific client needs
- Services solutions
- Service/Product benefits
- Summarization

- Action item
- Information processing

Fully develop each category, and be aware that the order of these steps will change with each contact.

Step 4: Know Your Client

Listen, listen, listen. To deliver an effective and acceptable response, listen to your client and prospective client and choose your response from one of your sales flow categories. To avoid disappointment when "asking for the sale," be prepared to initiate and complete each step in the sales flow.

Step 5: Label and Visualize Success

Frequently, salespeople do not know what to do after the sale is closed. Overcome this barrier by labeling "your style." How do you want your clients to see you? How do you see yourself? Create a positive image and visualize the success you will gain with your new or newly defined style.

Step 6: Accept Change

All professional accountants and consultants enjoy their fair share of success and failure. An ever-changing environment can create cyclical gaps that spread your successes even further apart. To ensure continued success during any change, it is important to track and note the tools, styles, and deliveries used to create previous successes. Then, when a new development is encountered, success can be achieved by simply adjusting the current plan.

Step 7: Closing

Only after working through the first six steps and practicing the plan should the professional expect to close more sales. The results of hard work will accumulate and result in a sustained increase in business.

What is the problem with this approach? Plenty—it is *tough.* It takes intelligence, a strong desire to succeed, a complete knowledge of the business and its products and services, and an understanding of the art and science of selling.

The prospecting informational seminar is a great relationship marketing tool. Exhibit 10.6 contains guidelines for developing, implementing, and benefiting from seminars.

EXHIBIT 10.6
The Prospecting Informational Seminar

Teaching Prospective Clients to Become Clients

1. *Make the topic timely for the prospective client.* Do not fall into the trap of selecting seminar topics because they are of interest to you or your salespeople. Get inside the heads of prospective clients and figure out what they are interested in. For example, one accounting firm developed an excellent seminar, "Smaller to Mid-Sized Market Financing—Full-Sized Results." This is a pertinent topic for the business executives and owners of one of their niche markets.

2. *Never run more than two hours.* Of course, no topic can be fully developed in such a short period. But a sales seminar is not a graduate-level course. Its purpose is to share important information in a way that demonstrates a firm's competence. Do it in a brief, concise period. Remember, the people you want to attend are busy. Respect their time by giving them top-quality information in the time they are willing to make available.

3. *Keep it businesslike.* Forget about food and liquor. Send the message that this is business. Serve coffee, juice, fruit, and Danish in the morning. If it is later in the day, soda and cookies are fine. You want to demonstrate that you have an important message. Make your topic the focus of the event.

4. *Make the information entertaining.* Businesslike does not mean dull and boring. If anyone gets bored, you have lost the prospective client, and your current clients may have doubts about continuing with your firm. A seminar should be an upbeat, enjoyable experience. Take a realistic look and determine if you can perform in an outstanding manner. Anything less, forget about it. If you cannot have someone else do it, join Toastmasters or 12-step groups and learn to give an excellent seminar. Remember, no seminar would be preferable to a bad seminar.

5. *Give them something they can talk about.* Seminar participants should leave with one or two important ideas they can discuss later. When this happens, they feel that the seminar had value.

6. *Keep sessions small.* There should be enough participants so no one is uncomfortable, yet small enough so everyone feels important. Depending on the topic, anywhere from 10 to 40 people can be appropriate. There may be occasions when 100 or more might attend, for instance, perhaps if you are having a noted speaker.

7. *Sending out invitations.* Send out many times more than the number of people you want to attend. If there are too many responses, simply schedule another session. The invitation is important in itself. Even if some people cannot attend or are not interested in the topic, sending the invitation lets them know about your firm and what you are doing. Call those on your list before the event. This will increase the attendance if you need it.

8. *Promote your expertise.* For example, if you have lots of experience guiding businesses through their budgetary process, a seminar is an opportunity to demonstrate your knowledge of the key issues. It also gives you a chance to forge an image as the expert in a specific field.

9. *Tell them everything you know.* The more you tell them, the better. Candor impresses prospective clients, and lets them discover what you know. Listeners can spot fluff and puff. If they think you are trying to make a sale by withholding information, you will never do business with them.

10. *Avoid anything that sounds like a sales pitch.* Yes, there is one sale that must be made at a seminar. Participants should come away believing that you know what you are talking about and that the message has validity for them. This is quite different from turning a seminar into a sales session. If you do a good job at the seminar, there will soon be opportunities for getting the business.

11. *Allow no one to leave empty-handed.* Brochures and sales materials should provide additional information. Prepare folders and have them ready at the end of the session.

12. *Do on-the-spot evaluations.* Have an evaluation form for everyone to fill out before leaving the seminar. The questions

might include: How would you rate this seminar? What did you find most or least helpful to you? What can we do to improve the seminar? If you would like additional information, what is of particular interest? Would you like to be on our mailing list? What need do you have at this time that you think we could help with? Be sure to collect the forms before your participants leave the room.

13. *Do additional follow-up.* Every participant should receive an appreciation letter within 48 hours of the session. This letter should refer to the individual's comments on the information form. The letter should also set forth how you are going to work with the prospective client in the weeks and months ahead and that you will be staying in close touch through newsletters, e-mail, other seminars, and personal contact.

Source: The Accounting Guild.

The Accounting Guild has prepared and makes available "Seminar-in-a-Box" presentations. These are for professional accountants to use as the basis of their own seminars and are on a variety of topics. Contact The Accounting Guild for a listing of the seminar materials and other professional materials for accountants and consultants.

The seminar is an efficient way to demonstrate the accounting firm's ability to do consulting and create and build meaningful relationships. More than many other activities, it is an effective—even essential—technique for identifying prospective clients, building a prospect database, and creating a positive selling environment.

THE IMPORTANCE OF VERSATILITY

Above all else, accounting professionals need **versatility.** Versatility means that we adapt to our clients and circumstances. In so doing, we have opportunities to act, not merely react, by truly understanding how our clients are motivated.

There is an old saying in accounting that goes, "People do business for their reasons, not ours." This statement merits remembering. It means that clients will not do business with us merely because we want them to. They have needs to be met before doing business with anyone. Clients will do business for their individual reasons. It is up to us to determine what those reasons are.

In the final analysis, that old and wise saying means simply that we must find the need and satisfy it and not merely pitch the features of our services hit or miss. We must not be only accounting professionals. We must become professional accounting consultants.

Before we start, let's make sure what being a professional accounting consultant for our clients really means. For openers, it means making a commitment, as we did with our Agreement in Exhibit 10.5. That commitment is to become a student of people and human nature. After all, if we are to become consultants, or counselors in effect, we must deal with many different types of people. The marketplace is our playing field, our artist's canvas. To become as productive and effective as possible, we have to learn as much as we can about people.

Next, you must agree to constantly put your knowledge to use. Just one exposure will not make you an expert, but practice might. Robert Benchley said, "A little knowledge is a dangerous thing," and Benjamin Disraeli said, "The wisdom of the wise and the experience of the ages are perpetuated by quotations." Overconfidence can lead to real problems. Fortunately, putting your knowledge to use is fun and easy to do. The unwillingness of people to practice is why there are so few real accounting professionals. One of the purposes of this book is to change this mindset.

The next step to becoming a professional accounting consultant is to absorb product and services knowledge as if it were a favorite treat. Look at every morsel of accounting and business information as being worth its weight in gold, because it is. Establish sources inside your own firm, at the software publishers and developers, computer manufacturers, and the trade press. The Internet presents a virtual gold mine. Use all sources to their best advantage. Do this and do it correctly, and soon your clients will know where they can go for their information. To their consultant—to you.

If you do these things, you will be successful. Why? Because you will have a working understanding of what motivates your clients, and you will have the expertise to follow through.

CREATIVE FOLLOW-THROUGH

As we discussed, accountants need certain sales and people skills to make the follow-up process lead to a sale. These skills are not complex or hard to learn, but they play a vital role in determining the most effective type of follow-through. Get to know the prospective client's hot buttons—triggers that may persuade the prospect to buy from your firm. Make certain that with each follow-up, new information is presented relevant to the prospect's needs and hit those hot buttons. When following up, be prepared for anything. This requires flexibility and creativeness in style and presentation.

To ensure maximum impact, ask yourself five questions about your follow-up technique:

1. Are you sincere in your desire to help the client first and put your sale second?
2. Are you direct in your communication?
3. Are you funny? People love to laugh. A laughing prospective client is more likely to buy.
4. Are you friendly? People buy from friends before they buy from salespeople.
5. Are you selling benefits? Prospects are interested only in how they can benefit from your services or products.

Sales Objectives

The objective of follow-through is to build the relationship along with the sale. Think of each follow-up as a new sales adventure—a new opportunity to make the sale. Plan each follow-up contact as though this is the one that will do it.

Here are some lead-in lines to start the conversation:

- "I thought of a few things that might help you decide . . ."
- "Something new has occurred that I thought you might like to know about . . ."
- "There has been a change in the status of . . ."
- "I was thinking about you, and called to tell you about . . ."
- Do say: "I sent you some (name the material) the other day, and it wasn't completely self-explanatory. I wanted to go over a couple of things with you personally; I'll need about five minutes. Have you got your appointment book handy?" (Don't say: "I called to see if you got my letter/information/whatever." If the prospective client does not want to talk to you, he can just say, "No, I never got it." Where does that leave you? Back at square one.)

Tools of the Trade

Sales tools are the most underemployed weapons in the selling process. There are everyday sales tools like the phone, fax, e-mail, letters, brochures, and literature, but the professional accountant needs out-of-the-ordinary tools to entice the prospective client to engage the firm over the competition.

Make these tools part of your sales plan:

- *A personal note.* A handwritten note (greeting-card-sized, imprinted with your company name and logo) is far more effective than a typed business letter in convincing the prospect you care.
- *A package of letters from satisfied clients.* One third-party endorsement is more powerful than 100 sales pitches.
- *An endorsement from a mutual friend.* A friend of your prospect is far more influential than you are. The friend can smooth the way or find out the real reason you cannot get an appointment or make the sale.
- *Something in print.* A copy of a favorable article gives you an additional reason to contact the prospective client. Send articles about your business or, better yet, about the prospective client's business or, best of all, about the prospect's personal interests.
- *An invitation to your facility.* Bring the prospective clients to your home field. Make the visit memorable with enthusiastic greetings from you and the staff, great food, and some type of memento. Ask yourself, "Will the prospective clients go back to their offices and talk about this visit?" If not, change it so they will.
- *Specialty item.* Send a handy or unusual item that will be used, seen, and talked about. This can be anything from a jar opener to a T-shirt.
- *A meal.* Meetings in a nonbusiness environment are the most powerful. They enable you to get the personal information that leads to a relationship.

Employ traditional sales tools creatively:

- *Telephone.* This is the second most powerful sales weapon (personal visits are the first). Calls can arrange meetings, give information, and close the deal. However, calls can grow tiresome and often go unreturned. To make the most of the phone, never call without a purpose, and never hang up without setting the next meeting or contact and confirming it.

- *Fax.* A fax is still a priority document. Fax a referral letter, a top-10 list, a cartoon, or a page from your appointment book for next week with the open times circled.
- *E-mail.* Use the Internet to attach something the client or prospective client would find interesting. It is not so much a matter of what is sent, but that it is thoughtful and consistent.
- *A plant, flowers, or other tasteful gift.* You will be amazed at how even a small gift can change an attitude.
- *Networking events.* Arrange to meet the prospective client at a networking function. A social meeting can speed up a business relationship. Social business engagements, such as trade association meetings, Chamber of Commerce events, and sporting events, are the heart of business life.
- *Send a provocative letter without being provoking.* Ask questions or make statements that make the prospective client think. Do not sell anything but an appointment.

No Sale

Sometimes all the follow-through in the world does not result in a client relationship. Either the prospective client is still in the decision-making mode, has decided no, or has begun a relationship with a competitor and has not told you yet. Find out the reason, and you will understand what it may take to get the sale.

Take a risk, take a chance, use your creativity. Do not be afraid to make a mistake, do not worry about rejection, and *do not quit.*

On Track

No matter how well you handle it, your follow-through will not pay off unless you keep track of your efforts. The best follow-through tracking system has three components:

1. *Contact management.* There are many programs designed for contact management and sales follow-up. GoldMine is simply the best available. When you have all your information on a computer, your mind is free to create. That is part of the secret of sales achievement.

2. *Business card file.* Write prospective clients' personal and business information on the backs of their business cards. Transfer the information to your GoldMine program as soon as possible.
3. *Daily priority planner.* Use this in conjunction with any system to keep your appointments and notes.

Your ability to follow through determines your success in building a successful accounting and consulting business. It is said to take an average of seven exposures or follow-ups to close the sale. What is the secret to getting to the seventh try? *Persistence.*

ENTREPRENEURIAL SALES

Entrepreneurial sales skills can be achieved by taking more than one course in marketing. Marketing is not complicated—unless you take several courses in it. (This is said somewhat tongue-in-cheek, since the author majored in marketing along with accounting courses at the Bernard M. Baruch School of The City College of New York.)

Goals

- Create demand for your services indirectly (through means other than direct advertising).
- Get the business community to have confidence in you as a respected, high-caliber individual.
- Instill confidence in your firm within the business community. Earn a reputation for such high-quality performance that people talk about it.
- Establish yourself as an expert. Why just be in the accounting field when you can be perceived as on top of it?
- Be seen and known as a leader. Speak in front of an audience, or get involved in a group and lead them.
- Separate yourself from the competition. Get in front of the pack (in a dog team every position but the lead has the same view), and set a standard.
- Gain professional stature. Your image is defined by others. Your outreach determines your image.

- Build your image and the image of your accounting business by being a consistent, positive performer, by associating with quality things and people, and by always delivering what you promise.

Reach Out

- *Get in print.* Ads do not work as well (or as credibly) as an article about you or your accounting firm. One story about your firm will attract immediate business and has immeasurable residual value when reprinted and mailed to prospective clients and current clients.
- *Get on the broadcast media.* Get interviewed. TV or radio talk shows, even if they are local, can have a large impact. One evening news report can lift you from unknown to known in your market area—and the credibility is unmatched. Get copies on videotape (the best is the professional broadcast quality tape from the television station or studio) or audiotape (from the radio station) for later duplication and distribution.
- *Get published.* Write about your market niche specialty or expertise. The more you publish, the more credible you become. Your best vehicles are local business journals, local newspapers, city magazines, trade publications (of your target industries), and newsletters relevant to your clients (newsletter editors are always looking for contributors).
- *Publish a newsletter.* Having a difficult time getting into print? Publish yourself. Put in timely and helpful information, then get it professionally designed and edited. You can also use desktop publishing software in-house and have it edited professionally for maximum impact. Target your present and potential clients, and every influential person you can think of for your mailing list.
- *Speak in public.* Use business and civic groups to get your message out. You do not have to talk about accounting—you just have to make an impact. If you are a powerful presenter, they will assume you have a powerful business. (Need to polish your speaking skills? Join your local Toastmasters chapter.)
- *Give a seminar at your prospective client's business or trade association.* A one-time, no-cost look at your skills and expertise will land business, build confidence, and earn respect.
- *Network with the right people.* Be seen and get known by those who can have an impact on or can become clients of your

accounting business. **Directed networking** is the fulcrum of entrepreneurial sales. Networking is inexpensive, great one-on-one exposure, productive, time-effective—and fun.

- *Get involved in the community.* Volunteer where you feel you can be most effective. Select a well-established, well-respected, apolitical organization. Meet with the leader. Ask about the best way to get involved, and what kind of impact you can have.
- *Join the Chamber of Commerce.* It is the single most powerful business organization in your community, so get involved. Meet with the leadership, attend every networking event you can, exhibit at its business fair, and make a five-year plan to get on the board of directors.
- *Join a trade association.* Team up with accounting professionals in different niches, and learn from direct competitors in other parts of the country. Contact The Accounting Guild which provides excellent assistance in enabling you to network with professionals nationally and learn from the success of others.
- *Join the trade associations relevant to the market niches you have chosen to develop.* You will be an associate member with a chance to affect your clients and others. Attend meetings regularly, get involved, and speak to or lead a group. Magnify your impact by developing a reputation for helping others get business (through leads and referrals).
- *Join an executive business group.* Developing relationships with other respected business people can only lead to opportunities.

Exhibit 10.7 outlines activities that you can engage in to enhance your reputation and spotlight your business when others are seeking accounting and consulting services.

EXHIBIT 10.7
Making Your Mark in Professional Accounting and Consulting Checklist

1. *Be willing to give of yourself.* It is not the only way, but it is the best and most lasting one. Becoming a resource is much more powerful than being perceived as a salesperson or accountant. People will want to be around you and pay attention to what you say and do if they believe it is valuable to them and their business.

2. *Get others to help you.* List the people you think can help you or help you connect, and ask for their support. The easiest way to get support? Give it first—without keeping score.

3. *Do everything with a creative flair.* This makes the time and effort you contribute worth remembering. Memorability is a vital link to building market awareness. Here are some creative ideas:

    - Instead of the standard introduction, come up with a brief 30-second "commercial" about what you do and how you can help others. Deliver it after you have asked the other person what he or she does.
    - Get the very best business card for yourself and the firm's staff. It is the firm's image. Every time it is given out, it makes an impact. Engrave it, foil-stamp it, logo it, professional graphic-design it, or multicolor it. Here is the acid test: If recipients do not say "nice card" when they receive it, get it redone.
    - Give away an advertising item that is novel—something people will talk about or show to others.

4. *Combine outreaches:*

    - Use your charity to spotlight you in the community as a spokesperson.
    - Donate a scholarship to your best client's trade association.
    - Give a talk and donate the speaking fee to your charity.
    - Make a donation in honor of a significant event in a client's life.
    - By combining outreaches, you create a steady flow of your image (in the paper, on television, in your newsletter, etc.) to your target market. This helps you stay in front of the people you want to do business with.

5. *Dedicate time to making it happen.* Again, persistence is the secret. Do not do anything once, and then sit back and wait. You must keep plugging, without expectations of instant results. If you are good, have patience and your phone will ring.

Source: The Accounting Guild.

One Step at a Time

First, make a plan. You cannot make a lasting mark without one. Write out your objectives and what you expect to get from each outreach. The best plan is a solid mix of strategies.

Seek professional help. Yes, the phrase does sound funny; however, it refers to professional business assistance. Your best initial investment is to buy professional assistance. Paying a public relations professional for an hour or two and bouncing ideas around is a worthwhile use of funds. It is better to have $500 worth of professional advice than a $500 worthless advertisement that gets no response. The Accounting Guild has excellent professional advice that is especially suited for the accountant and consultant.

Go Slow for Best Results

To get the fastest (and best) results, go slow. The business community is wary of a flash in the pan. Low heat takes longer to cook, but the result always tastes better and you never get burned.

Become known as a person of action, a person who gets things done, a leader. It is not just a reflection on you—it is a reflection on your accounting business and the services and products you offer. It is something you cannot place a value on or buy, but it can make the difference between a thriving business and the alternative.

11

CLIENT PERSONALITY STYLES

This study of client personality styles will boost you on your way toward becoming a student of human nature. In addition to providing insights into your client base, it will provide some interesting slants on other aspects of your professional and personal lives as well. Remember the bicycle? Your front wheel is about to get a great deal stronger.

PERSONALITY STYLES

The charting of personality or social styles was pioneered by Dr. Carl Jung who postulated that most human behavior could be plotted on a grid formed by two axes. These two axes were driven by responsiveness and assertiveness. Each of these two words can have several connotations, so for clarity, we will define them this way:

- **Responsiveness: The degree of control one will exert over his or her own emotions.**
- **Assertiveness: The degree of control or influence one will attempt to exert over others.**

By gridding these two characteristics with their opposites, Dr. Jung came up with four quadrants, as shown in Exhibit 11.1.

Responsive people are typically more emotional than others. They are more animated when talking, often using gestures. They tend to be intuitive and have a knack for picking up on the feelings of others. This type is somewhat impulsive and tends to make decisions based on "gut feelings" rather than strictly on facts. For example, they are impulse buyers, and when shopping for a particular item, they may come home with several.

EXHIBIT 11.1
Grid of Personality Quadrants

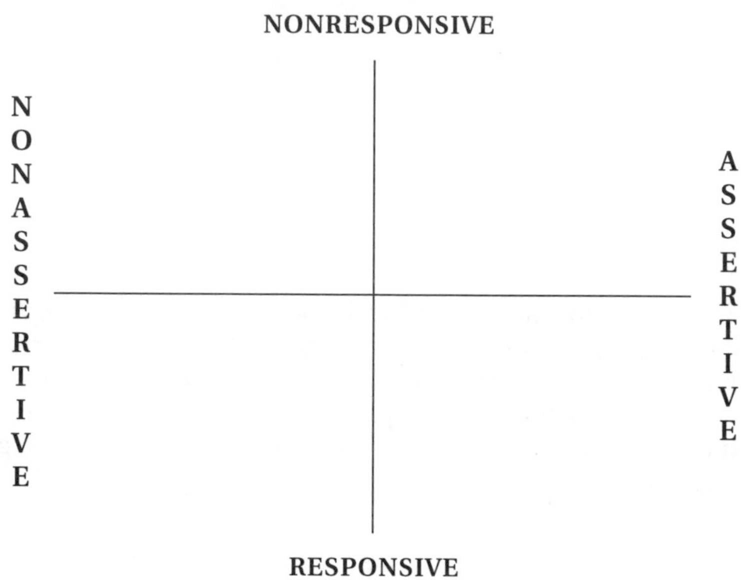

Nonresponsive people are less emotional in most aspects of life. Their decisions are more cerebral, more thought out. They may appear harder to get to know, a bit more reserved. People in this group seldom shop on impulse, but rather, are more likely to be comparison shoppers. They tend to be logical in their thought processes and will dress somewhat conservatively, preferring less trendy styles and muted colors. Although often unintentional, they usually will not come across to others as warm, open, and emotional.

Assertive people like to take charge when they are in a group. They seem more opinionated than others. This may not be true, but the nonassertive person may just prefer not to share opinions, whereas the assertive person is most willing to. Assertive people walk quickly—they are in a hurry to get there, even if lost. They are usually goal oriented and take the achievement of their goals very seriously.

If you have ever been at an intersection with a traffic light when the driver behind you was honking the horn the very millisecond that the light turned green, there is a good chance that you had an assertive driver behind you. Assertive people may or may not care what you think, but they will make sure that you know what is on their minds. They will attempt to influence you to their way of thinking.

Nonassertive people simply worry less about influencing others. They are happier waiting at that traffic light for a second, instead of appearing impatient over something so trivial. They appear to be more relaxed and serene. When walking together, the assertive person may have to wait for the nonassertive person to catch up and then fume about it. Nonassertive people are usually less outspoken (though not necessarily less opinionated) and may even appear shy. They can also be goal oriented, though they will beat themselves up less if a goal is not achieved and probably will not be in the habit of writing their goals down.

Dr. Jung termed the resultant quadrants: **Thinkers, Sensers, Feelers,** and **Intuitors.** These names may have had clarity from a behaviorist's point of view but were a bit confusing for accounting professionals. Industrial psychologists Drs. David Merrill and Roger Reid as well as numerous others placed the following four terms into common usage:

1. Analyticals
2. Drivers
3. Expressives
4. Amiables

The material can be very useful as long as you keep in mind that none of this is intended to be in any way manipulative. The intent is to further your understanding of people, how to work with them better, and more important, what motivates them to take action. You will learn the distinction between working with people and dealing with the public.

The labels are not designed to be judgmental. There is no better or worse category among the styles. In any randomly drawn group of 100, roughly 25 will be found in each category. Keep in mind, however, the story of the person who placed one foot in a bucket of boiling water while the other foot was encased in a block of ice. On average, the person was comfortable. If the group is gathered by profession or industry, it is no longer random and the results may differ.

A practical application where you may indicate your personality style is shown in Exhibit 11.2. You can approximate the grid in your notebook or make a copy of the page to protect your privacy.

EXHIBIT 11.2
Practical Application

On the grid below, place an X on the north/south axis above the centerline if you tend to be **nonresponsive,** or below the centerline if you think you are more **responsive.** Think on balance, on average, not merely at work. Putting your X in the middle is a **nonresponse.**

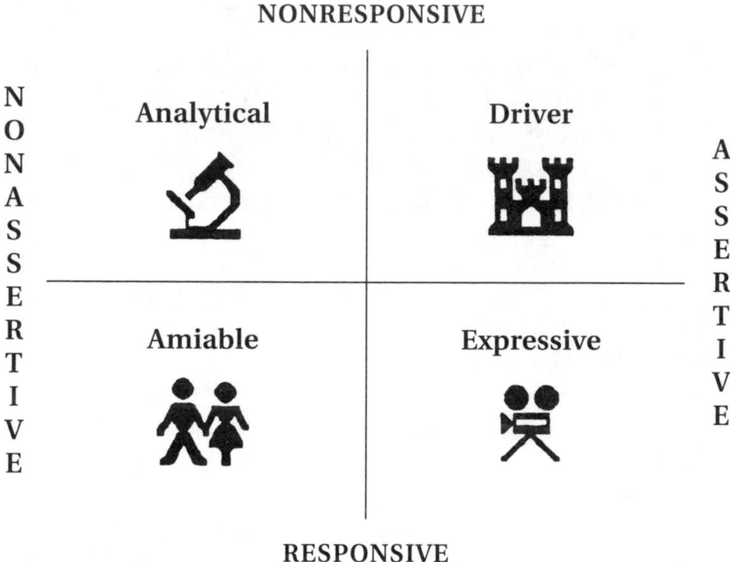

Let's repeat the previous exercise. An enhancement to Exhibit 11.2 is offered below in Exhibit 11.3. This time find the appropriate spot on the east/west axis to place your **X.** Do not let ego or some preconceived idea get in your way. **There is no better or worse place on the grid.** The only bad place is a false one, because it will skew much of the remaining exercises for you if you are not honest with yourself.

Once completed, a line connecting your two marks would occupy one quadrant of the grid.

EXHIBIT 11.3
Practical Application—Phase Two

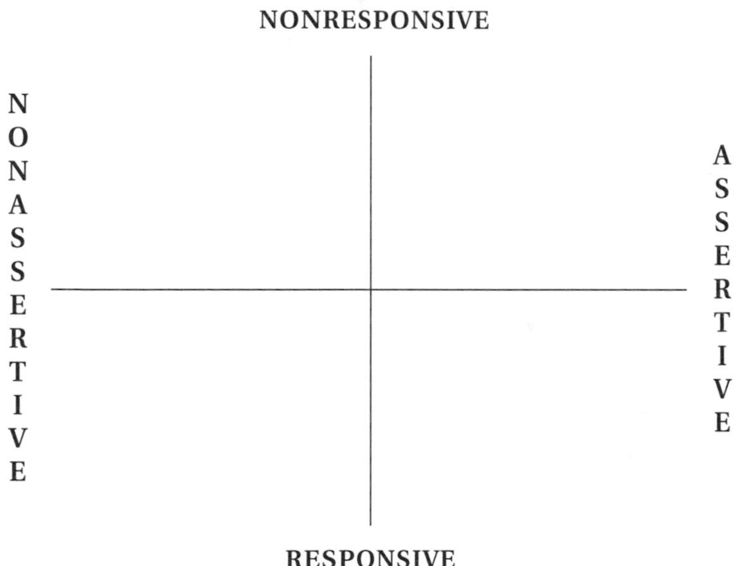

The Analyticals

On the nonassertive side in the nonresponsive quadrant, we find our analytical clients, without whom we would likely be back in the caves. The analyticals are procedural and orderly people who pay great attention to details. They are society's functional perfectionists, making certain that our software is upgraded and that our rocketships lift off and return safely. They are quality conscious and love to have as much logic and data as possible to produce first-class results.

Analytical types often seek careers that allow them to work with facts and figures within an organized, clear-cut framework. Examples of career paths include accounting, law, medicine, the sciences, computers, certain aspects of the military, and finance.

On the downside, analytical types are generally less intuitive than the other styles so they are less quick to pick up the "vibrations" of other people's feelings. Likewise, they are often uncomfortable in expressing their own feelings and may seem somewhat aloof—not to the extreme of the stereotypical "absent-minded professor" perhaps, but enough to make them hard to know as individuals. Exhibit 11.4 shows the location of the analytical personality on the grid.

EXHIBIT 11.4
The Analyticals

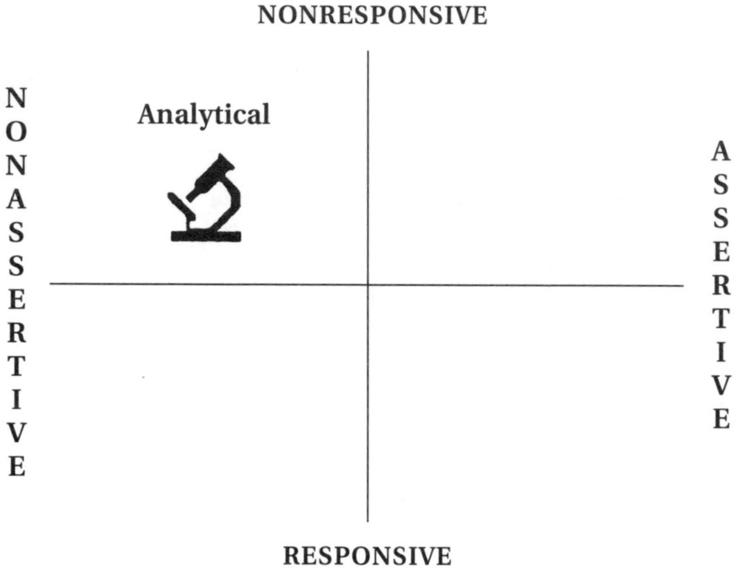

	NONRESPONSIVE	
NONASSERTIVE	Analytical	ASSERTIVE
	RESPONSIVE	

The challenge in dealing with an analytical is a result of their love of facts, of data. They want to make the best possible decision and therefore do not make them quickly. This slowness in decision making can make them appear to be indecisive and noncommittal. This is a frustrating state of affairs for the professional accountant, but a mistake in perception can lead to real difficulties later.

Does this sound like anyone you know? Most of us know someone like the classic analytical type: our doctor, our attorney, or we ourselves may well display many of the characteristics.

You may recognize some of these features in yourself, even if you did not fit into the analytical box on the grid. This is because we all display some of the traits of each personality style at various times, making most of us hybrids. There are very few people who perform true to their style in all facets of everyday life. However, bear in mind that on balance, virtually everyone has a distinct and identifiable style. You can plan your client sales calls and vary your approach to deal appropriately with each type of client or prospective client.

The Drivers

The assertive and nonresponsive box on the grid indicates the drivers of our world. Drivers like to be in charge. They frequently are high-energy, impatient, results-oriented people. They are usually very time conscious. Since they strive to be in charge and in control, their careers often lead them to the executive suites of companies. They are also entrepreneurial, willing to take big risks that offer big rewards. This type is concerned with the macro scheme of things, the big picture. They do not do well with details, preferring to leave them to others.

Drivers make things happen in the world—that is their job. When the analytical type asks, "How?", he or she uses the scientific method to find the answer. The driver type would probably not be able to sit still long enough to do that. They would much prefer to have one or more analytical personality types at work and would probably be pushing them, saying, "How? I don't care how . . . just get it done."

High-profile corporations attract the driver-type personality. Senior executives in computer software companies and other high-pressure businesses are often drivers. Examples of this type include self-employed entrepreneurs such as builders and realtors. Law enforcement, sports coaching, some types of teaching, and the military officer corps are all occupations which might attract driver personality types.

What is the downside for the driver personality type? Like their counterparts on the non-responsive axis, they can seem impersonal. They may like you, but business is business, and they would prefer to be more businesslike. In short, they may appear somewhat aloof and impatient without even realizing it. The driver type does not often stop to smell the roses. That does not get the job done as far as they are concerned. Exhibit 11.5 shows the location of the driver personality on the grid.

The Expressives

This corner of the grid is both responsive and assertive—quite a combination! Many people tend to see themselves in this quadrant, often inaccurately, because it is a fun place to be. The expressive personality types are outgoing, life-of-the-party people who love to be the center of attention. Like the driver personality types, expressives are results oriented but, unlike their nonresponsive neighbors, are strongly relationship oriented as well.

EXHIBIT 11.5
The Drivers

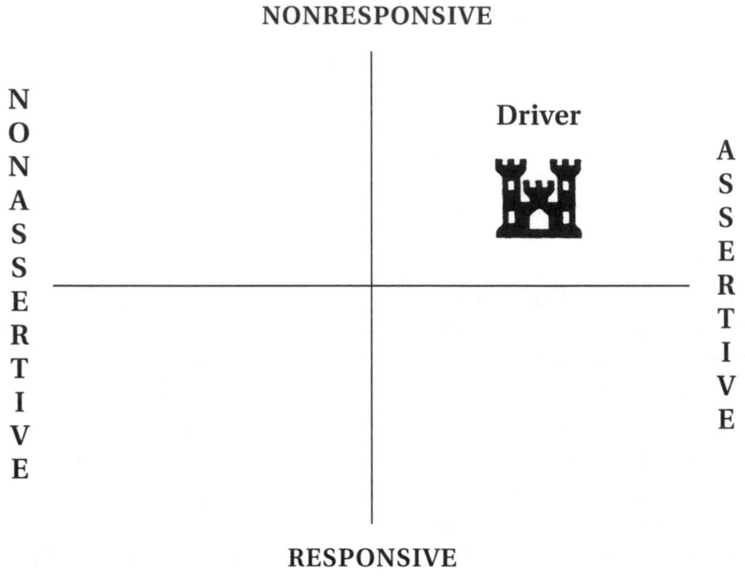

NONRESPONSIVE

NONASSERTIVE

Driver

ASSERTIVE

RESPONSIVE

The expressive personality type is a willing and charismatic leader, naturally enthusiastic and motivational. When it is needed, they are effective at dishing out praise as well as discipline. Because of their strong results orientation, they hate to lose and will do anything in their power to avoid failure. This does not mean they will avoid taking risks. They are very willing risk takers. This may be because of the edge that challenges put on life and the additional thrill of victory that risk taking brings.

The occupations that attract expressive personality types are those associated with good and enthusiastic verbal skills, such as sales. In addition to sales, we find expressives in high-risk work, such as acting, entertaining, politics, athletics, and others that involve some sort of "performing." They really need some form of stage to provide an outlet for self-expression.

The downside for the expressive personality type is mainly in the trait of being a poor listener. Listening is often called the single most important attribute for the successful professional accounting salesperson. The absence of listening can lead to a multitude of problems. When the client is the expressive, he or she is content to do most of the talking and the professional accounting salesperson should be content to do most of the listening. Exhibit 11.6 shows the position of the expressive personality on the grid.

EXHIBIT 11.6
The Expressives

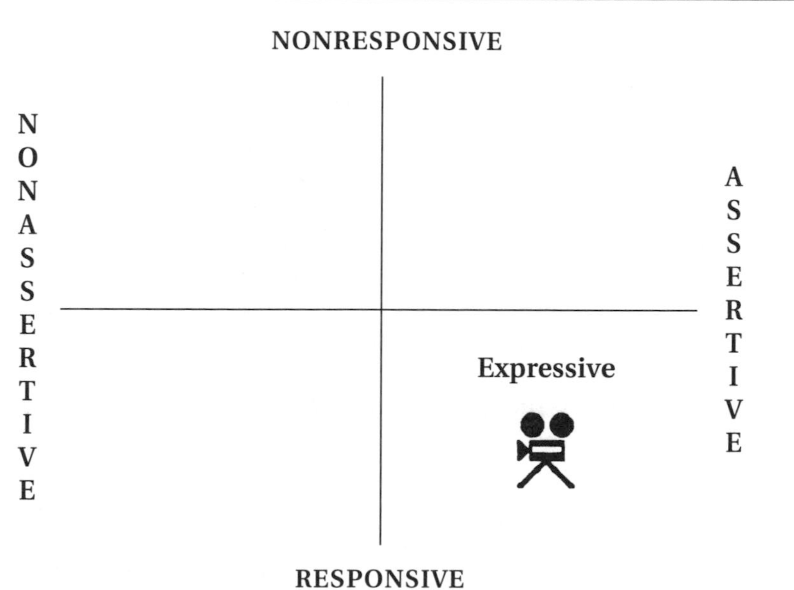

Professional accounting salespeople can effectively guide the interview. They can control it simply by asking questions. The expressive personality types are happy to talk about any subject. They can convey information to help accountants determine the clients' needs. This makes developing a strategy much easier. There is an old adage that says that, "Nobody is easier to sell than a salesperson." Assuming that the salesperson is an expressive type, it is easy to see why.

The Amiables

The final quadrant is composed of the nonassertive but responsive social style, the amiables. These are the people we really like to be around. They are warm, open, friendly, and supportive. In addition, they are concerned and caring and, most important, they are good listeners.

Amiables genuinely care about you and your point of view. They may seem less opinionated than the driver and expressive personality types, but this is not necessarily so. Amiables are less inclined to verbalize their opinions. They are the perfect foils for the expressive types—expressives are happiest when talking, and amiables are happiest when listening.

Sometimes, amiables come across as being shy and this is often true. They can also seem wishy-washy, but this is usually because they can see both sides of an issue more clearly than others.

A particularly endearing trait of the amiables is their natural ability to be team players. They prefer to work as part of a group to achieve a common goal. Amiables will expect their share of the credit for a job well done, but will seldom be pushy enough to call attention to themselves.

Amiables are often found in socially oriented occupations. Service industries, such as food service, hotel resorts, and gaming, attract them as well as social work. Customer service areas within businesses and other highly personal jobs are frequently held by amiable personality types.

The downside for amiables is an inability to share their true feelings, especially if those feelings are negative. If an amiable is a prospective client, this can be a real problem. It makes it difficult to find out what the client's true objections are. You may have the most difficulty getting a commitment from this personality type. They will say yes to appease you and make you happy. Unfortunately, they are saying the same thing to every other accountant who comes in the door. It can be a real challenge trying to do business with them. It requires your professional touch, applied on a consistent basis. Exhibit 11.7 illustrates the amiable personality in the lower left quadrant of the grid.

CLUES FOR SPOTTING PERSONALITY STYLES

There are many clues to help you determine a client's style. Keep in mind that it is an acquired skill—it takes practice. After a while, it can become second nature and you will have a valuable tool at your disposal. Clues are especially available in the physical aspects of the client's office.

Analyticals usually dress conservatively, staying well away from trendy, faddish styles. They generally prefer sensible clothes that will be acceptable for years, if not decades. The "preppie" look was probably the answer to the analyticals' prayers. Analyticals wear classic button-downs and wingtips, the wools and natural shoulders that have been good business styles for generations.

EXHIBIT 11.7
The Amiables

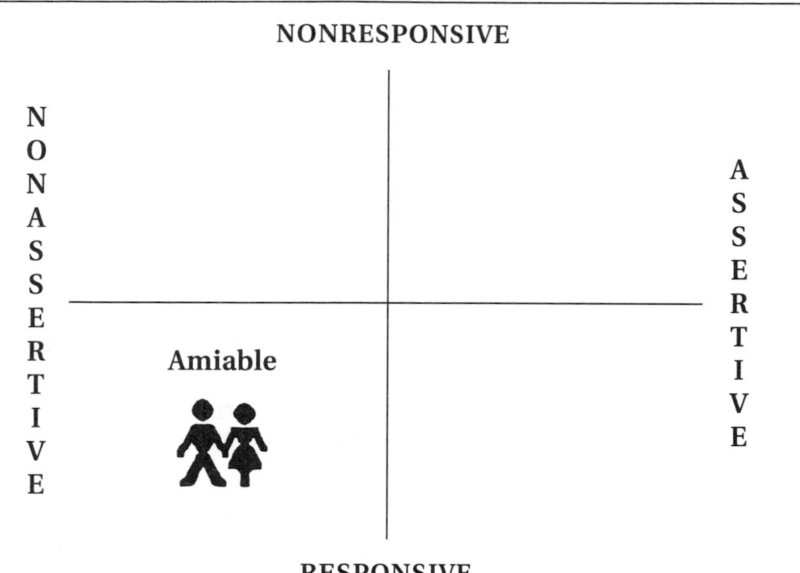

Drivers are a different story. They realize that the right clothes can enhance the perception of power and authority. They will often opt for dark colors with sharp contrasts, like navy suits with white shirts and red ties. They will seldom wear earth tones or pastels for business wear.

Expressives also like a powerful look but with a great deal of individuality. European-cut suits were tailor-made for expressive personality styles along with white-on-white shirts, contrasting collars, and saddle shoes. They will have larger collections of glen plaids and earth tones than the driver personalities and will dress very much for the seasons.

Amiables care a lot about their appearance and regard it subliminally as a means of self-expression. They like the bright, warm colors and the subdued ones as well.

Offices and Decor Relating to Personality Types

Analyticals like simple and efficient environments, even to the point of being spartan. Their efficient and practical surroundings will include few live plants and pictures, but you may find some charts and graphs in evidence. These may relate to sales volume or business reference material. There will usually be a desktop computer at hand.

A messy desk usually identifies analyticals. They like to keep their data handy at all times. Even though their work area may be messy, they will usually know where everything is.

It is a different story for the drivers. Left to their own devices, drivers like to surround themselves with symbols of control and trappings of authority. Look for heavy, massive, dark wood desks and credenzas, bookshelves, awards, degrees, and clocks. They like to keep their desks clean to enhance their efficient image and to make room for their computer monitor and keyboard.

On the drivers' walls, you might find pictures of things, such as boats, cars, or airplanes. Another indicator of a driver is a photograph of the subject receiving an award from the boss or shaking hands with a celebrity. You might also see family studio portraits, probably in somewhat formal poses. There may be some plants, perhaps a small tree in the corner, but the drivers will almost certainly not have the responsibility for putting them there or for caring for them. Drivers may have amiable secretaries who are responsible for the plants, so do not be fooled by a single incongruity.

Expressives will create offices as highly individualistic as they see themselves. You will find warm to bright decor and modern (though not cold) furniture. Other clues will be bold, perhaps even hard-edged, abstract art on the walls and large imposing plants around the room.

You may also find a chart or two, probably dealing with sales quotas and results, and you might also find sports trophies and humorous artifacts. If there are pictures, they will probably be of people rather than things, and there will be an overall "feel" of welcome and comfort to the room.

Amiables have warm offices, though maybe a few degrees cooler than the expressives. Amiables like warm colors, wood furniture, and lots of live plants, which they probably water personally. Look for pictures of people and places that evoke pleasant memories. Family pets will probably be represented, too. This personality style prefers the serenity of a neat desk. If amiables have a say in the art on the walls, it will probably be landscapes, seascapes, or perhaps an enlarged old sepia-toned photograph of the city in a more innocent time.

Solving the Personality Style Puzzle

Once you have had an opportunity to gather as many clues as possible, put them together to form conclusions. This is far easier and less mechanical than it sounds. It is important to understand what the clues are. It is more important and valuable to understand what they mean, that is, how they relate to the axes of the grid.

The proper placement of the clues on the grid determine the entire analysis. Since the grid is composed of only two main components, it becomes fairly easy to put the clues to work. You have to answer only two questions:

First, ask yourself, "From the clues that I've seen, is this client or prospective client warm, open, and emotional or more guarded and reserved?" This will establish the north/south axis of responsiveness.

Second, ask yourself, "Do the clues indicate that this person is outspoken, hurried, and forceful or more relaxed and contemplative?" This will establish the east/west axis or assertiveness.

Once you have those two points on the grid identified, you have solved the puzzle. You can readily decide the client's personality style and plan your approach accordingly. (See Exhibits 11.8 through 11.11.)

EXHIBIT 11.8
Identifying Personality Style Clues Exercise I

For the following clues, answer: Assertive, Nonassertive, Responsive, or Nonresponsive:

1. Take Charge:
2. Animated:
3. Reserved:
4. Intuitive:
5. More logical:
6. Impulsive:
7. Impatient:
8. Serene:
9. Comparison shopper:
10. Results oriented:
11. Warm:
12. Distant:
13. Careful:
14. Persuasive:

15. Sharing:
16. Shy:
17. Intimidating:
18. Cool:
19. Time conscious:
20. People oriented:

EXHIBIT 11.9
Identifying Personality Style Clues II

For this set of clues, answer: Analytical, Driver, Expressive, or Amiable (some may have more than one answer):

1. Orderly:
2. Controlling:
3. Empathetic:
4. Loud:
5. Entrepreneurial:
6. Shy:
7. Spartan:
8. Big picture:
9. Team player:
10. Effervescent:
11. Details:
12. Light woods:
13. Bright colors:
14. Earth tones:
15. Massive desk:
16. Disorganized:
17. Time conscious:
18. Inviting:
19. Dominating:
20. Procedural:

EXHIBIT 11.10
Answers for Identifying Personality Style Clues I

Please complete the exercise before reading the answers (it works better that way).

1.	Take charge:	**Assertive**
2.	Animated:	**Responsive**
3.	Reserved:	**Nonresponsive**
4.	Intuitive:	**Responsive**
5.	More logical:	**Nonresponsive**
6.	Impulsive:	**Responsive**
7.	Impatient:	**Assertive**
8.	Serene:	**Nonassertive**
9.	Comparison shopper:	**Nonresponsive**
10.	Results oriented:	**Assertive**
11.	Warm:	**Responsive**
12.	Distant:	**Nonresponsive**
13.	Careful:	**Nonassertive**
14.	Persuasive:	**Assertive**
15.	Sharing:	**Responsive**
16.	Shy:	**Nonassertive**
17.	Intimidating:	**Assertive**
18.	Cool:	**Nonresponsive**
19.	Time conscious:	**Assertive**
20.	People oriented:	**Responsive**

EXHIBIT 11.11
Answers for Identifying Personality Style Clues II

Please do the exercise first.

1.	Orderly:	**Analytical**
2.	Controlling:	**Driver**

3. Empathetic: **Amiable**
4. Loud: **Expressive**
5. Entrepreneurial: **Driver**
6. Shy: **Amiable**
7. Spartan: **Analytical**
8. Big picture: **Driver**
9. Team player: **Amiable**
10. Effervescent: **Expressive**
11. Details: **Analytical**
12. Light woods: **Amiable**
13. Bright colors: **Expressive**
14. Earth tones: **Amiable**
15. Massive desk: **Driver**
16. Disorganized: **Expressive**
17. Time conscious: **Driver**
18. Inviting: **Amiable**
19. Dominating: **Driver**
20. Procedural: **Analytical**

If you had 20 or fewer correct answers, you need to go back over the material again. Do not be discouraged—nobody expects you to be an expert the first time out.

If you had 10 to 25 correct, you still need to review.

If you had 25 to 30 correct, you are picking it up fast.

If you answered 30 or more, bravo!

You will find that the more you work on categorizing personalities, the more natural it becomes. Before long, you will share a common descriptive language with others who have made the effort. You will wonder why everyone in accounting sales is not using this highly professional technique for understanding clients, prospective clients, and ourselves.

12

SELLING ACCORDING TO PERSONALITY TYPE

APPROACHES

You have learned how to analyze the personality styles from the available clues. You have probably started to form new approaches to prospective clients with whom you are trying to do business. Also, you should have some new insights as to why you may have been experiencing difficulties with them. This is where you learn to put your personality type identification skills to work.

Different personality styles view different things as being important; therefore, they have to be treated differently. For example, would you call on drivers and spend 15 minutes chatting about your summer vacation? Not if you want another appointment. They just do not want to spend their time that way.

By the same token, would you swing right into your business discussion with amiables without first exchanging pleasantries and personal asides? Amiables would think that you are cold and perhaps do not like them.

People are not the same. They *must* be treated as individuals. The accounting professional recognizes this fact and gives it the respect it deserves.

Getting to the Client

Those who have never sold might think that this is a strangely titled section. Of course, you have to get to the client—who else does the buying? Nobody, but that has nothing to do with the problem of getting to the decision makers.

The decision makers are often well protected. Such protection may be in the form of rows of desks peopled by intermediaries. There may be a number of individuals who must be consulted before a buying decision can be made. Often, the chief protector is the dedicated, competent, tough-as-nails administrative assistant, who asks killer questions like, "May I tell her what this is regarding?"

Determining How and by Whom Decisions Are Made

The most obvious and proven method is to seek out the management of the prospective client. The best way to go about getting the information is by setting up an appointment. That sounds easy, but it may not be.

Dealing with Intermediaries

Usually, you will have to deal with intermediaries. You call or drop in with the intention of seeking an appointment, not expecting to speak with or see the people in charge. It is often an insult to even ask to see them without an appointment. It is important that assistants realize that you will respect the boss's time and are businesslike. Why? Because assistants are putting themselves on the line for you by scheduling an appointment. How would it look if the boss came out afterward and said, "Why did you schedule that person?"

If the assistants are at risk, who could blame them for asking questions about your purpose? While there may be standing orders to exclude salespeople, it is very rare to have professional accountants included in that restriction. Make an innocent comment to an intermediary, such as, "Your office is beautiful. Was it professionally decorated?" (Be sure to be truthful in your comments.) Such a comment can elicit a wealth of information about prospective clients. The more you learn, the better you can prepare for the call.

Make certain that assistants perceive you as purposeful and professional. It could mean the difference between getting the appointment and getting the cold shoulder. One safe tack to take is to limit the time commitment involved. If you are being phony and insincere, or are otherwise trying to use the assistants to get to the decision makers, one thing is certain: The assistants will recognize it and deal with it appropriately.

If you are making the appointment over the phone, you obviously cannot get the clues from the office that will help you prepare. The individual who answers the phone may be a good source of information.

Whether over the phone, in person, or in writing, treat support people at the business genially and with respect. You are there for the long haul, and there may be times that their assistance is needed.

Learn the first names and something about each individual you encounter at the prospective client. Not only does this make the business relationship less impersonal, it really helps make it more fun.

Entrepreneurs are frequently workaholics and spend an incredible amount of hours on the job. This tendency transcends personality style—there is very often just too much to do inside a normal workday. Therefore, your prospective clients may be accessible before the staff shows up and after most people have gone home. A good time to call may be 7:30 A.M. or 7:30 P.M.

Depending on the hour, turn the intrusion into a positive: "I'm sorry to bother you at this hour, but you've been so busy that I've had a very hard time getting to talk to you—that must be why your business is so successful. Can I have a few minutes of your time today (tomorrow)? We have something new that you should know about. Can I stop by at 9:00 A.M. or would 10:00 be better?"

You might want to set an appointment for very early or very late. The same reasoning applies here that applied before. Winners do not worry much about hours, and winners like to do business with other winners.

Exhibit 12.1 is an outline for you to use in identifying and categorizing your recent prospective clients. Following the directions will yield insights into the changes in approach that will convert your prospects into clients.

EXHIBIT 12.1
Practical Exercise Drawn From Your Experience

List some of your current or recent prospective clients that have been the toughest to get started with. To the right of each, note specific items in your approach that you will or would have changed in trying to engage the account.

Prospective Client Name: ________________________________

Changes in Approach: ________________________________

____

____

____

Prospective Client Name: ______________________________

Changes in Approach: ______________________________

____

____

____

____

Prospective Client Name: ______________________________

Changes in Approach: ______________________________

____

____

____

____

Of the prospective clients you listed above, put a check mark to the right of the prospective client's name if it is *still* a prospect. If some of them are checked, there is a ready-made proving ground for some of the information that was studied. If the prospective clients have already been converted into clients, congratulations!

THE SALES INTERVIEW

Regardless of the number of calls you have made on a client, a sales interview is necessary—not only necessary, but vital to all parties. Why? Because in the changing world of accounting and business services, needs change as rapidly as the technology. Just as the sum of your professional knowledge is shaped by the industry's movements, the client's requirements are also affected.

Reflect for a moment on this famous line: "There is nothing permanent except change." Care to venture a guess as to when it was written? A good guess might be Ben Franklin, which would make it around 200 years old. The correct guess would be Heraclitus, in the fifth century *before Christ!* No, change is not new, only some of the changes.

What Is a Sales Interview?

A sales interview is nothing more than a fact-finding session with your client or prospective client. Its purpose is to determine current and future needs so that you may act to meet them.

Should I Follow a Specific Format?

Absolutely not! That is a mistake most sales training and college marketing courses make. They restrict students to a format of the instructor's own device, not recognizing the inherently high individuality of talented professional accountants. Everyone in the field for any length of time is conducting sales interviews, often without knowing it.

The purpose of this section is to heighten awareness of the process and not necessarily alter any style or approach that works. The important thing is to get the information in a constructive, professional manner and not get caught up in the procedure.

Do I Have to Do a Formal Interview on Every Call?

Not per se, but fact-finding is needed on every call. Remember, knowledge is power in business. What you may have learned that your competitor has not could make an enormous difference in your approach and in your performance.

When to Conduct a Formal Interview

The most obvious time to do a formal interview is on the first call or on a prospective client that has not committed to doing business. The time that most competitors will overlook is at or before the time that you think you are really doing well. When overconfidence about a client arises, your guard can slip. You may think that you have got a lock on the business. At that time, you should hear a clear signal that it is time to put the antennae up and do some fact finding. If you do not, it is certain that someone else will, and you will be left wondering why you did not get the business.

Differences between Informal and Formal Interviews

A formal interview has the interview as the sole or main purpose of the call. Informal interviews are often part of a maintenance call and are generally conversational in nature. The discovery of needs is the keystone to successfully selling accounting services.

What is needed? Nothing that you would not normally take on a business visit—effective listening and questioning techniques and something to write on. A small portfolio is an excellent way to carry product illustration sheets, needs analysis forms, and handouts, as well as a writing pad and pen. Do not take a briefcase or a large purse. They can be awkward and suitcase-like.

THE FORMAL INTERVIEW

A formal sales interview means that fact finding is the central purpose of the call. To start, open the portfolio and say, "Do you mind if I ask you a few questions and take some notes?" That is a professional way to proceed. Get into the heart of the matter, showing the prospective client that you are there to listen and learn and are interested enough to write down what is being said. Remember the various personality styles. They can help set a direction when conducting the interview.

The Analyticals

Analytical-style prospective clients like to talk in finite terms. Remember, when dealing with analyticals, the key word is *data*. Analyticals require facts and figures before they make decisions. They will talk about numbers, statistics, individual processes, industry trends, and other precise matters. Not ready talkers, they frequently need to be drawn out. They require less small talk than the other personality styles and prefer a crisper, more concise interview. It is really easy to find out who does what within the prospective client's business. Analyticals will often tell you right away. This is helpful if you need to call on them in the future or if you should be talking to someone else in the business on a regular basis.

Analyticals will have a good handle on who performs which function because they probably had a lot to do with organizing the business. When dealing with analyticals, your facts should come from a credible source. When talking about the economy, for example, you should refrain from giving your personal economic forecast or prophecy about interest rate scenarios. Unless you are a credentialed economist, the analytical personality style does not want to hear your opinion. Give this prospect the latest information from your internal sources: "Our research department feels . . ." is a much more effective statement for the analytical style.

Analyticals love to have things in writing. After any discussion, follow up with written material and be sure to follow through. The novice accountant seldom does, but the professional accountant never fails to follow through. Analyticals do not respond well to having their space invaded. They are not particularly "touchable" and often have a strong sense of territory, which they do not want encroached. Do not place your personal items on their desks. Coffee cups, portfolios, purses, and briefcases in an analytical's territory immediately send up the ALERT system. You will lose effectiveness rapidly. If you sense that you are losing an analytical's attention, check to make sure that you are not invading his or her space.

Analytical Personality-Type Summary

1. Make appointments whenever possible. Analyticals do not like surprises.
2. Avoid invading an analytical's "space."
3. Aside from a handshake, avoid touching them.
4. Be prepared to support your statements with facts and figures.
5. Cite expert opinion whenever possible.
6. Follow up in writing whenever you can.
7. Try to have something specific for them when you call.
8. Keep an eye out for technical information specific to their business, appropriate to their level of expertise and interest.

The Drivers

Drivers are results-oriented people. They will happily share stories. They do not have the same good grasp on the detailed inner workings of the business that analyticals have, because the driver type delegates responsibility. However, they will be well versed on the accounting system. Because drivers like to control, it may be difficult for you to discover who makes decisions on selecting accounting software. Drivers are extremely time sensitive. In order not to waste their time and to show your respect for it, it is best to work with them by appointment. Further, your appointment should have time limits. A powerful technique to use is: "I need 20 minutes of your time. Is Tuesday at 10:00 good or would 11:00 be better?" This example shows purposefulness and respect for their schedule. It gives them a choice and allows them to make the decision.

Dress appropriately when calling on drivers. They prefer a crisp, businesslike look. They want to do business with "members of the club"—their circle of high achievers—and your appearance can have a lot to do with their acceptance of you.

If you have mutual acquaintances, mention that you know them or that you do business with them. This can enhance your credibility and hasten your acceptance. Drivers like fast-moving meetings. If you are making a presentation and you are satisfied that you have addressed the most critical needs sufficiently, close. Emphasize the bottom-line benefits in dealing with your firm. Try a closing statement like: "It looks like we have a basis for doing business. I'd like to get started right away with the needs you have determined now. If I can take the list of requirements with me, I can save you a lot of time."

These prospective clients may have objections that will have to be overcome before getting started. These objections will usually emerge after the first attempt at closing and can be addressed at that time. It is relatively easy to know where you stand. They do not have to like you to do business with you—they just have to accept you professionally. Look sharp, be decisive, be forceful without "competing" with them, and you are on your way. A simple rule to remember: Drivers like to deal with other drivers.

Driver Personality-Type Summary

1. Always set appointments with a time limit.
2. Dress conservatively, but sharply.
3. Be forceful and dynamic in your presentation.
4. Mention common acquaintances.
5. Tell success stories of your other clients.
6. Drivers like to make decisions. Give them options.
7. Limit small talk.
8. Do not encroach on personal space.
9. Close quickly and often.
10. Use results-oriented benefit statements.

The Expressives

Expressives are the easiest to get talking. One or two open-ended questions can give you everything you wanted to know about the prospect's business. At times, they can wander way off the track, and you may need a few closed-ended questions to get them back on the subject. Unhappy if stuck working with details, these prospects are great delegators. Nevertheless, they may not admit they are not the ones you need to see on a routine basis. If you sense that this is the case, ask a closed-ended question. Make sure you participate in an appropriate amount of small talk, unless it is absolutely clear that the prospect lacks the time.

Schedule appointments with expressives to show that you consider their time valuable. You may find that once you begin your presentation, if they are enjoying it, their time orientation goes right out the window. You will know they are enjoying their time with you because they are doing most of the talking. Thus, if you are with an interested expressive, you will be fighting back the urge to interrupt.

Employ all your effective listening techniques. Acknowledge comments with nods and other good reactive signals. If the prospective client gets significantly off the track, ask an open-ended question to get back on track. If a situation is right for humor, use it. Expressives admire a quick wit.

Remember that "The one who listens, controls." Expressives are delighted to let you control. That is an enormous tool to have at your discretion. With effective listening and questioning techniques, you will find out what you need to know to do business with the expressives.

Expressives are very results oriented. Therefore, your closing statement should appeal to that. At the same time, it should strike them on a human level:

> "Mr./Ms. Client, I really believe that we are a firm with whom you will like doing business.
>
> In our discussion, I've shown that I can offer the services and products that will keep your business's accounting and business planning needs satisfied, now and into the future.
>
> How about if we get started right away? I'm anxious to show you and your colleagues what we can do!"

This example includes an initial belief statement as well as a benefit statement. Dynamic, positive, enthusiastic presentations and closes will always be more effective with expressives.

Expressive Personality–Type Summary

1. Make appointments whenever possible.
2. Be personable, not overly serious.
3. Be attentive and interested in personal anecdotes.
4. Pick up conversation starters from clues around the office.
5. Remember, expressives prefer to do business with people they like.
6. Use open-ended questions to guide the conversation.
7. Use positive, dynamic, and personal belief and benefit closing statements.

Do not try to out-express expressives. They will do things for their own reasons, not yours. Let them be the center of attention.

The Amiables

Amiables will be fairly open during the interview. They will genuinely want to help you be successful, particularly if they like you. Use open-ended questions. These require amiables to talk more than they might under normal circumstances. Appointments are always recommended for initial calls on amiables. Make sure to allow time for small talk. These types always enjoy being with vivacious people. Amiables are often among the most frustrating to deal with if there are problems. They will strive to avoid unpleasantness and confrontation and genuinely want to spare your feelings. As a result, they become uncomfortable, you lose business, and you may never understand why. The best way to avoid having this happen is to bring issues out in the open in the most nonthreatening manner possible. They may feel that because they are the prospective client, it is not their job to tell you when you have erred—and they would be right.

> "Mr./Ms. Client, I really need your help. For some time now I've felt that there might be a problem in earning your business. I sincerely want and need your business. You would really be doing me a favor if you can tell me where there is a problem."

This is an example of a sincere and heartfelt request for business. Closing a presentation to amiable types can be a real challenge because their commitments are often not firm. They will not take a hard close. That is okay because the accounting business is built more on relationships. Give amiables reasons to do business with you and ask them for business. In many respects, these prospective clients require the most selling. But when they do get on your side, they are there for the long haul.

The Amiable Personality–Type Summary

1. Allow time for small talk.
2. Be genuinely interested in these clients as people. They will detect insincerity.
3. Take the lead in getting conversations started, looking at clues for icebreakers.
4. Emphasize "team" themes.
5. If you suspect problems, address them early. Do not let them fester.
6. Thank all clients for their business, but especially the amiable-type clients.

SELLING UNDER PRESSURE

Each personality type will respond differently under tension or pressure. When asking for a business commitment, you are putting that prospective client under pressure. You should have a good idea as to how each particular type of client or prospective client might react under that pressure.

Listen

Effective listening is one of the easiest sales techniques to master, but it is one that is very often overlooked by accounting professionals. What could be more critical during a sales interview than effective listening? Ultimately, it is probably more important than the quality of the questions asked. Almost everyone prefers to be looked in the eye when they are talking. It is the best way to indicate interest and attention. It is especially powerful when combined with a sensible amount of note taking. Write your key thoughts with minimal loss of eye contact. This shows strong interest. Reserve most of your note taking for moments when you want to show that a particularly strong nerve has been hit. This adds emphasis to the fact that you are paying close attention. It is vital to relate more to your prospective client than to your note pad!

When asking questions, maintain strong eye contact. This may be difficult if you need to resort to notes. Take a few minutes, perhaps while waiting for the appointment, to go over the questions that must be asked. Use intelligent body language to show interest and encourage the prospect to continue. Nod occasionally, adding phrases like "I see," and a simple "Uh–huh" are things we normally do while listening. They are positive signals that you are paying attention. Leaning forward is another good signal. It keeps you from appearing complacently comfortable, slouching back in your chair. Crossing your legs is a good way to show that you feel at ease and are comfortable, but once again, avoid giving the impression that you are in your favorite chair at home.

Clarification

Clarifying is the consultative selling counterpart to "closing" in other types of selling. In the sale of most tangibles and intangibles, the sale is made when the salesperson closes and the prospect says "Yes." That is seldom the case in consultative selling. In this type of selling, the objective is not to get just one sale, but rather to have continuous sales through the development of a long-lasting professional relationship.

In clarifying, the professional is isolating one or more client needs and attaching a commitment to their satisfaction. It becomes a tacit understanding, between the professional and the client, that if the specified need is met, the professional will receive the business.

There are common technology and financial problems facing all businesses. They are all crying out for help—a plea the professional accountant can answer. Reflecting on the pleas that you hear in your client meetings is an excellent way of clarifying something that you may not have understood. It can also help identify needs. "Did I understand you to say that . . ." is a good closed-ended lead-in to get the prospect to restate a point.

Remember why you are there. You are there to gather the information you need to put together an effectively tailored proposal. It is easy to get lost in personal asides and small talk, particularly with the more responsive personality styles.

If you discover that you are doing most of the talking, you have blown it. You have to get the conversation back on track. Otherwise, you will have had an enjoyable but thoroughly unproductive appointment.

Finding the client's needs and then fulfilling them is key to your business success. Exhibit 12.2 presents an identification of needs checklist.

EXHIBIT 12.2
Checklist: Needs Identification

- ❑ **1.** Make sure the client's needs are understood.
- ❑ **2.** Get a commitment from the prospective client that if the needs can be satisfied, the professional accountant will get the business.
- ❑ **3.** State and restate the next action by each party.
- ❑ **4.** Prepare and present the solutions to meet the needs in the sales proposal.
- ❑ **5.** Follow-up and strengthen the relationship.

Analyticals are constantly under pressure. They do not make decisions well. Because life is a constant flow of decision making, they are under pressure a good deal of the time. To deal with these pressures, analyticals have developed an effective defense mechanism. They simply avoid the decision. When you ask an analytical for business, you may get an answer like, "I want to think about it." Another favorite tactic is, "Give it to me in writing." In this way, not only have they prolonged the decision, they have requested additional information to analyze. You know you are dealing with an analytical type when you question them as to the result of adding one and one and they answer, "I'll get back to you next week."

Drivers are very direct people and, under pressure, will respond in a very direct fashion. If you have not convinced them that they should be doing business with you, they tend to become autocratic. A favorite phrase for the driver type is, "We'll do it this way." In this way, they reestablish their own authority position and put you off. The good news is that you always know where you stand, and you can readily use your reflecting techniques to try again. Drivers admire tenacity and will respect you for not giving up.

Expressives use an emotional defense mechanism. Rather than avoiding the issue or becoming autocratic, the expressive type will confront and attack your point of view. They may say, "I don't agree," or "You're wrong!" What they are really saying is that they do not have enough information to see it your way. It is up to you to regroup and try again.

Amiables do not like confrontation. If they are not convinced, they will seldom become bossy or aggressive. Instead, they are more likely to acquiesce. They know that this is the best way to satisfy you and get you off their backs. It is probable that the commitment is not valid.

Unless you are careful, you may leave thinking you will see some business. It is probable that every other competitor that has come through that prospective client's door has gotten the same treatment. If it seemed too easy, it probably was and the commitment will not stick.

IF THAT DOES NOT WORK . . .

Each of the personality types have an alternative style reaction that comes into play if they are subjected to further pressure. If avoidance has not worked for analyticals and they are backed into a corner, they will emerge from that corner in a very assertive mode. Taking a cue from driver types, the prospects will become autocratic. At that point, it is probably best for you to schedule another appointment and promise to bring some additional information that will support a decision to do business with you.

The driver types will become noticeably analytical if not ready to commit. They will seek to avoid the issue by asking for some additional information, posing a question that you cannot answer, or by changing the subject. You can assess at that point whether you should continue to pursue the matter or pack up and set a new appointment. Chances are good that the drivers may decide the matter for you by mentioning that your time is up and another appointment is waiting.

You may have noticed that the driver types and the analytical types traded styles briefly along their shared axis on nonresponsiveness. The expressive types do the same thing with the amiable types along their shared axis of responsiveness. If the expressives' tactic of attack fails to relieve the pressure, they will appear to give in.

As with the amiable type, you may want to believe that you are inherently superior personality and charm has won the day. This may not be the case; the commitment may just be intended to get you out the door. One avenue to take is to test the commitment by setting a time understanding as to when to begin the needs assessment.

The amiable types are full of surprises. If you continue to push after they have already given in, you are likely to be facing an attack from them. Not in the physical sense, of course, but if an amiable style does get pushed too far, you may have to drop back and punt in order to defuse the time bomb.

Use your good common sense when you apply pressure on a prospective client in a closing situation. You know you will have to ask for the business in some way, but as a real pro, you will use all of your skill and experience to nurture and sustain a lasting relationship.

Body Language

It is useful to understand the signals that are being sent by the prospect during the interview. Even though the professional is intently listening, thereby controlling the interview, the ice must be broken in most cases. Later on, when doing a sales presentation, you must also observe the prospect's nonverbal signals. They can very often provide some solid clues to monitor how you are doing.

The prospective client's posture indicates how well his or her attention is held. There is often a desk in the way; a high-back desk chair is an invitation to lean way back, and such factors blur potential clues. An interruption in the normal posture is a strong clue. For example, if the prospect is talking and suddenly sits upright when making a point, it is an important one. If the professional is talking and the same thing happens, a nerve has been struck. A call may start with the prospect's hand on the desk, the back straight. This can hardly be considered relaxed; the prospect is clearly not at ease. After some small talk, prospects should loosen up and relax their posture. When that happens in an interview situation, your prospect is open and willing to talk. If it does not happen, there may be a problem. Use your powers of observation to nip problems in the bud, and do not be afraid to discuss the prospect's concerns. Those concerns may grow into objections and could become more difficult to address properly at a later time.

Keep your eye on the long term. Just because you do not walk out of the prospective client's office today with a signed agreement does not mean that you will not tomorrow. Use the people knowledge that you are gaining to understand your prospective client; then, kick in the turbo drive, using your superior product knowledge as a resource. With practice, dedication, and hard work, you will soon be turning in that bicycle we started with for a racing model.

A comprehensive progress exercise is presented in Exhibit 12.3 to determine your ability to identify the personality types of your prospective clients.

EXHIBIT 12.3
Comprehensive Progress Exercise

For each of the following 50 descriptors, match one or more from the following:

- Analytical
- Driver
- Expressive
- Amiable

1. Aggressive, dynamic:
2. Warm, "touchable":
3. Open and emotional:
4. Likes small talk:
5. Respects an aggressive close:
6. Likes to do most of the talking:
7. Prefers an efficient, simple office:
8. Is intently interested in what you have to say:
9. Likes to delay making a decision until all the facts are studied:
10. Prefers to get right down to business:
11. Will say "You're wrong" when pressure is applied:
12. Wants to avoid confrontation:
13. You may never know why you are not receiving promised business:
14. Likes dark, massive office furniture:
15. For the first call, you should make an appointment:
16. You should never get "right down to business":
17. If the first stall was not effective, will attack your position:
18. Will seek to avoid your close:
19. Is extremely time conscious:
20. On technical matters, prefers the opinions of "experts":
21. In a sales interview, you need to draw them out:

22. The hardest style to get a true commitment from:
23. Will be your longer appointments:
24. Likes pictures of things:
25. Will have a clean desk:
26. Is a bit messy, but knows where everything is:
27. Wants to know that you really believe:
28. Likes lots of plants in the office:
29. Dresses in dark colors:
30. Include a strong, bottom-line benefit statement:
31. Include a positive, people-oriented benefit statement:
32. Are more likely to get along with a driver:
33. Like to be shown that your claims are true:
34. Often need to like those they do business with:
35. Likely to have a closer relationship with the end user:
36. Is the best listener:
37. Would prefer to drive a black Mercedes:
38. Would prefer a Volvo and would keep it until it wears out:
39. Likes bright colors:
40. Prefers neutral tones:
41. Does not often stop to "smell the roses":
42. Speaks easily and comfortably:
43. Often found in technical and precise fields:
44. Have firm handshakes:
45. Share the axis of nonresponsiveness:
46. Are easily recognizable as real "people" people:
47. May unwittingly hurt or offend others:
48. Is outgoing and somewhat impulsive:
49. Is quiet until feelings become too strong:
50. Share the axis of assertiveness:

(Answers appear in Exhibit 12.4)

Discovering and Identifying Needs

The interview process leads to the point of identifying what the prospective client really wants. You can use a formal interview or an informal interview. The informal interview is simply asking good questions in a more conversational context. You must now synthesize the data into information so that a sales presentation may be planned.

Is price alone the paramount consideration? Accounting is a people-oriented profession. The name of the game is people helping people to meet their business goals. Price may be farther down the list than one might suspect.

A Few Words About Your Personality Style

It is difficult to alter your personality. It is easier to modify it to increase one's versatility. If we fail to adapt to fit the needs of our clients and prospective clients, we are probably wasting our time in the accounting field. A few words concerning your own individual style are in order.

Analytical types, being naturally nonresponsive, need to work on being more conscious of the feelings and perceptions of others. Remember to say, "How are you?" and mean it, a little more often. People may occasionally find you enigmatic. That has worked well for Mona Lisa, but it can be very trying on real-life relationships. In a nutshell, you probably need to express your feelings more because others may have a hard time learning who you are and how you feel about things.

Driver styles should work on being more attuned to the feelings of others. Few will have a problem knowing where a driver type stands at any given point. In the extreme, this overassertiveness can make the driver personality style seem impossible. Slow down a bit and tune in more to the world around you. This is important in personal relationships. It is also very important in business. People do not like to be overwhelmed or to feel they will not be listened to.

Expressive types often feel that they have it all. You love life, people, business, achieving, and relaxing. You do have a shortcoming in that you do not like to listen. Most people are not content to be in the audience forever. You will ultimately lose them and be forced to look for others. People really like being around you and vice-versa. Listening is not necessarily easy, but it is rewarding. People *need* to be listened to and will do what has to be done to have that need fulfilled in both their business and personal lives.

Amiable styles are "people" people and love to be around them—not to be entertained (expressive types take note), but to *listen.* At some point, however, you too must be heard. Express your opinion more often. Become more assertive in getting your point of view across.

Exhibit 12.4 provides the answers to the comprehensive progress exercise in Exhibit 12.3, which determines your ability to identify the personality types of your prospective clients.

EXHIBIT 12.4
Answers to Comprehensive Progress Exercise

Please do not look at these answers before completing the exercise in Exhibit 12.3.

1. Driver, Expressive
2. Expressive, Amiable
3. Expressive, Amiable
4. Expressive, Amiable
5. Driver
6. Expressive
7. Analytical
8. Amiable
9. Analytical
10. Analytical, Driver
11. Expressive
12. Amiable
13. Amiable
14. Driver
15. Analytical, Driver, Expressive, Amiable
16. Expressive, Amiable
17. Amiable
18. Analytical
19. Driver
20. Analytical

21. Amiable
22. Amiable
23. Expressive, Amiable
24. Driver
25. Driver, Amiable
26. Analytical
27. Expressive, Amiable
28. Amiable
29. Driver
30. Driver
31. Expressive, Amiable
32. Analytical, Driver, Expressive
33. Analytical
34. Expressive, Amiable
35. Amiable
36. Amiable
37. Driver
38. Analytical
39. Expressive
40. Analytical
41. Driver
42. Expressive
43. Analytical
44. Driver, Expressive
45. Analytical, Driver
46. Expressive, Amiable
47. Analytical, Driver
48. Expressive
49. Amiable
50. Driver, Expressive

A checklist of the steps to be accomplished during every prospective client interview is presented in Exhibit 12.5. The sequence of each step is not as important as the completion of all of the components.

EXHIBIT 12.5
Interview Review and Checklist

- ❑ Fact find on every call.
- ❑ Conduct formal interviews periodically with all active accounts.
- ❑ Carry something appropriate to write on.
- ❑ Be mindful of personality styles when asking questions.
- ❑ Use open- and closed-ended questions to guide the interview.
- ❑ Use effective and active listening techniques to encourage open, frank dialogue.
- ❑ Be aware of your own and the prospective client's body language. There are often strong nonverbal statements being expressed.
- ❑ Do not be afraid to discuss the prospective client's strongest concerns.
- ❑ Reflect the needs that have been identified.
- ❑ Use the clarifying techniques to gain a commitment.
- ❑ State and restate the next action for mutual understanding.

> "I keep six honest serving men, They taught me all I knew: Their names are What and Why and When, and How and Where and Who."—Rudyard Kipling

Exhibit 12.6 affords you the opportunity to reflect on what you learned about yourself since completing the self-discovery exercises.

EXHIBIT 12.6
Reflection

Look back at the self-discovery exercises you wrote in your personal three-ring binder. Discuss in a few paragraphs what you have learned about yourself since you completed those questionnaires.

Would you change any of your answers? Are you satisfied that you have truly been open and honest with yourself in answering this question?

SIZING UP PROSPECTIVE CLIENTS

Experienced professionals have learned the hard way that some clients are not worth pursuing. No matter how much money is at stake, if the terms are not right, you are better off biting the bullet and walking away. One bad client could jeopardize your business. When you are young, ambitious, and hungry for business, that is hard to live with.

Let's look at one accountant's experience with a medium-sized beverage distributor that had left another accounting firm after some type of disagreement. The accountant proposed installing a client–server accounting system to monitor and track certain specialized types of transactions on a multidepartmental basis. The previous accounting firm had prepared a subset of the system.

The new firm, along with a computer hardware partner, built the system according to the client's specifications as prepared by the former accountants. It functioned as planned. However, the client's specs were inappropriate for its desired goal. The client's executive steering committee that requisitioned the accounting system did not know all the business processes interacting between the departments. Consequently, six months after the implementation, the system was not producing the required results. It was seen as a failure—one that was blamed on the new accounting firm.

Distribution was a key market niche for that new accounting firm. Each time they tried to work with a beverage distributor, they would be questioned about that last project that did not go very well. They were perceived as a failure, and it hampered their ability to win new accounts.

Another accounting firm went after a prospective client where the scope of the engagement was well over its head. As a result, the firm was severely penalized. Furthermore, the accounting firm had purposely limited business to a specific vertical market within a single state, with word-of-mouth as the primary marketing vehicle. The prospective client thought the accounting firm was responsible for more system development on another project than it actually was. This was not immediately clear and was not explained by the accounting firm. Word spread quickly when the project began unraveling. The accounting firm started getting calls from other current clients that heard they were blowing a big account. Not only was the big fish getting away, but the accounting firm was jeopardizing its smaller clients as well.

The lesson is to develop an unwavering policy of screening all prospects before accepting them as clients. Ask the tough questions:

- How will our services help you improve your business?
- How will our relationship be enhanced?
- Are we competent to satisfy this client?

If neither the client nor the accountant can give satisfactory answers, do not take the business.

13

MAKING EFFECTIVE SALES CALLS

NOTHING HAPPENS UNTIL SOMEBODY SELLS SOMETHING

Why in the Internet age of mass media, databases, telecommunications, advertising, and direct marketing do you need to sell? More to the point, why should you, a highly trained and skilled accountant, spend your time selling when your expertise is in accounting, taxes, computer software, and business consulting, not in selling or marketing?

The current accounting paradigm relegates selling to an activity that detracts from the professional role for which the accountant was trained. It removes the accountant from the profession's traditional skills and knowledge base. And the time spent selling is not billable! The underlying theme behind this thinking in the minds of accountants is, "What if I'm not successful at selling? What will I have to show for my time?"

Selling is very expensive. In the accounting profession, the cost of a sales call (i.e., meeting the prospective client, preparing a proposal, presenting the proposal, etc.) can range from several hundred to thousands of dollars. There is significant pressure on partners and accountants in general to be highly productive—either high billings or bringing in a lot of new business. Time spent marketing and selling brings no guarantee of new business.

Why sell? The answer is basic, despite the costs and risks involved. Nothing communicates—solves client problems—like one-on-one/eye-to-eye communication. And nothing sells professional accounting solutions like the professional who provides them.

While selling is expensive and risky, to stay in business the professional accountant needs clients. Professional selling is the key to building any accounting business. In the final analysis, nothing happens until somebody sells something.

Professional selling is the process of satisfying client needs with your firm's services and products through a process of relational communication. Underlying this definition is the concept that in order to succeed, any business must satisfy the needs of its customers with superior services. For accountants, such services run the gamut from traditional accounting write-up, auditing, and tax compliance to niche services such as technology consulting and business valuations.

Quantify Your Sales Goals

1. What is the sales (revenues) goal for the year?
2. Who else in the accounting firm knows the sales objective?
3. What would happen if each member of the firm knew the goal?
4. What could each do to achieve the goal?

The Truth about Keeping Score

What gets measured gets done—but only for a little while. In the past, performance charts served as scoreboards. They led staff to believe that Big Brother was watching, and they felt like a management edict. Since there is no scoreboard for the new open-book management, the big picture numbers may be something other than actual sales or profits. For example, performance indicators might be an index measuring client satisfaction scores and the firm's actual performance compared to forecast.

This sends the staff the message that the scoreboard is displaying the firm's business success and is, thus, an indication of job security, bonuses, and opportunity. Another big difference between old and new scorekeeping is that now the staff gets involved in setting targets, creating the boards, and figuring out what rewards or bonuses to give themselves if they succeed.

Most important, the new scorekeeping is a dynamic phenomenon. The goals and metrics change. The staff learns to think in new ways and to start asking the kinds of questions a business owner would. Scorekeeping in action becomes a tool that gets people focused on the sales figures that achieve the goal. Scoreboards force a level of accountability that is often missing in small businesses. The real value of the scorekeeping process comes over the long haul. People learn not just to watch numbers but to take responsibility for them. Employees incorporate the scorekeeping process into their year-in, year-out approach to the accounting business.

In the final analysis, scoreboards are no more than a tool for encouraging good management practices like goal setting, budgeting, performance management, and mutual accountability. They increase the employees' understanding of how they can move the numbers along, as well as their involvement in doing so.

The Sales Process

The following are the 10 steps of the sales process:

1. Develop opportunities.
2. Set up appointments with prospective clients.
3. Plan the sales call.
4. Create credibility with the prospective client.
5. Identify prospective client's concerns.
6. Develop solutions to those concerns.
7. Overcome objections.
8. Justify pricing (create the perception of value).
9. Get the client to sign on.
10. Keep the client.

Develop a Sales Environment

Accountants' negative attitudes toward selling may be the biggest obstacle to effectively selling accounting services. Contrast this with the attitudes of those entering the financial services industry (insurance, banking, personal financial planning, etc.). For a long time, accountants did not have to sell. Today there is a major convergence between the two industries.

When the first edition of this book was published in 1984, the typical accountant could concentrate on accounting. To be successful 15 years ago, an accountant did not have to worry about building a sales environment, employing professionals who could also market and sell, develop creative sales techniques, or be client-centered. In 1991, with the publication of the second edition of this book, marketing and new business development was understood to be a promotion-based activity—newsletters, seminars, public relations, institutional advertising, and the then-emerging phenomenon of personal computer (PC)-based accounting. To a great degree, professional selling was still not required or practiced by accountants.

The explanation for this collective accountant's state of mind was that the demand for accountants' services was greater than the supply. The realities of the accounting industry as it enters and moves into the new millennium is that the supply of accountants far exceeds the demands for their traditional services. Clients are more sophisticated than ever before. Through the use of PC-based accounting software, they can perform many, if not most, of the basic accounting and tax functions that once only accountants knew how to do. The new environment demands a professional who is well trained in identifying client needs and who knows how to satisfy those needs.

Sales Environment Factors

The need for sales intelligence mandates a thorough knowledge of your sales environment. The key factors which must be researched and mastered include the following:

1. Defining the sales task
2. Having the right people sell
3. Having the right market niche to fill (sell)
4. Preparing the staff to sell
5. Facilitating selling
6. Measuring sales performance
7. Rewarding sales performance
8. Developing sales management

The Sales Cycle

A major reason for the time involved in building a client relationship is that both buying and selling are lengthy processes. If you are to be effective in selling your services, you must unite both processes.

The Decision Cycle

The Decision Cycle has a beginning, middle, and conclusion. The essential information that is needed to bring the cycle to a successful outcome is outlined as follows:

1. *Problem recognition.* The client may know that an annual audit is necessary because of lender requirements. Potential tax problems may have arisen from IRS inquiries. Nothing really happens until the prospective client becomes aware of some existing or potential problem.
2. *Needs description.* The prospective client begins to translate the problems into the needs that you will eventually have to satisfy.
3. *Information search.* The amount of information the client will seek about how to satisfy the needs will vary according to personality style. It also depends on the importance and complexity of the need and whether the prospective client had previous experience in making such decisions.
4. *Services specification.* This is an important step for larger clients who issue requests for proposals or who have a very formal process for evaluating vendors. An increasing number of clients are requesting proposals from their professional advisors. Much of the increase comes from the client's desire to obtain a fair price. At the same time, it permits you to demonstrate your understanding of the client's problem and offer a solution. Regardless of the formality of the process, the client ultimately will develop some idea of what she or he believes is an adequate solution to the needs.
5. *Evaluation of alternatives.* The client then narrows the field of competing services and products. This process depends on the amount of differentiation between the services and products offered by the marketplace to satisfy the needs.
6. *Vendor search.* The client evaluates the solution providers.
7. *Vendor selection.* The client decides which competing firm will provide the services and products. This step may also include specification and price negotiations.
8. *Purchase decision.* The actual step in which the client decides that your services and products and firm are appropriate. At this stage in the process, you should have a signed engagement

letter that outlines the scope of your work and how your fees will be determined.

9. *Performance review.* Once the purchase decision has been made, you should expect that your performance will be reviewed. Many accountants take the initiative and use a client satisfaction survey. This provides a mechanism for the client to review the firm's performance. It is both a way of cementing a long-term relationship and improving future work satisfaction.

10. *Post-purchase behavior.* Most prospective clients gain information about your firm from current clients. Dissatisfied clients may be very vocal with their friends and acquaintances. Satisfied clients are, and always will be, your best source of new clients.

CORE COMPETENCIES

To thrive in the fast-changing accounting business, owner–managers must frequently review what their firm does best and measure those skills against what clients value. In other words, whether the firm makes money mostly from write-up and tax work or strictly from software consulting contracts, management must know what it is good at and what makes the practice tick.

Assuming you are good at what you are currently doing, the question becomes: What is the essential information needed to plan for continued success? For the answer, start by examining the firm's organizational strengths, and identify the differentiators that make the firm unique.

As an accounting firm owner, you must understand what business you want to be in and what competencies you will offer. This knowledge will allow your firm to better differentiate itself in the marketplace, to give the firm's prospective clients a clear reason to become clients.

Figuring out your core competency can be almost as difficult as implementing it, because core competencies are not a laundry list of the services that are provided. They are the one or two things the firm does *particularly* well and, ultimately, the ones that will make it successful.

Start by listing your firm's capabilities. Then, categorize each capability and rate it for strength and importance. "Importance" is what has the most direct and significant impact on your firm's competitiveness.

CORE COMPETENCIES

Most accounting firms' skill sets fall into three buckets:

1. Technical
2. Sales
3. Infrastructure

Technical skills encompass areas like accounting systems design, product integration, and programming. Sales skills cover product selling and consulting services. Infrastructure capabilities may include internal training and management information systems.

To make this core competency audit pay, you must be painfully honest. The problem is not simply identifying what the firm does well. It is also recognizing what the firm is doing poorly and having the courage to eliminate it. Exhibit 13.1 provides you with the steps to conduct your own competency audit.

EXHIBIT 13.1
Steps to a Competency Audit

1. Itemize your accounting firm's capabilities.

2. Categorize these capabilities as primary, critical and core. (**Primary** capabilities are the basic qualifications for doing business—e.g., internal training or management skills. **Critical** capabilities are skills that have the most direct and significant impact on competitiveness—e.g., accounting system software certification or help desk. **Core** capabilities are the result of strong and synergistic critical skills—e.g., accounting system network engineering, combined with help desk and customer training, create the core competency of business systems service integration.)

3. Rank the capabilities in a hierarchy of ascending complexity, with primary capabilities at the bottom, critical capabilities in the middle, and the core competencies at the top.

4. Target promising new core competencies by mixing and matching different clusters of the accounting firm's critical capabilities, while weighing each combination's potential to satisfy the future needs of clients.

Source: The Accounting Guild, Original research study, 1999.

Is the Competency You Have Identified Truly Core?

- Does it provide potential access to a wide variety of niche markets?
- Does it make a significant contribution to the perceived client benefits of the end product?
- It is difficult for competitors to imitate?

THE IMPORTANCE OF BEING PERSISTENT

How successful can you be without being persistent? If you or your firm offered tax preparation and charged minimum wage rates, you could do a lot of business but not be successful. You and your firm would not last very long either. Success is where everyone wins.

In the real world, we find out daily what the true meaning of success and persistence is:

> To go on resolutely . . . in spite of difficulties.

And there is never a shortage of difficulties.

Franz Kafka has said, " . . . Only our concept of time makes it possible for us to speak of the Day of Judgement by that name; in reality it is a constant court in perpetual session."

To be more positive: The tests of business life are not made to break you . . . but to make you!

It is hard going out there every day. Because it is so hard, there are not many people who are willing to do it. To risk rejection and failure every single day is appalling to most people. That is why for the professional accountant the rewards can be much more substantial than in less demanding lines of work.

Consider just how rare truly professional accountants are. They must have intelligence and grace under pressure. They need poise and a good appearance to be accepted. They require the perspective to understand the big picture and the ability to control ego. They must have the ability to master a wide range of products and services. Accountants need the skill to creatively handle a variety of unforeseen situations. They must have the personal stability and the emotional fortitude to hear "No!" over and over again without taking it personally. Primarily, they must have an exceptionally high need to succeed, to achieve, and to keep themselves motivated and "out there" day after day.

An amazing number of your competitors fail to display the versatility needed to be true professionals, especially in dealing with clients and prospective clients as people. Many may have the skills, but not the drive, to persevere. Your job is to have it all—the product knowledge, accounting skills, the people skills, and the desire to succeed that connects all the factors.

Is persistence alone enough to promise success? No, of course not . . . But its absence is *more* than enough to guarantee failure. On this subject, Charles, Baron de Montesquieu (1740), said, "Success depends on knowing how long it takes to succeed."

MISTAKES ACCOUNTING SALESPEOPLE MAKE

The benefits of learning from your mistakes have been lauded many times, or even better, to learn from other's mistakes. The following mistakes made by other accountants can provide valuable lessons.

- They are more focused on their own agenda than the client's. They concentrate on their sales process instead of the client's buying process.
- They sell too fast—they get to the "close" before the client is ready to commit.
- They focus on what they have instead of on what the client needs.
- Overaggressive selling. Clients are tired of self-focused sales pushers.
- They call on prospective clients who do not appreciate their value. They call on a prospective client who is price focused and not value conscious.
- They fail to identify sufficient client needs before making the presentation.
- They fail to identify behind-the-scenes decision makers. In accounting services, as much as 90 percent of the sales process happens when the salesperson is not there. It occurs when one decision maker sells other decision makers on a particular course of action.
- They submit proposals that lack information crucial to selling those behind-the-scenes decision makers.
- They fail to learn about the prospective client's business.
- They fail to identify the cost to the prospective client of doing nothing. For many accounting salespeople, the primary competitor is the prospective client's decision to "wait."

- They assume the prospective client recognizes its own needs.
- They fail to address the client's fear of commitment.
- They fail to find a compelling reason why a prospective client should buy from them.
- They confuse "telling" with "selling." If good questions are asked, prospective clients sell themselves. It is the ultimate sales skill.
- They fail to develop multiple sources of leads and develop relationships with business partners.

EDGE OUT THE COMPETITION

Here are 10 proven strategies to beat the competition.

1. *Be more accessible.* Your clients should be able to contact you whenever and however they like. An e-mail address or Web site can open up a whole new selling market. In addition to your primary phone and fax numbers, give your clients your beeper and cellular phone numbers.
2. *Improve sales cycle management.* Higher billings are a by-product of efficient contact management and follow-up. Be sure to qualify and prioritize prospective clients carefully to avoid wasting time on prospects with little profit potential.
3. *Be an asset to your clients.* Develop lifelong client relationships by showing clients you are willing to do more yourself. What will your client gain from an alliance with your firm? Show your prospective clients a list of no-charge services your firm can offer to differentiate yourself from the competition.
4. *Be innovative.* Innovators are welcome assets to any organization. Find out all you can about your client's business. Suggest new solutions to old problems and additional services your clients can utilize. If the prospective client complains about a problem, pay close attention and find out how your firm can help. Stay on top of new problems and new solutions for them.
5. *Save your clients' time.* Time is money for you and your clients. Return calls quickly. Anticipate client questions and be prepared to answer them. Monitor changes in your clients' businesses to make recommendations that help them make speedier buying decisions.

6. *Act decisively.* Give clients confidence in your knowledge and ability by making decisions without undue hesitation. Few decisions come with a guarantee, so do not let fear keep you from making an informed choice. Even decisions that prove unwise are better than appearing confused, too afraid, or too uninformed to take action at all.
7. *Personalize correspondence.* Give clients individualized attention by personalizing letters, proposals, invoices, and literature packages. A handwritten message on an invoice, for example, shows your clients you care about their needs even after they have signed the engagement agreement.
8. *Look for new niches.* Many accounting businesses succeed because they fill a need that no one else does. What does your firm do better than your competition? How can your firm offer services, products, or expertise that everyone wants but few firms have? Even if your firm excels only in a specialized market, do what you can to make it the best at something.
9. *Think beyond the big sale.* It is not easy to sign a big client, but cultivating a number of smaller clients can yield big results too. A great many smaller clients offer better word-of-mouth promotion potential than one large one, and they may yield more repeat business.
10. *Communicate warmly.* It is not always enough to be polite. Enthusiasm is contagious, so generate some and share it with a client. Instead of using a "cold" approach to business letters, infuse your correspondence with warmth. When you appear to truly enjoy your job, you will help reassure your clients that you are serving them to the best of your ability.

THE 80/20 RULE

The 80/20 rule is a bit of a mystery. Nobody seems to know just why it appears to be consistently true. Nobody knows who noticed it first, although it is sometimes attributed to the Italian economist, Vilfredo Pareto. It applies to many aspects of many businesses, not only accounting and consulting, and there are several interesting things it can tell us about the importance of persistence.

The 80/20 rule states that: "80 percent of our business comes from 20 percent of our clients." It has corollaries as well. One of the more intriguing ones is, "80 percent of the business is done by 20 percent of the professionals."

What is really significant about this aspect of the 80/20 rule is this: Almost half of all accountants make one call and give up. One quarter of all accountants make two calls and give up. 80 percent of the prospective clients become clients after the fifth call. Therefore, we can conclude that only 20 percent of the accountants make more than five calls!

This is a pretty incredible statistic, isn't it? In the accounting business, we know that our competition is calling on our clients on a regular basis, but they frequently are not making "real calls." Merely dropping off a firm's brochure or business card at the receptionist's desk does not qualify as a sales call—that is just a "show and go." The 20 percent that are doing 80 percent of the business are making five or more quality calls before they are writing engagement letters.

That speaks very eloquently about the importance of persistence, doesn't it?

Have you ever given up on a prospective client before the fifth call? If you have, do not worry about it. We all have for various reasons. Maybe we did not know what to say after discussing our service features, benefits, and pricing, or maybe the prospect raised objections we could not counter. The important question is: Knowing what you know now about people, statistics for sales call results, and how to communicate on sales calls, will you ever quit before the fifth call again?

If Montesquieu was right, if we need only know how long it may take to be successful, what reason is there for us not to give it more than five solid calls?

CALL RELUCTANCE

> "When I was young I observed that nine out of ten things I did were failures . . . So I did ten times more work."—George Bernard Shaw

The reason everyone has quit before the fifth sales call or even before the first is that there are times when anything seems better than making a sales call. Sometimes we would prefer to chance a visit to the dentist. This is a natural feeling but a counterproductive one if you allow it to get out of control.

When you experience call reluctance, you are feeling precisely the same emotions that keep most accountants out of the sales arena. It is a fleeting shell shock, a delayed stress. Because it does not leave most people, it works to your advantage. Why? Because you are a professional and you know that it is fleeting and can take steps to deal with it.

The best way to deal with call reluctance is to recognize it for what it is and plan around it. It is an emotional reaction to the possibility of failure—"stage fright" by another name. And aren't we really performers in a sense? Our stage is the prospective client's office, and our craft is selling ourselves.

If your plan for the day includes a sales call to a prospective client who causes call reluctance, start the day off with a client that you know is usually an easier one. Pick one who is genuinely happy to see you, where you have developed a good level of trust, not just friendship. By making your first call on a client who really views you as the expert, you will find that you are bulletproof for the rest of the day. No one will get you down or scare you off and you will actually look forward to a joust with your toughest prospective client.

This is an especially good tactic if you are facing a current client who may feel frustration over a particular problem that your firm could not get resolved and the client wants to unload on you. Becoming the "dart board" sometimes goes with the territory, but it is seldom enjoyable. Do not schedule those calls for the first thing in the morning. Try to make them for later and make a "friendly" call early.

Call reluctance is a fear. The smart, honest professional recognizes that call reluctance is expensive because it costs productivity.

You have fears because you are human. You can accept and deal with them because you are intelligent. You can conquer them because you are a professional.

Exhibit 13.2 provides a format for you to identify clients and prospective clients who you feel are among the toughest you call on.

EXHIBIT 13.2
Do a Quick Analysis of Some of Your Clients/Prospective Clients

---

Toughest—I really do not look forward to calling on these:

(Name)	(Location)

1. ______________________________
2. ______________________________
3. ______________________________
4. ______________________________
5. ______________________________

6. ______________________________

7. ______________________________

8. ______________________________

9. ______________________________

10. ______________________________

Exhibit 13.3 provides a format for you to identify your friendliest clients and prospective clients with whom you feel terrific after completing calls.

EXHIBIT 13.3
Friendliest Clients

Friendliest—I always feel terrific when I finish these calls:

(Name)	(Location)

1. ______________________________

2. ______________________________

3. ______________________________

4. ______________________________

5. ______________________________

6. ______________________________

7. ______________________________

8. ______________________________

9. ______________________________

10. ______________________________

Exhibit 13.4 is an outline to assist you in correlating the previous two lists. You can identify those of your friendliest clients and prospective clients that are located nearest to each of your tougher prospective clients.

EXHIBIT 13.4
Correlation between Friendlies and Toughies

Now correlate the lists and see which "Friendlies" are located nearest each "Toughie."

(Toughie)	(Nearest Friendly)
1.	
2.	
3.	
4.	
5.	
6.	
7.	
8.	
9.	
10.	

If you have been in your territory for a while, the odds are that your "Friendlies" outnumber the "Toughies" by a substantial margin. If you are new to the field, do not worry. There are many potential "Friendlies" out there waiting to meet you.

MANAGING YOUR CLIENTS

Many glib sayings and pronouncements have sprung up around the concept of client satisfaction. One of the most common is this gem:

- Rule #1: The client is always right.
- Rule #2: If the client is wrong, see Rule #1.

Any firm that attempts to keep clients happy by catering around the clock to each and every demand is going to find out the hard way that the client is not always right—not by a long shot. Accountants are keenly aware that all the client-handling expertise in the world does not help the bottom line when the client is just plain hard to handle. Sure, dissatisfied clients can hurt your business, but spending too much time and effort attempting to satisfy extremely demanding clients can hurt your business too.

What is an accountant to do? The quick answer: Learn to discern the satisfiable clients from the unsatisfiable clients and steer clear of the latter. The not-so-quick answer that will ensure satisfaction among your clients, without putting you either out of business or out of your mind, is this: Develop a reliable system of managing your clients that begins before the first sales call and extends throughout the relationship with your client.

This is a system that is rarely, if ever, in place at the founding of an accounting business. As an accounting business grows, a client analysis system is not only useful but mandatory. The niche markets that most accounting firms operate in are "closed, tight communities," either geographically or vertically constricted, or both. Clients who have had a bad experience with an accounting firm will tell others. Many potential clients will hear about it. Closed communities also inherently limit a client pool. Merely to survive, most accounting firms have realized that existing clients must contribute to the revenue stream. Half of the typical accountant's income is generated from long-term existing clients, so if you do not have good client relations, you are not going to be a successful professional accountant.

Developing and maintaining a base of satisfied clients has nothing to do with pretending that clients can do no wrong. Proper client management involves a combination of assessment and presentation. The process begins when potential clients are still prospects, and continues through the sales cycle, implementation, and into the support relationship. The early stages are the most important, because the best way to be rid of difficult clients is to avoid them in the first place.

Assessment

Assessment is done as early as possible in a potential client relationship, ideally, as soon as a lead arrives for screening purposes. Small and start-up professional accounting firms usually do little if any screening of leads—a lead is a lead, after all. This attitude must change once client management is the goal.

Managing your clients begins in the prospecting process. Make sure the prospect is a good fit. Compare the prospect with your best clients, those who offer your firm the best return on dollars spent.

Accountants that are not used to much financial analysis of prospective clients might be looking simply for businesses that operate in the appropriate niche market, with, perhaps, a quick check on general financial conditions and approximate state of their technological needs.

A far better way to begin the client management process with a prospective client is to have in hand a conglomerate profile of your best clients. Look at as many characteristics as you can devise that help define who these clients are and how they spend their money, as well as how you spend your money on them. Include such things as frequency and amount of services billed, distance from the firm's office, length of sales cycle, and marketing expenditure required to obtain the original lead.

Presentation

After screening out unsuitable prospects, focus attention on the most promising clients. Begin the sales effort with a client management mentality. That will influence how you act while meeting the prospective client and what is emphasized in the presentations.

If there is one key to the process of client management, it is found in the word *expectations*. From the outset of the sales cycle, the accountant must accurately determine the prospective client's expectations. Expectations must be addressed in two areas.

First, there are technological expectations. Those expectations may be unrealistic if the clients do not understand the effort it takes to implement a complex accounting system. You cannot permit clients to expect that their problems will disappear with the tendering of a check to the accounting firm. Joining a health club will get you in better shape—if you go to the club. Clients must realize this before they sign anything in order to reach the goal of smooth client relations, happy clients, and, ultimately, tidy profits.

The second area in which expectations may run on the rocks is the nature of the service: how much the accounting firm, for the quoted price, will and will not do to provide the promised solutions. It is no great mystery as to how clients are thus illuminated. The accountant just needs to tell them. Be clear. Do not say it in an offhand manner. Say something like, "Sit down and listen very carefully. This information will make or break our ability to provide you with what you need and your ability to use what you're buying effectively."

Clients must be made to understand exactly what you are going to deliver. Delineate everything—not just a description of the financial statement compilation and accounting software configurations, but exactly how many hours of implementation are included, exactly when the clock starts for billing additional support and services, and so forth.

If in the middle of setting expectations, prospective clients are just not understanding them, that is the best time to walk away. You have got to walk away from those who have the danger signs. They are the perfect clients for your competitors.

The final portion of a comprehensive client management process is the ongoing assessment of your client base. This determines the level of support you should be offering and identifies problem clients in the making. Track your support time and costs and compare those to what the client is adding to your revenue.

The goal is not to lose the client, but sometimes it may be unavoidable. The savviest accountants learn to recognize as quickly as possible which "high-maintenance" clients are better dropped than served. Client management gives the accounting firm an objective, business—not emotional—level of knowledge that some clients are not worth the trouble. Exhibit 13.5 is a checklist to assist you in managing your client business relationships.

EXHIBIT 13.5
Checklist: Client Management

- ❑ Begin assessing client potential from the first meeting and continue throughout the relationship.
- ❑ Build profiles of your best clients, and use them when assessing prospective clients.
- ❑ Set client expectations at realistic levels, both in technology areas and in contractual agreements.
- ❑ Be the catalyst for client training; otherwise, the clients' use of the accounting systems and their rapport with you may never reach its full potential.
- ❑ Analyze existing clients' long-term potential and invest accordingly.
- ❑ Be prepared to walk away when you are not communicating.

Source: The Accounting Guild.

BOTTOM LINE

Fifty percent of all accountants make one call and quit. Twenty-five percent of all accountants make two calls and quit. Eighty percent of all prospective clients become clients *after* the fifth call. Eighty percent of all the accounting business is done by twenty percent of the firms.

Are you going to be one of those twenty percenters?

14

BASIC BUSINESS SERVICES

THE VALUE OF THE ACCOUNTING MARKET

Accounting services, including client write-up work, tax preparation and consulting, bookkeeping, internal audits, systems audits, and real-time audits, produced $38 billion in revenues for the nation's accounting industry in 1998.

Consulting services, including litigation support, pension consulting, administrative and management consulting, total financial solutions (computer hardware and software), and valuation consulting, totaled $78 billion in revenues in 1998.

Business accounting services, including payroll services, human resources, staffing, workers' compensation, benefits administration, back-office business needs, insurance, financial services, securities equity, equity markets, corporate compliance services, and specialty markets, such as health care, manufacturing, entertainment, real estate, federal and state governments, higher education, energy, estate/financial planning, financial education, credit and banking services, and information technology, was $250 billion in 1998.

SMALL BUSINESS IS BEAUTIFUL—MEDIUM IS BEST

For more than 20 years, a debate has raged over small business's contribution to job creation and the entire U.S. economy. One side holds that small companies create most of the new jobs; the other, that small businesses play only a minor role in job creation. The data that have been collected, analyzed, and studied reveal that each company-size category generates jobs on about the same proportion to that category's share of total employment. In other words, firms with 500 or more employees employ half of the U.S. workforce and generate half of the new jobs.

A tiny fraction of the businesses that started during a given time period account for most of the job growth that follows later. This pattern will vary by industry sector and by stage in the business cycle, but the hazard rate for start-up—what organizational-studies people call the *liability of newness*—is huge. Dun & Bradstreet economists think that the small number of start-ups that do grow are *born* large; the maturation of the 10-person garage shop into a big firm is extraordinarily rare. The author fully agrees. That was the good news. The bad news is that small businesses also show the highest rates of gross job destruction. The employment levels are more volatile at small employers.

There are two basic processes that lead to job creation. One is a natural or base level of turnover among existing businesses: One restaurant folds and another takes its place, perhaps in the same location. This process accounts for perhaps 75 to 80 percent of the turbulence among firms. The second process involves the redistribution of jobs across industry sectors: a typewriter-repair shop closes, but a shop that recharges laser-jet printer cartridges starts up.

The Small Business Administration (SBA) definition of *small business* as one with fewer than 500 employees is part of the interpretation problem. More than 90 percent of all businesses in the United States employ fewer than 500 employees.

Millions of corporate employees who were laid off during the late 1980s and early 1990s are now running their own businesses and are part of the small-business statistics. These comparatively new microbusinesses (under five employees) reflect the move from an industrial to an information economy, from a manufacturing to a service economy. These are relatively young, technology-dependent, and service-oriented firms with national or international reach. The ratio of revenues to employees is extremely high by historical standards, which accounts for unexpectedly high wages.

This is only the beginning of the exploration of the emerging role of small business. These are also the early stages of understanding what will be required of the accounting industry as it works toward prosperity in the new economy. The cumulative effect of rapid change on our businesses makes even the newest and smallest businesses infinitely more complex. This complexity aids the growth of the accounting business.

As useful rules for managing in the new economy emerge, the roles of the professional accountant and consultant are being refined and redefined. A significant demand for professional accountants and consultants exists from prospective clients who are desperate for additional support and services.

There is an important direct correlation between the opportunity to build the accounting business an accountant wants and the ability to deliver what clients want. Understanding what clients want typically leads to an expansion of services and capabilities far beyond the scope of traditional services. The more services that an accounting firm gives a client, the longer the firm will retain that client.

For example, if the firm provides only annual tax return service for a client, the firm is quite vulnerable to competition. If the firm provides tax service and financial statements on a regular basis, the odds of the client switching accountants will go down.

Add to those services meaningful consulting, such as financial planning, business performance monitoring, technology consulting, strategic planning, or financial management, and the result will be a more loyal client.

CLIENTS YESTERDAY, TODAY, AND TOMORROW

Accountants have long wrestled with the question of what to do about the small-business client. The accounting profession has for the most part ignored the needs of most segments of the small-business sector. This is largely a matter of economics. In the second edition of *Starting and Building Your Own Accounting Business*, the author wrote that, "the key to your success as an accountant is low cost. If you can offer your services at a price small businesses can afford, your earning power will be unlimited. Similarly, the higher fee structure of traditional CPAs opens vast possibilities for building a successful accounting business." In this third edition, the author now believes that serving the small to medium-sized market is the key to maximizing earnings and professional satisfaction.

The personal computer (PC) has revolutionized the way business and accounting is done. There are now more than 10 million registered users of Quicken, QuickBooks, and QuickBooks Pro who are performing (if the software is actually used) in-house what used to be done by accounting firms. Millions more use Peachtree, One-Write, Dac Easy, Simply Accounting, M.Y.O.B., and a host of inexpensive and even generic low-end software.

An analogy of this phenomenon is that of the blacksmiths and stable owners at the time the automobile reached a critical mass. Horses and carriages and their service facilities were replaced by more automobiles, garages, and gasoline service stations.

Today, the professional accountant's time and resources are limited. Accounting firms are operated in a manner designed to maximize earnings and satisfaction. There is not much satisfaction or money to be found working for the majority of smaller businesses that do not appreciate the value of quality work and will not or cannot pay what the services are worth.

It may be politically incorrect to advise against working in the small-business segment, but it is economically correct. The start-up or young accounting firm should concentrate its efforts on building a future with the "rapid risers" (see Exhibit 14.1) category of small to medium-sized business. These are the fastest growing businesses and are the most likely to be considering changes in relation to their present business growth, professional service providers, and financial and accounting systems. This group of businesses are the most likely to adopt new technology. They are the most receptive to the services that an excellent professional accounting firm can provide.

A medium-sized business has the resources to afford the fees that quality services demand. The real difference between small and medium-sized businesses is that there are more zeros on the checks the accounting firm receives. In starting out, if the accounting firm cannot get the medium-sized clients, it should prospect until smaller businesses are found that have growth potential and then help them get to the medium-sized business. Many large, lucrative clients have an accounting firm who worked with them from the start and can now be termed "childhood business friends."

EXHIBIT 14.1
Checklist: Small to Medium-Sized Business Category

❑ 1. *Moms and Pops.* Concentrated in automotive, retail, and restaurant businesses, this segment represents 30 percent of the overall market. This category has generally been in business the longest (over 10 years), has the fewest employees (average 14), and the lowest computer use (40 percent).

❑ 2. *Other professionals.* Local or statewide professionals (doctors, lawyers, insurance agents, etc.) comprise 26 percent of the total market. About 60 percent have been in business over 10 years; only 13 percent added employees in the last 12 months. This category considers computers important and has a high rate of use (85 percent).

❑ 3. *Steady pacers.* These businesses represent 32 percent of the total market. They are predominantly in retail, wholesale distribution, and construction. They are generally younger and larger, with an average of 19 employees and regional geographic coverage. More important, steady pacers are rarely satisfied with their current level of business and continually seek growth opportunities.

- ❑ 4. *Rapid risers.* This group represents the youngest (46 percent under 10 years), the largest (average 24 employees), and the fastest-growing companies. They are mainly in the service sector for health care, hospitality, and business. Rapid risers are most likely to be unhappy with their current business growth and have national ambitions. They are also the most likely to adopt new technology. But, unfortunately, they represent only 12 percent of the total market.

WINNING BUSINESS SERVICES CLIENTS WITH VALUE

Your clients and prospective clients face an increasing number of choices in the accounting services that are presented to them. Their perceptions of quality, service, and value affect their selection. Although price is always a factor, clients usually will go for the proposal that maximizes the delivered value.

Clients are most satisfied when their requirements are met and elated when their expectations are exceeded. Professional accountants who have fulfilled these expectations and needs will profit from increased billings, regular business, and enthusiastic referrals.

As an accountant, you can play a major role in defining and delivering high-value services, products, and systems to target clients. To win clients with value, use the following process.

Client Feedback and the Market

Use informal and formal methods to obtain feedback. Informally, observe emerging industry trends by monitoring competitors' service and product offerings, listening to clients' questions and problems, reviewing complaints, holding one-on-one talks with staff and watching for recurring difficulties that may signal an opportunity to deliver greater value.

Then, use formal research to confirm your observations and corroborate new information about changes in client behavior. The most common research methods are telephone and mail surveys, personal interviews with clients, and focus groups with clients to pinpoint opportunities that would influence your service offerings.

Target Niche Markets

Categorize clients according to their position in a buying cycle. For example, is the prospective client a start-up? An existing business without an accountant? An existing business that is looking to change accounting firms?

Customer-Satisfaction Orientation

Make all personnel aware that complaints must be resolved rapidly and to the client's total satisfaction if it is a client you wish to retain. The client is not always right.

Quality Obsession

Quality has two dimensions: First, clients must perceive quality as functional in that it solves a problem and offers a tangible advantage. Second, quality must convey superior value compared to that delivered by competitors or there is no competitive advantage. Further, quality is not limited to billed services exclusively. It also applies to the value of assistance, software application, timeliness, and friendliness of the receptionist.

Innovation

Accounting ideas and recommendations are legitimate only if they are implemented. Cross-functional teams are the best means for setting an idea in motion. Regardless of the size of the accounting firm or the number of individuals on the team, the group should be empowered to manage the client relationship, from needs identification to delivering an accounting solution.

Write-Up Business

Write-up service is a broad term used to describe a wide range of services. Generally, write-up services include:

- Recording cash receipts and disbursements, accruals, and adjustments to produce a general ledger or trial balance
- Preparing financial statements from general ledger or trial balance information
- Maintaining accounts receivable or accounts payable ledgers
- Calculating depreciation and maintaining fixed-asset registers
- Processing payrolls
- Calculating payroll tax deposits and preparing payroll tax returns
- Summarizing data required for tax returns

Write-Up Business Factors

The write-up business is not dead, and the CPAs and accountants who perform write-up are not a dying breed. Write-up is thriving in practices throughout the nation, and the volume of financial statement preparation being done from the proverbial shoebox full of client records is steadily increasing. The typical write-up engagement includes transaction summarization, after-the-fact payroll reporting, tax issues, bank account reconciliation, and financial statement preparation.

Write-up work does not command large fees, but requires time-sensitive processing, skilled staff, and some management effort. It is also not an expanding market for firms targeting the upper tiers of the small to medium-sized market niches. Many accountants point out that accounting staff that can perform these services are difficult to find and increasingly expensive. To offer these basic accounting services profitably, make sure that an engagement is really a write-up engagement. Differentiate between work that requires transaction summarization and after-the-fact payroll reporting and work that just needs transaction summary.

Engagements not requiring after-the-fact payroll reporting can be handled by workpaper tools, such as GoSystems Audit, AuditVision, and CaseWare. These have easy-to-use transaction summary capabilities and excellent financial reporting and tax return preparation features. Another substitute to a traditional write-up application is an off-the-shelf general ledger (GL) package. Firms that use GL packages for traditional write-up services develop skills that allow them to tie other services to these packages. This is a new service that can produce substantial revenues.

The downside is that GL packages typically contain many features not needed for write-up services. This means more complexity and may require additional staff training. Also, conversion is arduous if a decision is made to convert a client from another application.

Accountant's Relief by Micro Vision

Accountant's Relief is available in a 32-bit version for Windows 95, 98, and NT. It uses the Microsoft Access database. This provides excellent access to information and allows the use of the system's data with other applications. Access can enable the creation of virtually any report desired. Accountant's Relief creates complete, publishable financial statements, including cover sheet, report letter, table of contents, and footnotes. The user can preview the financials on the screen before printing.

The program provides efficient data entry for entering transactions. All entries are made in a spreadsheet format that is very intuitive. Five different kinds of adjusting journal entries (adjusting, reclassifying, federal, other, and potential) with capability for reversing and recurring entries. A comprehensive, fully integrated after-the-fact payroll module for federal and state payroll tax forms is supported by the software program. Payroll information is automatically rolled over to this program.

Accountant's Relief GL Link module imports data quickly and easily from virtually any accounting program that a client might use. Accountant's Relief comes preconfigured for most GL programs. Users can configure it to import data from any other GL program. Time-saving features include data entry in a familiar spreadsheet format, online technical support services for downloading updates and sending your questions electronically for faster response, and word processing capabilities for creating other documents. The program also includes workpapers, bank reconciliation, and analytical ratio analysis. The latest version also includes the ability to consolidate, departmentalize, and customize financial statements. The Tax Link option exports data to most tax programs.

Certiflex Dimension Client Write-Up by The Versatile Group

Certiflex Dimension Client Write-Up is a comprehensive accounting software program that integrates with Certiflex Dimension business accounting software and popular tax software. The program is a completely integrated write-up solution that is available in one package for one price without the need for additional modules.

The batch entry permits users to enter and edit all transaction types without changing screens. Data entry is further enhanced by shortcut keys to minimize keystrokes, use of a numeric keypad, and the ability to add employees, vendors, and ledger accounts "on the fly." It automatically increments prior reference numbers and dates. Also, the program keeps running totals by batch, journal entry, or hash totals.

The report writer adjusts to any level of detail. Certiflex Dimension includes multiple industry-specific charts of accounts and financial statement templates. The program lets users exclude accounts with zero balances, process multiple currency types, summarize account detail, and print financials for any period, day, or range of days. Reports can be printed for a range of clients or by a cycle number.

After-the-fact payroll and payables print federal forms, including 941s, W2s, W3s, and 1099s. The program reports employee and vendor history, including optional GL distribution, and manages up to 26 different earnings and deduction categories such as 401(k), tips, bonuses, and insurance.

Certiflex Dimensions' client control tracks client activity and management responsibilities (budget versus actual), contains a user-defined information database that helps manage key information on each client, plus each client's data location is user definable.

CPA-98 by Franklen Computer Systems

Franklen's CPA-98 is a Windows write-up program that conforms to true Windows conventions. It focuses on four critical elements of write-up: transaction entry that maximizes speed and accuracy; a report designed with power and flexibility to meet the needs of the client; a fully integrated and comprehensive after-the-fact payroll; reporting function and a sophisticated client integration function, import and export modes.

The financial report design offers flexibility in formatting financial statements, including schedules, column headings, calculations, ratios, historical trends, and horizontal reporting. The program provides line-by-line control using Windows true-type fonts to produce publication-quality reports. Financial statement layouts include current period, year-to-date, and budget comparatives. Financial statements can be reprinted for closed periods.

A client setup wizard makes fast and easy work of adding new clients. A work-saving client integration module allows for both import and export functions. CPA-98 has a graph wizard to convert financial data into color graphs and charts. The program produces quarterly and annual federal and state tax forms. It offers unlimited payroll earning types and payroll deductions.

Franklen's Checkman allows clients to write checks and interface data with CPA-98. The capabilities include magnetic ink character recognition (MICR) encoding, bank reconciliation, and full accounts payable capabilities. Payman is its comprehensive service-bureau quality payroll system.

CPA-98's import feature will download information from Quicken, QuickPay, QuickBooks, Lotus, and other ASCII files. Tax information can be exported to Lacerte, Turbo Tax, Pencil Pushers, and other major tax software packages.

EasyACCT Professional Series by Tax and Accounting Software Corp.

EasyACCT Professional Series provides an extensive suite of accounting firm applications that has write-up (including after-the-fact payroll), service bureau payroll, asset depreciation and management, bank reconciliation, and loan amortization. Transaction information is entered into the program using transaction, payroll, and sales journal screens. The system supports on-the-fly editing and addition of account, employee, and vendor information.

An unlimited number of clients may be processed through the write-up system. Each time a new client is brought onto the system, portions or the entire setup can be copied from an existing client. One unique aspect of this program is that account numbers may be renumbered regardless of the amount of activity that is assigned to them.

The program will create financial statements automatically, based on the chart of accounts' numbering scheme. Financial statements may also be created manually by using a nongraphical financial statement layout table. There is no provision to create a cover page, footnotes, or accountants' report within the statements. Free-form text of any kind will have to be created outside of EasyACCT.

The bank reconciliation module automatically matches and clears entries and calculates a "proof of cash." Extensive on-screen help is available for each data entry field. The program generates several helpful, easy-to-read reports that provide detailed documentation for each bank reconciliation.

To help professional accountants meet clients' in-house accounting needs, an EasyACCT Business System is available for small to medium-sized businesses to write their own checks, enter transactions, and handle other accounting activities. The client-created information can then be imported into the EasyACCT Professional Series.

Real-Time General Ledger by Universal Business Computing Company

Universal Business Computing Company (UBCC) offers a full line of accounting firm, commercial business, and contractor accounting software programs. Its applications handle processing on a "real-time" basis (hence its name) as opposed to "batch processing." Transactions are immediately ready for editing and information purposes without any "posting" requirements. Transaction information, including budgeted data, is available for five years.

The user interface is uncluttered and easy to use. Individual record locking can allow two or more people to function concurrently within the same data file. Its two data entry types are the traditional mnemonic-based menu structure and the prompted pull-down menu structure.

The system creates financial statements in a variety of formats, including 12-month, five year, side-by-side, and multiple locations across-the-page comparative formats. Predefined financial statements are available for comparative financial statements, compilation reports, and statements of cash flow. Changes made to report format carry through to all other reports using the same format. However, the software offers no easy provision for creating a cover page with a table of contents or accountants' report letter. Similarly, all footnotes must be created outside of the program.

QuickBooks, Quicken, Peachtree, M.Y.O.B., and most other low-end accounting software can be extracted from clients' computerized accounting systems and integrated into UBCC General Ledger and Bank Reconciliation applications through their Universal Importer. There are more than 13 different payroll modules available separately for those firms with heavy-duty processing needs. A drawback is that UBCC sells the different payroll modules separately, which may make them significantly more expensive than other systems.

WinCABS by Client Accounting Systems

WinCABS is a fully Windows-integrated software package offering a robust set of features. The standard package allows for after-the-fact entry of payroll. An additional data conversion module allows easy access to data within popular accounting software programs such as QuickBooks, Quicken, and M.Y.O.B. It also exports to most popular tax packages. The standard package allows for the importing of ASCII text files.

The chart of accounts allows for an account number with up to eight characters and offers additional nonposting memo accounts. When posting transactions, the user may choose from up to 12 journals, eight of which are completely user definable. Form 1099 totals are automatically created for any data entry that is associated with a vendor. Up to 300 subsidiary companies may be consolidated into one GL account. These consolidations may include accounts from any company contained within the system.

Users can write custom reports through a built-in graphical report writer. Creating new reports is facilitated by the program's ability to borrow report formats from other client companies. There are seven sample companies included, whose templates may be borrowed to establish unique layouts. Groups of reports may be bundled so that a complete financial statement may be printed with one mouse click. Payroll processing is accomplished through the after-the-fact payroll module that is included in the basic system. Users can generate W2s, 1099s, and even magnetic media reports. The program automatically calculates FICA, state disability, and Medicare taxes during data entry. The standard 941 and 940 reports may be printed as desired.

WinCABS is a good choice for accounting firms striving to remain on the cutting edge of accounting technology. The package allows presentation-quality financial statements and is a good example of how accounting packages are using the additional functionality available in a Windows environment.

Write-Up Plus by UniLink Software

UniLink has embraced the concept of offering a suite of products designed for the use of a professional accounting firm. Write-Up Plus is a companion to the software publisher's practice management and general accounting modules. The software is exceptionally well documented, with clear explanations for all processing procedures.

The system provides fast setup for clients, while also handling all of the complexities of the most demanding clients. Its financial report templates and comprehensive report formatter enable the user to customize financial statements. However, producing cover letters and footnotes for financial statements could prove difficult, because the word processor that is included does not offer spell checking. If "too much information" is entered, a "buffer is full" message could be received, which will not allow the user to enter any further footnotes or text. The chart of accounts structure may accommodate up to 10 digits divided into three separate segments. The main account structure may not be larger than five digits, and, once established, the structure cannot be changed. When combining or copying client files from one entity to another, care must be taken to use the same account structure because dissimilar numbering schemes cannot be combined. Accounts may contain nonfinancial data, such as units of production or special computations for displaying totals on the statement of cash flows.

Accountants can use a CashLink application in the client's place of business for transaction entry, print accounts payable and payroll checks, and to reconcile checking accounts. CashLink information can then be imported into Write-up Plus for additional processing. An import utility option allows the user to link with Quicken, QuickBooks, Peachtree, and most general low-end accounting software programs.

UniLink has a qualified reseller program that offers a discount to accounting firms that resell their applications to clients.

Write-Up Solution II by Creative Solutions Inc.

Creative Solutions offers a series of popular packages designed for the professional accountant marketplace. Each is integrated with Creative Solutions's family of accounting practice productivity software. The Write-Up Solution II program has innovative features that enhance data entry, provide good connectivity to other software packages, and include write-up practice management features. The system also comes with excellent documentation that offers both reference tools and tutorials.

The program offers an extensive set of predefined sample clients and reports. Proportional fonts and borders are included to give a professional flourish to the financial statements and transmittal letters. A Quick Start Formatter allows the user to set up financial statements within minutes. Another Creative Solutions product, Checkbook Solutions, can be used by clients to process accounts payable, payroll, and accounts receivable information. Checkbook Solutions information is then imported to Write-Up Solution II for additional processing and reporting. The professional accountant can also pass back any updated information, such as changes to the employee data file or chart of accounts, to the client.

Posting transactions to the system is accomplished through a streamlined data entry screen. The software will remember and automatically recall the last transaction amount for specific vendors or employees. The user can set posting to occur in real time or only when a general ledger report is run.

Write-Up Solution II offers tools directed at enhancing write-up practice management. An activity log tracks the processing status of all clients on the system. The activity log is a very useful tool for showing the last processing date for each client. Operator time is tracked by the system and can be entered into Creative Solutions' time and billing application for further processing. Creative Solutions offers a wide range of software training, including hands-on training in major cities, on-site training, teletraining, and videotapes.

Conclusion

Before deciding on any of these write-up packages, the professional accountant should consider the firm's investment in computer hardware and other software applications. If the firm, like most others, is heavily invested in Microsoft Windows, Microsoft Office, and Microsoft BackOffice, then it makes sense to focus the search on those packages with Windows interfaces.

Request information, including an evaluation disk, from the producers of the software in which you are interested. The information in this section was based on the latest programs available at the time of preparation. New features may now be offered as well as the release of new Windows versions.

Important write-up features to consider include:

- Large number of end users
- Support for native Windows 98 or NT
- Ability to generate presentation-quality financial statements
- Flexible importing and exporting
- Flexible chart of accounts
- Ability to easily change prior transactions
- After-the-fact payroll processing
- Custom graphical report writer

A list of software publishers of the write-up programs previously described is presented in Exhibit 14.2. Additional sources for current information are contained in Accounting Today, Practical Accounting Magazine, Accounting Technology Magazine, AccountingNet.com, and Faulkner & Gray's ElectronicAccountant.[1]

[1]Accounting Today, Accounting Technology, Practical Accountant and Electronic Accountant can be found at www.electricaccountant.com. AccountingNet can be found at www.accountingnet.com.

EXHIBIT 14.2
Client Write-Up Software Resources

- Accountant's Relief, Micro Vision, Hauppauge, NY, (888) 735-4334, www.mvsinc.com
- Certiflex Dimension, The Versatile Group, Dallas, TX, (800) 237-8435, www.tvginc.com
- CPA-98, Franklen Computer Systems, Inc., Glendale, CA, (800) 821-1790, www.franklencomputer.com
- EasyACCT Professional Series, Tax and Accounting Software Corp., Tulsa, OK, (918) 493-5900, www.taascforce.com
- Real-Time Accounting Software, Universal Business Computing Co., Taos, NM, (800) 827-8610, www.ubcc.com
- WinCABS, Client Accounting Systems, Culver City, CA, (800) 350-7696, www.clientaccounting.com
- Write-Up*Plus, UniLink, Jackson, WY, (800) 456-8321, www.unilinkinc.com
- Write-Up Solution II, Creative Solutions Inc., Dexter, MI, (800) 968-8900, www.csisolutions.com

FUNDAMENTAL BUSINESS DECISION

The write-up practice is getting pinched by low-cost software, particularly Intuit's QuickBooks software, which has turned a traditional accounting mainstay service into a low-growth area. Yet the marketplace has presented a silver lining by spurring a demand for accounting knowledge. Accountants can exploit (in the finest sense of the word) the marketplace by becoming a virtual chief financial person or a cyber chief financial officer and assist clients to manage their businesses by understanding the financial accounting data they have amassed with their low-end accounting software. Accountants can educate business clients on how to transform data into useful information.

In many cases, accountants are using the financial statements as the starting point for consulting services, instead of using them as a final product. They are reviewing clients' data files on disk and providing controllership services. What used to be the end product is now the means to accomplish greater client business performance.

AFFILIATE BUSINESS SERVICE BUREAU

Accountants are advised to consider setting up a separate business service bureau entity to perform accounting and bookkeeping functions, such as write-up and payroll preparation. By outsourcing this work from the parent accounting firm, each entity is freed to concentrate on areas of the accounting business that are best handled separately.

THE ACCOUNTING GUILD

Payroll preparation is a wedge to attract write-up business. This in turn expands into doing financial statements, after-the-fact payroll, and tax returns. For those looking to develop the traditional practice or a service-bureau subsidiary and want personalized assistance in setting up their business, the author presents a seminar for accountants to receive training on how to better market their services to target write-up clients.

Accountants tend to make up their own excuses when they are not doing well. The Accounting Guild's aim is to provide accountants with the skills and translate those acquired skills into new business. The Guild starts out by assisting the accountant in goal setting and establishing parameters for the business and provides a wide range of services, including sample engagement letters, sources for leads, instructions on how to train telemarketers and accounting salespersons, and, perhaps most important, how to close a prospect.

TAX RETURN PREPARATION

Tax return preparation is a major component of any accounting business. The opinion of the author, based on more than 20 years of experience, is to concentrate only on the tax returns of the clients' principals and managers in addition to all tax returns required for the businesses. The business returns will either be some form of corporate return or information return for partnerships, S corporations, and forms of limited liability corporations. For nonincorporated businesses, Form 1040 with Schedule C will be required for the sole proprietorship, and Schedule E for others with K-1 income. Returns for the management personnel of the client business will be done as an accommodation and the business not solicited. The type of business this book is promulgating is not based on high-volume, low-fee tax preparation.

These returns will require considerable care, thought, and time, and should be billed at the appropriate professional rate which covers time, costs, and profit. The other type of returns, which take time away from the ongoing business, do not bring the billing rates of practice and will detract from the time available for marketing, which results in a large lost opportunities cost.

IRS Market Segmentation

The Internal Revenue Service has instituted a market segment specialization program. This program was established to make IRS audits faster and more geographically consistent and was designed to level the playing field. As a result, IRS audits are no longer the hit-or-miss propositions they have been in the past. The heart of the program is to train or retrain revenue agents to become "experts" and perform more effectively in specific market segments. The IRS publishes Audit Technique Guides. These are available through its Freedom of Information Act reading room in Washington, D.C., and from the IRS Internet Web site. In focusing on specific businesses, the booklets provide step-by-step guidance on how to conduct audits and deal with the issues that are specific to a particular industry.

The mortuary audit guides, for instance, familiarize agents with common industry terminology such as embalming, cremation, and mortuaries. They also cover state laws and health codes, insurance coverage, characteristics of the cemetery business, and internal controls.

The guides focus on a number of areas (listing follows). The guides aim to reduce taxpayer burden, result in quality audits, and create more professionalism in the agent ranks. With this program, the IRS and the public and accountants win. Market segmenting alerts accountants and clients as what to expect from an audit and alerts the clients in those segments to prepare for the possibility of an audit. The guides and listing of target markets give the professional accountants additional expertise in the field and spotlight market niches to cover.

IRS Market Segmentation Guides

- Air Charters
- Attorneys

- Bed and Breakfasts
- Gasoline Retailers
- Mortuaries
- Taxicabs
- Trucking

Exhibit 14.3 lists the specific types of business activity that the Internal Revenue Service has identified for market segment specialization.

EXHIBIT 14.3
IRS Target Markets

- Auto dealerships
- Check cashing industry
- Coal mining
- Commercial fishing
- Entertainment
- Garment contracting
- Grain growers
- Grocery retailing
- Health care
- Insurance agencies
- Laundromats
- Life insurance
- Ministers
- Mobile caterers
- Music industry
- Passive activity losses
- Pizza restaurants
- Real estate construction
- Reforestation
- Rehabilitation tax credit
- Sales—door-to-door or by phone
- Travel agencies
- Wine industry

National Association of Computerized Tax Processors (NACTP)

In 1969, mainframe computers operated by six service bureaus were the only computerized link to tax preparation. These competing service bureaus joined together to create an organization that would help the entire industry grow. Its immediate goals were to create standards in tax processing and form alliances with federal and state agencies to work together toward preparing compliant tax returns. The NACTP now numbers approximately 65 companies from all spectrums, including tax preparation software, electronic filing processors, tax form publishers, and tax processing service bureaus. Nearly every tax preparer in the nation uses a PC to prepare client returns, and many are participating in the electronic filing program.

Popular Tax-Related Web Sites

- The Internal Revenue Service, www.irs.ustreas.gov
- Internal Revenue Bulletin, www.fedworld.gov/ftp/irs-irbs
- IRS Forms, www.irs.ustreas.gov/prod/forms_pubs/index
- National Association of Computerized Tax Processors, www.nactp.org
- Schmidt's State Tax Directory, www.taxsites.com
- Taxlibrary.com, www.taxlibrary.com
- PricewaterhouseCoopers Tax News Network, www.taxnews.com/tnn_public
- Research Institute of America, www.riatax.com
- Nelco, www.nelcoinc.com

A list of a few of the many tax preparation software providers along with their telephone numbers and Internet addresses is presented in Exhibit 14.4.

EXHIBIT 14.4
Tax Preparation Software Providers Resources

It is beyond the scope of this guide to report evaluations of the many tax software programs available. Each of the software providers listed will be delighted to furnish you with descriptive materials as well as an evaluation disk to help you decide on the particular program to use.

- **Alpine Data Inc.,** Montrose, CO, (800) 525-1040, www.alpine-data.com
- **AM Software,** Kansas City, MO, (816) 741-7848, www.amtax.com
- **Arthur Andersen & Co.,** Sarasota, FL, (800) 872-1040, www.arthurandersen.com
- **ATX Inc.,** Washburn, ME, (800) 944-8883, www.saberpro.com
- **CCH Inc.,** Torrance, CA, (800) 457-7639, www.cch.com
- **CLR/Fast Tax,** Carrollton, TX, (800) 327-8829, www.clr.com
- **CPASoftware**, Pensacola, FL, (800) 272-7123, www.cpasoftware.com
- **Creative Solutions,** Dexter, MI, (800) 968-8900, www.csisolutions.com
- **Drake Software,** Franklin, NC, (800) 890-9500, www.drake-software.com
- **Intuit,** San Diego, CA, (800) 446-8848, www.intuit.com
- **Lacerte Software Corp.,** Dallas, TX, (800) 765-4065, www.lcsoft.com
- **Micro Vision Software,** Hauppauge, NY, (800) 829-7354, www.mvsinc.com
- **Tax & Accounting Software,** Tulsa, OK, (800) 998-9990, www.taascforce.com
- **Taxbyte Inc.,** Moline, IL, (800) 245-8299, www.taxbyte-usa.com
- **TK Publishing,** Orlando, FL, (800) 323-2662, www.taxshop.com
- **Universal Tax Systems,** Rome, GA, (800) 755-9473, www.taxwise.com
- **Xpress Software,** Columbia, SC, (800) 285-1065, www.xpress-software.com

15

CONSULTING, PARTNERING, AND THE INTERNET

An increasing number of accountants, CPAs and non-CPAs alike, are entering the consulting business. Whether they enter because of client demand or competitor pressure, the consulting part of the accounting business is so new and so different to these entrants that there is little basis in their experience for managing it well.

While the complexities of the accounting consulting business are real and many, there are some decisions an accountant can make to help increase the prospects for success. One of the basic decisions is the decision to resell products, both computer hardware and accounting-related software. For years, the accounting profession mindset has been to sell professional time. Product sales were seen as liabilities. Many CPA traditionalists struggled with the concept. They had ethical questions. How could they buy at one price and resell to clients at a higher price? How does the accounting firm afford the costs of carrying inventory? How does the accountant control the process and manage the additional necessary staff?

Because of these questions, many accounting firms would only perform needs analysis and prepare software request for proposals (RFPs) and searches, going to extremes to be sure the client selected the best solution. Then, the accountants referred their clients to relative strangers, software and hardware vendors. These vendors often went out of business a short time later. And, when the project went sour, the client called the accountant.

CHANGING ECONOMICS

The changing economics of the personal computer (PC) hardware and software business further complicated the problem. When mid-range accounting systems cost $30,000 to $40,000, spending $5,000 on the needs analysis and search made sense. Now, those same or more powerful system capabilities cost $3,000 to $8,000.

How does an accountant justify asking a client to spend $5,000 to select a few thousand dollars in highly standardized hardware? Wouldn't it be wiser to spend most of that money on implementation? That rationale became the selling strategy of the nonaccountant segment of competition, the value-added resellers (VARs). They knew a few accounting packages widely available to anyone with a resale tax certificate. These resellers with a bare minimum of accounting expertise would quickly size up the prospective client and provide a "fit" very similar to the practice of selling shoes. Some resellers who knew software programs modified source code, while others helped clients change procedures to better conform to a package's standard features. Rather than determining the best system to serve the client's needs, the client's procedures were modified to meet the packages' limitations.

SOLUTION SELLING

Accounting firms sold solutions to needs instead of selling products. They were "on the inside" working with their clients, making change happen, creating ongoing relationships, and adding value to the products and tools that they did sell. These are the very things that professional accountants and consultants strive for in dealing with their clients.

The accounting firm that sells a one-stop solution controls the accounting computerization process. They know the quality of the software and its publishers and what hardware works best with which operating system and application software. The accountant knows the people involved on the project and their commitment to client service and where to find them if needed. The accountant controls when resources will be on site and ready. The accountant decides when and if more resources are needed, so the client's expectations are met from start to finish.

Selling full solutions allows the professional accountant and consultant to gain control of the process and retain the profits that others would otherwise make from the accountant's projects. In today's marketplace, accounting consultants can competently configure, order, set up, install, and implement the products and expertise of an accounting system and give the necessary training.

The accounting firm does not usually need additional people to move to a full reseller–consultant mode. For the technical demands that small to medium-sized businesses deal with, hardware and software distributors can help with configuration and operating system details and third-party on-site technical service support. Some of these distributors are Ingram Micro, Tech Data, and Pinacor (a listing of leading distributors is in the Distributor Partnering section of this chapter). Once you decide to be in this business, commit to it. Do not "straddle" your core people—dedicate and train them. Once dedicated and trained, the accounting firm will find that the more it does, the easier and more profitable this part of the practice will become.

BENEFITS OF OFFERING COMPUTER CONSULTING SERVICES

Computer consulting services are an addition to the traditional professional services of tax, audit, and review work and not a replacement or redirection. The size of the businesses requiring this type of service has increased in direct relationship to the change in the capability of the computer hardware and software. The reasons for providing these services really do not change according to the size of the accounting firm. Often, the smaller the firm, the more important these abilities prove to be.

Financial Considerations

The greater breadth of services offered brings new consulting service revenue from the existing client base. The additional time and expertise delivered to clients result in an increase in the billings for that time and expertise. Expertise has come to mean more than just an accountant coming up with the name of a software program. Knowing what software programs can do and whether they are the right solution for a business is the added value to the clients.

A growing number of accounting firms have developed practice segments built around the delivery of computer consulting services. Some of these firms are generating hundreds of thousands of dollars in revenue annually from the delivery of these services alone. Most of the engagements are with smaller companies, and most of these started with small, single-user implementations. As the experience grew, so did the size and complexity of the engagements. Network selection assistance and multiuser software installations are to be undertaken only by those consultants who have "earned their stripes."

Uncovering Additional Business

A properly implemented accounting system will very often point to other potential areas of concern in the client's business activities. For example, in implementing the system, some deficiencies in control of the client's cash flow may be uncovered, presenting the opportunity to advise the client on cash management procedures. This is beyond the scope of the original engagement and, hence, additionally billable. It also shows the client the level of the professional consultant's expertise and concern for what is in the client's best interest.

Very few other professional service activities match computerized accounting consulting as a means of attracting new full-service clients. Practice development opportunities abound, when you combine an active pursuit of computer consulting for non-client businesses with other activities.

Accounting Software Publishers

Accounting software companies have taken the lead to create special programs that address the needs of the accounting community. The programs offer, for varying fees and some without fees, demonstration software, complete software packages, technical support, training, product upgrades, and lead referrals. Some publishers provide sales and marketing representatives, who will provide assistance to the accountant in forming a working relationship with authorized resellers in the area or assisting with the authorization of the accounting firm itself.

Value-Added Reseller Relationship

A relationship, primarily in the client–server area, can give the accountant not only a source for the computer hardware, but also provide the client–server hardware reseller with a qualified, knowledgeable consultant to whom they can refer clients. The networking hardware resellers are not generally accountants and are not typically qualified to fully implement a sophisticated accounting system in a business.

Accountants offer their services and accounting expertise to the new software users to assist in many areas, such as the design of the chart of accounts and financial statements and the proper designation of cost/profit centers.

A well-designed and implemented accounting system means much more than a general ledger and financial statements. It can become an integral part of the client's management reporting and control system. Being able to help client companies get up and running with a minimum of trouble and duplicated effort puts the consultant in a very positive light in the eyes of management. The opportunity to provide additional services, including audit or review work on a continuing basis, frequently presents itself.

While building this relationship with resellers, the accountant learns the value of resellers' knowledge of client–server hardware and complex networking issues. These can provide value for the accountant's own client base. This gives the professional accountant/ consultant a significant level of comfort and confidence to refer clients to an organization that they know can and will give the appropriate advice and support on issues beyond the accountant's area of expertise.

The basic concept of this two-way relationship is simple. In practice, it takes both parties to make it work successfully and some continuing experience to make both feel confident with each other. As with many other business relationships, it is an investment that can pay good dividends if handled properly. In most cases, exclusivity of the relationship is not in the best interest of either party.

Practice Protection

Practice protection is another very important benefit of computer consulting services. Not only will accountants be providing an additional level of professional services to their clients, but they may also be preventing another firm from getting their "foot in the door."

Client–Server Computerization Candidates

The vast majority of companies that are candidates for client–server computerization have not yet made that investment. It is often overwhelming to many small and medium-sized business owners and managers. There is great fear and trepidation in making this type of decision. Also, there is a very large number of willing would-be partners offering their assistance in selecting the correct client–server hardware and networking system to these client companies.

Some of the would-be partners are accounting firms or consulting firms with accounting experience. In many cases, the independent consultants who contact these companies are strictly computer consultants with no claim to any accounting or operational expertise. While this is not an indictment of such consultants, they usually do not have the appropriate background to implement an involved accounting and management system into the day-to-day function of a business.

Those accounting firms that do offer computer consulting services do so within the normal ethical considerations of all accounting firms. This means that they will perform their duties with due diligence and provide as complete a service as they are able. This does not preclude them from offering additional services or even bidding on the continuing tax and audit work if asked.

Client's Financial Management

The general improvement of the client's financial management and control systems is part of the reason that the software has been selected. The mid-range to high-end accounting systems are designed in a fashion that brings in a level and type of control that is not possible or feasible with low-end systems. The ability to review, at any point during an accounting period, the financial picture of the business from cost of goods sold through the income statement and balance sheet is what truly makes these systems more than just an accounting system. They really do turn into decision-making aids and management reporting systems when installed properly with a complete understanding of the client's business activities.

The system will force a good and complete audit trail of all activities, making the review work easier. It will also allow for changes to current procedures to help in the flow of information under the guise of "the computer requires that it be done this way." If the system includes an order processing and inventory control function, then those areas will benefit greatly from an increased control and reporting capability. The overall benefit to the company can be to better manage their entire realm of activity and, thus, potentially be more profitable. An additional benefit to the client is that the data are more reliable and easier to track. Accountants who can give this level of return to a client have not only done their job, but proved to be worthy business advisors and not merely historians.

ADDITIONAL SERVICE OFFERINGS

There are many additional service offerings that can be developed through and provided by the computer consulting practice of an accounting firm. Many of those offerings will require a level of technical knowledge and investment beyond what most firms will want to make.

However, that does not mean that the accountant should not investigate such things as custom report development, telephone support, training for new personnel, version upgrade assistance, and linking the accounting system into other software products or available third-party specialized systems.

The reasons for providing computer consulting services are many and varied. The benefit to the clients and the client relationships are obvious. The potential for additional revenue generation from these nontraditional services is considerable. The potential practice development opportunities are certainly worthy of consideration.

COST–BENEFIT CONSIDERATIONS

Of course, there is a cost for all of the benefits in establishing an accounting/consulting program. It is necessary for the accounting firm to make a commitment in dollars (for client–server hardware, software, and training), in time (for learning the software beyond the training phase and the opportunity costs), in personnel (for the people taking on this responsibility), and in resources (a partner-level person will have to oversee the development, and manage the operation).

The bottom line is: Can the firm afford not to make the investment?

DEVELOPING A SOFTWARE CONSULTING BUSINESS

As we have said, a pressing need for any emerging and middle-market business is automated client–server financial and operational systems to support their activities. The majority of these businesses do not have the resources to successfully implement these systems without some level of outside assistance. The challenges are many for any professional accounting firm beginning this type of practice.

A basic step is to contact Microsoft Corporation and inquire about their Direct Access program, which is designed for consultants and service providers. Microsoft Corporation does not produce accounting software per se, but as the largest software corporation in the world it has a profound effect on the accounting industry. You can learn a great deal from their materials and then undertake the development of a formal practice plan.

CONSULTING PRACTICE PLAN

As with any new business venture, firms interested in developing a consulting practice should develop a formal plan that, like a business plan, defines the mission and goals of the practice. The plan forces the professional accountant to think through all aspects of the new venture. It will set a direction and a benchmark against which progress can be measured. Without a plan, time and money may be invested in areas that do not meet the primary objectives for starting the practice in the first place. A formal plan provides the opportunity for others in the firm to evaluate and respond. For the practice to succeed, top management in the firm must support it. Upper managers are the people who will financially support the practice and assist in marketing the services to clients, prospective clients, and others within the firm.

Organization of the Plan

This is no rigid format for the plan, yet the following are the more critical sections to be included.

Practice Objectives

The plan must begin with a listing of objectives. Simply put, identify why the practice should be initiated. This exercise is important because these objectives will be the basis for later decisions. For instance, if it is determined that the primary objective is to acquire new audit and tax clients, then a different marketing approach may be incorporated or different services offered than if the sole reason was to generate more revenue.

Several common objectives include:

- Growing source of revenue
- Developing new audit and tax clients
- Expansion of services to existing clients
- Retaining superior staff
- Practice protection

As you get into this exercise, you will define a number of objectives. However, you should prioritize these objectives and use them as a guide when making any major decisions concerning the consulting practice. If the decision does not support the objectives, closely reassess the decision.

Define Supporting Goals

Once the objectives have been determined, develop specific goals for the new practice. The goals should be action oriented and reachable.

Sample goals might include:

- Complete 10 accounting system installations with average collected fees of $10,000.
- Develop six new audit and seven tax engagements as a direct result of the computer systems practice.

Note that the goals above include specific figures. If it is uncomfortable specifying a specific number, include a range. Including a range indicates the uncertainty of the goal. Updating the plan annually should bring greater accuracy.

Definition of Services to be Offered

At this point in the plan, the practice begins to take shape. It is here that the types of consulting services to be offered are defined. The types of services offered have a direct impact on the investment the accounting firm will be required to make in training and in staffing.

Some sample types of services include:

- Entry-level accounting/general accounting
- Development of software
- Design and implementation of local area networks (LANs)

Personnel Requirements

The personnel requirements for the consulting practice will vary depending on the type of services to be offered and the volume of work that is anticipated. Several key points will need to be addressed:

- Identify a practice coordinator (preferably a senior member of the firm) and determine the amount of this person's time that is to be devoted to this new practice area.
- Determine if staff will come from other practice areas (audit or tax) or if they are to be hired.
- For staff coming from other practice areas, decide whether their commitment is to be on an "as available" or a full-time basis.
- Determine the administrative support available to the practice.

- Determine the roles of each staff (e.g., marketing, implementation, programming, networking, etc.).

Training

Unless the firm plans to hire experienced consultants, an investment in staff training will be necessary. The plan should identify the number of training hours and costs that are expected for each staff member to undertake.

Marketing

Fortunately, there are a number of sound alternatives for marketing consulting services. An excellent source of consulting work is with existing audit and tax clients. Tap this source by talking with each client. Staff from the practice may very well be the best source of referrals, particularly in the first year. With experience, introductory seminars can be conducted. This is an excellent way to get exposure for the firm.

Economics

Finally, develop a pro forma operating budget. The budget should include estimated chargeable hours by staff, nonchargeable hours by category (e.g., training, vacation). Additionally, you will want your budget to include estimated revenues by project type and estimated expenses, both one-time and ongoing. In developing this plan, keep the following in mind:

- It may be necessary to bid aggressively on the first few projects to gain experience.
- Budget overruns are likely to be experienced for the first two or three projects.
- It is difficult to meet the same level of chargeable hours normally achieved by audit or tax staff, particularly during the first year when substantial training occurs.

FOCUSING ON SUCCESS

Over time, most accountants specializing in computer accounting software packages find themselves, whether by design or default, supporting two to five different accounting programs. There are inherent problems with trying to support more than two or three different accounting programs. First, significant time is required to stay current with the features in each package that are in a constant state of change and change dramatically when a new operating system, such as Microsoft 2000, is introduced. Second, it is often difficult to remember all the differences between programs. Third, if you are trying to support several different packages, you are less likely to develop advanced consulting skills with any single program.

Over the last several years, the major producers of accounting software have each made tremendous strides with their software programs, and then either merged or otherwise consolidated themselves into comparatively few surviving software producers. The accounting software market is as competitive as ever. This competitiveness has encouraged better accounting software with an ever-increasing number of features.

Accountants can select a few top-level accounting programs and build a successful consulting practice by centering their consulting activities around those two or three programs.

Benefits of Focusing on Two or Three Programs

The first benefit of focusing on two or three accounting software programs is the reduction in the amount of time required to stay current on just a few programs as opposed to many. The second benefit is the ability to develop high-level skills that have a greater perception of value to a prospective client. It takes a certain amount of time to get comfortable with the "core modules" that all clients use. These core modules are: general ledger, accounts payable, accounts receivable, and payroll. A large number of accountants who consult on several different programs find it advantageous to use each program's superior features or applications. They thus create the "best of breed" and deliver the best solution to the client.

Another benefit is the increased ability of the accountant to answer questions from clients on a timely basis. A consulting department can support a large number of consulting clients when the majority of support calls received can be answered without referring to a manual or calling technical support at the software producer level.

The fourth benefit of focusing on two or three packages is especially important to consultants within an accounting firm. The firm will have a greater comfort level if efforts are focused on relatively few software programs because the consultant's knowledge of the software is high, and the consultants have a better working knowledge of what the software is capable of doing.

The fifth benefit is that it is wise not to keep "all of ones' eggs in one basket." While many of the software program publishers make cases for representing a single software program, it does not make as much sense for the accountant as it does for the publisher.

There are programs that are specifically designed for almost every market niche that accountants can target. It is up to accountants to thoroughly research the software available to effectively and competitively ply their trade in that particular market. If you were to practice archery, you would not put one arrow in your quiver. So it is with accounting software.

Selecting Accounting Software Partners

A strong partnership program is essential for success as a consultant. The program should offer hands-on training "specifically designed for accounting consultants" and should have classes available at both the basic and advanced levels. The training should not only focus on how the software works, but should also provide a great deal of information concerning consulting practices, hints, and tips.

The consulting program should offer support to the accounting consultant. This support should be without charge. When negotiating with software publishers, remember that their programs are not "set in stone" and there is room to bargain. The software publishers, unlike Microsoft, have a lot of competition, so the professional accountant can and should bargain earnestly. It is not as if you were a Ford automobile dealer and you wanted to sell Chevrolets and Chrysler cars at the same dealership. Accountants, for the most part, are not franchised dealers for any software producer and are free and able to resell and consult with whatever software they wish. There are some software producers who demand exclusivity, such as Navision, but that is the minority.

Look closely at the software producers who boast of having thousands of consultants around the country. Typically, these packages have been distributed at no charge or as specials to CPAs in an attempt to bring the CPA on as a dealer for the product in the same manner as dish soap is marketed. The marketplace is then flooded with CPAs who are installing the software, but have no idea how to support the software user. This is true only in the low-end market and is another good reason to ignore that market. Client–server accounting software is the only game in town if profits are important.

Level of Commitment

Determine the software producer's level of commitment to keeping consultants updated. Check out the vendor's Web site. Call some of the listed participating consultants and accountants. Call some out-of-town participant accountants (for competitive reasons) and ask the owners about their experience with the vendor. The accountant should have no problem discussing the vendor since there is a geographic distance. There is always a lot to be learned from talking to customers. The software vendor should be able to keep the consultant informed on a timely basis about changes in the software package and replacing outdated packages that are in the consultant's inventory.

Software Vendor's Reputation

Software ratings by impartial sources are an important determinant in measuring the strengths of an accounting software vendor. Look for consistent releases of the software. Without consistent releases, the software program will not be included in current software ratings and will not be responsive to the needs of the users and consultants.

Another way to determine the reputation of an accounting software vendor is to visit with dealers and consultants for that particular software program, again preferably out of town. If the dealer or consultant has supported a particular accounting program for three or more years, that is a good indication of the strength of the software vendor and their commitment to the marketplace.

Third-Party Programs

Look for a software program with good third-party programs. These third-party programs encourage other software vendors to develop interfaces between two programs. It is impossible for a package to be "everything to everybody," and invariably the need arises to supplement a general accounting program with a vertical market program. The vertical program's interface with the general accounting program the client uses may be a benefit but may not be a critical need. Some of the vertical applications affect such a small number of general ledger accounts that it is very easy to journal entry the monthly changes to these accounts and bypass the direct interfacing ability. However, if the accountant is working with very few vertical market clients, the interface would be designed for those clients and the accountant would further solidify their value in the marketplace.

Strong Reporting Capabilities

An accounting software program must have strong reporting capabilities. The program needs to have not only a strong report generator within the general ledger, but also a strong report writer that allows access to all of the data within the client files. This allows the accountant to be creative in assisting clients to generate all needed management reports.

A portion of chargeable time each month can be spent developing specialized management reports, for which clients gladly pay. Another plus is the ability to leverage a report for use on other consulting engagements.

DEVELOPING STRATEGIC RELATIONSHIPS WITH VALUE-ADDED RESELLERS

There are many differences between computer consulting and the more traditional accounting services. One such difference is the need to work closely with one or more computer dealers. Because most accounting firms do not sell computer and networking hardware (a growing number do resell computer hardware and networking equipment and software) and do not have the time to stay current on the continual changes in computer technology, they have to evaluate the need to develop relationships with VARs.

The word *strategic* is defined as "a plan of action, especially for attaining a goal." Accountants' goals for consulting services are to:

- Provide an additional service to clients and prospective clients.
- Build the firm's image.
- Attract new clients to the firm.
- Make a profit.

The level of expertise and competence among VARs varies widely. Accountants must ask themselves whether the VARs they work with help to accomplish their firm's goals. VARs may provide the skills, experience, critical mass, and even marketing expertise that the accountants and their firms may lack. As accountants look for VARs with whom to work, they should put a premium not only on professionalism, ethics, and staying power, but also on solid skills and experience to complement the professional accountant. Look for a partner you both enjoy and respect, as significant time will be invested building the relationship.

Selecting a VAR

Professional Image

When selecting a VAR, find someone who has the ability to help attract and land new clients. Most client–server accounting software installations require the purchase of hardware, software, and consulting services by prospective clients. When meeting with prospective clients regarding an installation engagement, it is often helpful to be accompanied by VARs who look and act like professionals. Prospective clients are often reassured to know that there are at least two levels of support regarding their new accounting system.

Effective Marketing Skills

The VARs with whom professional accountants work should have the ability to market the accountants' services effectively to prospective clients. It is a given that others are often in a much better position to market your services and vice versa. VARs with effective marketing skills can assist accountants in successfully marketing the accountants' consulting services to current clients, potential clients, and also to other clients in the VARs' business.

Thorough Knowledge of the Products

Some of the worst consulting engagements possible are the result of VARs not knowing or understanding the products they sell. VARs may fall into the trap of trying to sell and support such a broad range of products that their knowledge of each product is limited at best. When evaluating VARs, ask about the training they have received and certifications they have earned concerning the products they are selling. The more VARs know about a particular product, the better they can demonstrate the product to prospective clients, and the higher the level of support will be to both clients and accountants.

Cultivate the Business Relationship

Once you have selected VARs to work with, take the proper steps to cultivate the business relationships so they are mutually beneficial. Put forth some effort to find out what the VARs' particular strengths are and look for opportunities to market those strengths. Take the time to outline for the VARs the particular strengths of your firm as they relate to services and vertical markets. Avoid exclusive arrangements in which you will send your clients only to them and they will send new clients only to you. Referrals should be based on the belief that the other party is the best qualified to perform the particular work.

Benefits of Working with VARs

The benefits of working with VARs can be many. VARs can be a valuable source of referrals. They can provide tremendous support to the consulting practice. VARs can help train the staff and can be a rich source of information concerning the ever-changing market of computer hardware and software.

Webster defines *synergy* as, "The combined action of two or more substances or agencies to achieve an effect greater than that of which each is individually capable."

As an accountant, ask this question, "Do I have a strategic relationship with a VAR that allows us to achieve a greater end result than that which each of us could achieve individually?" There truly is a synergy between an accountant and a VAR.

Exhibit 15.1 provides a checklist of the factors to be considered in developing a relationship between an accountant and a VAR.

EXHIBIT 15.1
Checklist: Accountant VAR

- ❑ *Always put the client first.* Do not get so caught up in trying to create a win/win scenario that the client is forgotten.
- ❑ *Create multiple VAR relationships* to build the right mix of skills to serve the clients. It is rare for accountant–VAR relationships to be exclusive.
- ❑ *Be open about these other relationships,* however, so no one is taken by surprise. VARs sometimes hire a staff accountant to become a direct competitor.
- ❑ *Enter into an accountant/VAR alliance slowly.* Carefully plan the first shared engagement or two with frequent meetings to discuss progress. Evaluate performance and note areas for improvement.
- ❑ *Think and act as a team,* both in front of the client and behind the scenes. If something should go wrong, focus on finding the

right solution and preventing future problems. Avoid finger-pointing at all costs!

- ❑ *Think long-term.* The accountant and the client must realize that the VAR needs to make a fair profit in order to remain in business and take care of the clients.
- ❑ *Do not dwell on balancing the lead referrals.* Avoid: "I gave the VAR five referrals, and the VAR only gave me three." Instead, focus on how you might work together to generate joint business.
- ❑ *Consider drafting a brief letter of understanding to further define the relationship,* including nondisclosure of client matters. Have specific letters for each project, as well, to define responsibilities.
- ❑ *Think of the VAR as a "virtual department" of your accounting firm.* The VAR is ready to provide services when needed to help your clients, but does not present a payroll drain when times are slow. If the VAR also sees your firm in that role, the potential for leveling resource utilization is great.

With eyes open, communicating your expectations, and with respect for each other's skills, accountants and VARs can create rewarding alliances. Everyone can win—especially the client.

DISTRIBUTOR PARTNERING

Partnering with a distributor is very much like working with a VAR, substituting the distributor in place of the VAR. The distributors have never given much attention to what the author has termed accountant/VARs although that is changing with the increased importance of client–server equipment and software. For unbiased distributor selection assistance, e-mail the author, Jack Fox, at The Accounting Guild: jfox1961@aol.com. Some major distributors to contact are:

- Ingram Micro, Inc., www.ingrammicro.com
- Tech Data Corp., www.techdata.com
- Pinacor Inc., www.pinacor.com
- Merisel Inc., www.merisel.com
- Hallmark Integrated Solutions, www.hmis.avnet.com

The software implementation checklist in Exhibit 15.2 provides a framework for developing your own customized workplan.

EXHIBIT 15.2
Checklist: Software Installation Implementation

One of the best ways to ensure the success of an accounting software installation is by developing and implementing a standard workplan. The objective of the workplan is to document each key step to be performed during the installation.

Key Categories

- ❑ **Client data:** items to be considered include:
  - ❑ **1.** Client industry
  - ❑ **2.** Existing client hardware
  - ❑ **3.** Computer experience
  - ❑ **4.** Accounting expertise
- ❑ **Recommended hardware:**
  - ❑ **1.** Type of computers used
  - ❑ **2.** Current operating system
  - ❑ **3.** Printers
  - ❑ **4.** Type of network used
- ❑ Modules to be installed
- ❑ Current review of client accounting procedures
- ❑ Installation procedures
- ❑ Standard administration procedures supplied
- ❑ Standard forms—a list of standard input forms to be supplied to the client should be identified

Summary

To assist in the installation and implementation of accounting software, prepare a workplan that should be tailored to the client's specific requirements.

Following the workplan's detailed instructions and operating procedures is vital to the success of the project. The training of client personnel at every step of a proper installation in all of the daily systems and user procedures is mandatory.

PROFITING FROM THE INTERNET

The Internet has become accounting's lifeline. Virtually all government agencies have a presence on the World Wide Web. Here, they provide up-to-the-minute information about taxes, corporate filings, legislation, and other critical accounting subjects. This information, which once was available only at great cost through third parties or very slowly from the government agencies themselves, is now immediate and without charge.

All of the major accounting associations and standards bodies likewise have information on the Web—the American Institute of Certified Public Accountants (AICPA), the National Association of Enrolled Agents (NAEA), the National Association of Tax Preparers (NATP), the Institute of Management Accountants (IMA), the Financial Accounting Standards Board (FASB), and dozens of others. All 50 state accounting societies either have a site on the Web or are moving to create one. The Web offers information needed to expand accounting services in business consulting, computer and technology consulting, and other value-added client services.

The ability to access information on demand has changed forever the way accountants research tax and accounting issues for their clients. But the impact of the Internet can be felt far beyond the realm of research. The accounting industry has moved aggressively to embrace the Internet, extending its traditional use of online services to help drive the growth of valued research, communication, and management resources on the Internet.

Internet Accounting Resources

- American Institute of Certified Public Accountants, www.aicpa.org
- Financial Accounting Standards Board, www.fasb.org
- Internal Revenue Service, www.irs.ustreas.gov
- National Association of Enrolled Agents, www.cals.com/naea
- U.S. Tax Code Online, www.fourmllab.ch/ustax/ustax.html

16

PRICING, CASH FLOW, PRACTICE DEVELOPMENT, AND MANAGEMENT

Of the many skills needed to stay in business, knowing how to set fees for your services is one of the most important. Yet, the underlying methods of setting fees are as unfamiliar to accountants as they are to other service providers, consultants, and other entrepreneurs.

Pricing plays a central role in how much one earns for the work he or she does, and in the psychological subtleties of accounting business relationships. Set prices too high, and valuable business may be lost. Lowering prices may attract assignments and projects that would otherwise have been lost. But too-low prices can also translate to working unnecessarily long hours, to earning less than one should for those efforts, and in the worst case, to earning less than is needed to turn a profit.

FUNDAMENTAL PRICING STRATEGIES

There are several strategies that can be used to set fees, ranging from asking for the going rates to raising rates until clients say "ouch." The bottom line is cost-based pricing—that is, fees that reflect what it costs to be and stay in business. (The option always remains to negotiate different rates at times.)

Cost-Based Pricing

Cost-based prices are relatively easy to determine. It will take some thinking, perhaps a few phone calls, and then some time with a business planning software program. It is an exercise all serious business people must do, once or twice a year, even if they also set prices by other methods. In return, the result is real, bottom-line information essential to both starting and building an accounting business.

While this step-by-step guide to basic fee setting is designed for the accountant, it applies equally well to any business that sells time and knowledge. There is nothing mysterious about the process to be described. Yet, a surprising number of self-employed individuals and smaller businesses have never done the exercise. After mastering the techniques, the accountants can add pricing assistance to their list of professional consulting services.

Calculating Costs

Too often, professional accountants underestimate the full costs of starting up and maintaining an accounting business. Just like the real cost of operating an automobile includes not only the purchase price, but also insurance, maintenance, repairs, gas, parking, tolls, auto-club membership, and an occasional car wash, operating an accounting business entails spending for recurring costs and fresh investments.

- *Business and office expenses.* An accounting business can be started on a shoestring, with only an answering machine and business cards, but it is hard to run one for long or make much money on that basis. Day-to-day expenses are part of the cost of being in business. Pricing must reflect these costs.

  With few exceptions, you will need to occupy and operate some kind of office, even if it is a room at home (this is definitely not a first, second, or third choice). Ongoing expenses include phone, utilities, postage, copying, stationery, office and computer supplies, and subscriptions. Regular investments must be made in office equipment and furniture, computer hardware and software, upgrades, filing cabinets, fax machine, copier, and more. There will also be business-related taxes, such as occupancy tax, sales tax, resale tax permits, and professional licenses and taxes.

  Excluding rent on office space, many home-based accountants report that phone bills are their biggest expense, followed by equipment purchases, like a new laser printer or a larger-screen monitor. It is also easy for memberships and subscriptions to add up to several thousand dollars a year.

  The good news, of course, is that all business expenses come out of pretaxable dollars. They are subtracted on the Schedule C for sole practitioners from gross revenues to yield the taxable net income.

- *Salary and personal taxes.* One rule of thumb for self-employment states that earnings should be about what they would be as a full-time employee—otherwise, being an employee would be a simpler way to go. Lower stress and higher satisfaction are supposed to be important benefits of being self-employed, but economic issues must often come first. The stress and satisfaction are also very related to the earnings. Another way to start setting the fees is to determine what "salary" is required, in annual, monthly, or weekly terms. Consider personal taxes when making the calculations.
- *Benefits.* As employees, most people receive benefits: health, life, and disability insurance; retirement, profit sharing, and other plans; and other items, whose values can be as much as a third of an annual salary. The amount withheld from an employee's salary is usually less than the benefits' cost, and is usually only a fraction of what a self-employed individual must pay.

Estimating Assumptions

For the purposes of this exercise, estimate business expenses of $90,000 per year, or $7,500 per month. And let's suppose a salary-equivalent of $100,000 a year. Further, assume that health, disability and term life insurance and other benefits will cost more than $750 per month or $9,000 annually (to earn the money for these benefits, after taxes, means about $15,000 per year for an unincorporated individual). Let's add $12,500 in annual contributions to a retirement fund. These contributions are exempt from federal income tax, but not from FICA, state, or other taxes, so add another $11,000 to benefits.

This amounts to annual costs as follows:

$ 90,000	(Business and office expenses)
100,000	(Salary and personal taxes)
26,000	(Benefits)
$216,000	Annual costs
$18,000	per month costs

Equivalent Salary

To make the equivalent of a $100,000 salary as an employee, the professional accountant must achieve annual gross revenues of more than twice as much. You can, of course, get by on less, but this is the amount you deserve to earn, and the fees should be based on this total.

Calculating Salable Time

Overestimating billable time is the first mistake many professional accountants make. To define self-employment as a job and a business, start by defining a realistic work scenario. From the 52 weeks in a year, subtract two weeks for holidays, two weeks for sick or personal days, and three weeks for vacation. You may not take all that time off, but it should be built into the fees so that you are not cheating yourself out of the same benefits you would get as an employee.

That brings the work year down to 45 working weeks per year, which is standard. However, that is not all billable, revenue-generating time. To start with, you will need to spend time marketing. Count on making phone calls, attending meetings, contracting, negotiating, going to professional and trade shows, writing follow-up correspondence, and the like.

One hour per day, every working day, is a standard estimate for marketing. The same amount of time or more is bound to go for administration, support, and overhead—reading professional journals, paying bills, installing and learning new software, doing taxes, reloading the machines, addressing envelopes for overnight services, and so on. That is about a quarter of your working time that you will not be reimbursed for. And there is no certainty you will get enough work to be busy all the time.

To be conservative, let's assume 40 working weeks per year, with six billable hours a day for a true total of 1,200 billable hours (as opposed to a common guess of 50 weeks at 40 hours per week, or 2,000 total hours). You may end up being able to sell more hours, particularly if you tend to do medium- to long-term jobs (four-week-or-longer assignments), so you could have 1,500 salable hours. But do not count on it. If you do not base your calculations on a realistic set of assumptions, you are looking for trouble, burn-out, and other unpleasant forms of life stress. For this exercise, let's use 1,200.

To calculate your basic hourly rate, simply divide your annual costs by the number of salable hours. That is $216,000 (annual costs) divided by 1,200 (annual billable hours) equals $180 per hour.

In other words, to pay yourself a salary of about $100,000, plus expenses, benefits, and contributions to your retirement fund, you will need to charge about $180 an hour. That may sound like a lot of money, but it is certainly in line with what other professional accountants and consultants charge. Many professionals in the large and medium-sized accounting firms charge far more. When fees are calculated in this manner, it points out that certain accounting work and types of clients that do not command this level of fee should be left for those who do not value their services as highly.

Obviously, there is a lot of leeway in this $180 figure. You may be able to go down to $135, $120, or even $100 per hour. For example, you may have minimal business expenses, defer depositing that retirement money, be willing to draw a much lower salary, or work more billable hours. Or you may find that your rate should be $250 to $300 per hour based on the competitive fees in your geographic area.

In any case, do not apologize for your prices if they are fair. They reflect the cost of your accounting business and related services, including all of your overhead.

ADDITIONAL PRICING STRATEGIES

Once the fee structure is known, other strategies to base prices on can be considered. These take into account factors like circumstances and bargaining strength:

- *Going rates.* What do competing accountants charge? What are prospective clients paying? Call them and ask, or have a friend call.
- *Until they flinch.* Raise fees periodically. Keep raising them in talking with new prospective clients until they question them. Also, leave opportunities to negotiate down.
- *Ask for a piece of the action (where professionally ethical).* Base the fee on a percentage of savings that the work creates. Get the arrangement in writing.
- *Paying for priority.* If a client needs immediate, mission-critical service, that is often worth 25 to 50 percent more. Do not be greedy, though. Try to let clients know in advance that fees will go up as time gets shorter.

Dealer's Choice

The six pricing strategies that follow provide a guide for you to establish a pricing strategy best suited for your business and client profile. It is more important to have a particular pricing strategy suited for your individual practice than no policy or one solely geared toward beating the competition.

1. *Cost-driven pricing.* Add a set percentage "fair return" over costs. (Example: Add 25 percent to the cost of all accounting software sold.) A problem with this is determining the base cost on which to add a fair return. Volume purchased from suppliers usually influences costs. Should savings or reductions be passed on? Cost-driven pricing sounds good, but often does not work.
2. *Customer-driven pricing.* This reflects market conditions, namely, what the competition is charging. The difficulties with this approach include: salespeople have a tendency to drop prices at the earliest sign of client resistance; there is no direct relation between the value of what is provided and the price that is charged; and the price may not yield a profit.
3. *Premium pricing.* Deliberately charging more than the competition based on high value-added considerations (real or perceived), such as better service, quicker implementation, or greater ability to provide a workable solution to a client's problem.
4. *Price lining.* Carrying software only in a specific price range(s).
5. *Skimming strategy.* Trying to get as much profit as quickly as possible before competition forms. A unique product or service is needed to make this work. For example, you are the only accounting value-added reseller (VAR) in your geographic area with a popular mid- or high-range brand of accounting software. The skimming strategy might be sustained for a short time, but the high profits will eventually attract competitors.
6. *Penetration strategy.* This is a race to win as much market share as possible in a short time. It is usually accomplished with low prices and making it up with high volume or eventually dominating the market and setting prices arbitrarily. This strategy can be profitable only if there are economies of scale and the firm is highly efficient.

It is always legitimate to have different sets of prices:

- Large corporations versus start-ups and smaller businesses
- Agencies, job shops, contract houses

- Regular clients
- Standard types of projects
- Nonprofits, charities, and other worthy causes

STAY IN CONTROL

Stay in control. You set the price, although clients may challenge it. Negotiating makes all the difference. However, without knowing what you have to charge, you cannot go out and sell. You will not know when to say yes, when to say no, or when to say, "Let's keep talking."

Likewise, you may want to cultivate a high-quality, high-price image. In this case, you may quote a high price for a client engagement, even though there is a likelihood of losing the client, just to maintain image.

One debate that keeps swirling around the accounting business is the fixed-cost-per-engagement versus billable-hours question. Most accountants favor billable hours. This is especially important in accounting software systems consulting where it is very difficult to estimate the required hours with any degree of certainty. The accountant cannot assume that any engagement is like getting a car repaired. The automotive book says it takes 2.5 hours to do something, and if your person is talented, it can be done in less time. Accounting services just do not work that way. Unforeseen problems can easily arise when too many things are beyond anyone's control.

KEEP EMOTIONS OUT OF THE WAY OF BUSINESS

Situations often arise that make one's blood pressure rise. Not only is that an unhealthy response, it is also bad for business. Getting mad does not make anyone any money. Taking problems personally and popping off is a recipe for disaster. Whenever a situation arises that puts emotions more in control than logic, postpone any action for a day to analyze the situation rationally.

For instance, an upset client called an accountant about problems with the implementation of an accounting system the firm had installed. The temptation to vehemently defend the work may have been the accountant's first reaction. Instead, the accountant promised to get to the bottom of the problem. As it turned out, some bugs in the operating system had not been completely solved. This had escaped the attention of the accountant technician at the client's site. The accountant and the firm could have lost an excellent long-term client relationship if the accountant had told the client off. The situation was salvaged because of a cool head.

GOOD SERVICE LEAVES A LASTING IMPRESSION

The ability to provide a high level of ongoing support to their clients is absolutely crucial to all successful accounting businesses. Accounting expertise, familiarity with clients' private financial matters, and the permanent nature of the professional accountant–client relationship helps distinguish them from the traditional sources of accounting software: retail computer dealers, mail-order sources, and computer consultants. Providing a high level of support does not necessarily mean that the professional accountant will have a high volume of support calls. It does, however, mean that the firm's clients are entitled to expect a great deal of competence from their accountant. Focusing on efforts to build a practice that delivers that level of competence transcends the question of fees.

Unlike the one-time software product sale or the brief computer consultant's engagement, an accountant's effective practice integrates into the client's business on a continuing basis. As such, firms using a value-billing approach achieve better financial results. On an hourly basis, it is difficult to bill out all of the firm's initial learning curve, setup time, sales time, and support time.

ENGAGEMENT LETTERS AND CONTRACTS

Having an engagement letter or contract (agreement) for services will go a long ways toward preventing misunderstandings with clients. Customize each engagement letter to correspond to the exact terms agreed upon.

Presenting the Agreement

Obtaining the engagement is more than signing on the dotted line. It is not just another step in the process, but rather the outcome of all your steps combined. Before the final step of presenting the prospective client with the engagement letter, review the problem areas, and confirm the solutions discussed to alleviate the problems and the fees for services. Always present value, not cost, as an aid in overcoming price objections.

The Price Is Not Always Right

The key to succeeding in the accounting business is to convincingly convey the value of your services to your clients and have them know it is well worth the price. Clients buy value, not price. In the client's mind, your price is simply the monetary number at which they can acquire your value. If the value is perceived as higher than the price, they buy. If the value is lower, they do not buy, or you get "the price is too high" objection. No one ever buys on price alone. The first step in presenting your fees to a prospective client is to assure yourself that you are delivering value far exceeding your price.

Never apologize for your price. Present every fee proposal with conviction. Anything less will invite the client to either question the value or feel they can beat down the price. When presenting price, build the value first.

Anytime negotiations force the fees to be lowered, try to get a concession of your own in return. This prevents the appearance of compromising your value. For example, "I could lower the fee, if you can live with starting on the project two weeks later." If you have to lower fees to get a particular engagement, do not give in too soon. It might indicate that a bigger discount could have been had.

CASH FLOW FINANCIAL FUNDAMENTALS

Many accountants suffer from an insidious mood disorder. The symptoms are manifested by a dark gloom, bordering on clinical depression that appears and goes into remission in direct relationship to the accountant's bank balance. Money management is an ongoing dilemma for most business people, and accountants are not immune by virtue of their profession. The problem is that there is seldom enough in the till to manage keeping both revenue and cash flow on the plus side.

Accountants should not have difficulties managing their finances. By the same token, physicians should never get sick and insurance people should not have accidents. While the accountants are more technically savvy about the theory and practice of business activities, their own business affairs often suffer. Accountants are too busy generating revenue to be able to dedicate the resources needed to track their own finances effectively. Perhaps the reason is that accountants run service-oriented businesses. Unlike supermarkets or auto dealers, where the products are tangible items sold at set prices with patterned histories, accountants sell things like audits, compilations, and accounting systems. These products (if they can be considered as such) are typically sold based on a variable pricing strategy, which is determined by the variable costs associated with providing them. Consequently, tracking something as simple as working capital is quite complex for the accountant.

Defining Cash Flow

Cash flow is defined as the income of a business plus accounting deductions not paid out, such as depreciation, depletion, and amortization. An accountant has a more simple view, namely, the excess or shortfall of cash in-flows (receipts) less cash out-flows (disbursements).

Do not confuse cash with profits. Anyone who calculates profits by simply deducting expenses from revenue often discovers that the profit shown on paper does not exist in reality. If they have expenses unpaid and receivables uncollected, they may make a paper profit but lack the cash to pay bills and themselves.

Common Accounting Business Cash Flows

Cash in-flows include monies received from:

- Sales, services, and products
- New debt
- New equity investment
- Sale of fixed assets
- Bad debt recovery

Cash out-flows include:

- Overhead
- Cost of goods sold
- Wages, salaries, and commissions
- Taxes
- Marketing expenses

Of all the business hurdles accountants and all business people face, cash flow is potentially the most harmful to their business health. Studies have reported that 60 percent of all businesses that failed did so because they ran out of cash. However, that is a misleading statement because running out of cash was a symptom and not the cause of failure. It would be like saying that 100 percent of all deaths were attributed to the cessation of breathing.

Accountants make their living by investing in and supporting new technologies, so laborious or not, it is important that they keep a close eye on finances. If accountants' investments are made on the false assumption that more money is available than truly is, a disastrous downturn results.

Accountants who are struggling to get their finances in order, and other accountants who want to make sure they do not get in the same situation, need to know about some basic accounting practices.

Overhead

Start with the most rudimentary data: your overhead. It is important to know your expenses each month, because every investment decision is affected by that figure. Your overhead consists of all the fixed costs not directly connected to your services or products. That includes such things as insurance, rent, and maintenance. These items are considered fixed because their amount is never affected by the level of revenues generated. If office rent is $3,000 a month, a great sales month will not change the rent.

There are, however, some fixed costs that vary from one payment period to another. Utilities are considered fixed costs by definition. Their variances have nothing to do with the level of business that flows through the accounting firm. Yet, they will obviously vary.

Total fixed costs can be tabulated in one of two ways. First, add the unchanging monthly expenses. Then, either determine an average monthly cost for the utilities or take the month in which the most was paid in utilities—perhaps a cold winter month when more heat and light were consumed—and use that as the model. Padding the utility expenses on the high side will leave some margin for error on other items.

When adding the fixed costs, remember to factor in payments that are made on an other than monthly schedule. Water bills may be due semiannually. The same is often true for automobile insurance on your company vehicles. If you forget to add them, your overhead figure will show a greater cash flow than you actually have.

Variable Costs

Measuring variable costs is a little tougher to do. These are expenses that change based on your business activity. Your cost for purchasing computer hardware and software for resale are variable cost items. Money spent to configure, install, and support your products and services are also variable costs. Travel expenses you accumulate while serving long-distance clients would also be listed under variable costs.

Depending on the type of accounting practice you operate and how long you have been doing it, these costs can vary considerably. Let's say you have recently added another accounting system for the mid- to upper range of client–server accounting clients. As a smart business person, you researched the market and determined how much of an investment of additional computer hardware and initial software would cost. However, in your enthusiasm, you forgot to consider a few things: training, additional storage space, and training class space.

Only one of your three accounting software technicians is proficient enough to support your new business. That means you must invest in training. The addition of the accounting software to the firm's offerings requires the firm to train client personnel. A decision must be made to expand the training class space or find temporary training facilities on an as-needed basis. A room with six to ten computers carries a rental cost of about $1,000 a day at independent training facilities.

There was also a miscalculation as to how much space is available in your storage space. Arrangements will have to be made to rent storage space now and then, depending on demand. Those are just basic examples of unexpected expenses. The best thing to do is use a direct costing or activity-based costing method. These accounting strategies consider costs directly connected to a project. From the moment anyone begins work on a client account, all time, materials, and expenses incurred should be recorded to that client project.

Collections

The average number of days a firm takes to collect its receivables is called days' sales outstanding (DSO). The higher this number, the more money is tied up in receivables, which means less cash available for other things. To calculate:

$$\text{DSO} = \text{Average Receivables} \times 365 \div \text{Annual credit sales}$$

Average receivables (days' sales outstanding) are multiplied by 365 to provide a per-day calculation. According to industry reports, the median DSO for accounting firms is 57 days.

Analyzing the Results

By being conscientious about tracking costs, some very valuable information is available upon the completion of each project. Some simple arithmetic can determine the return on investment. If direct costing was used, add total costs on a particular project, then subtract the sum from the revenue generated by the same project. The difference is the net income or your return. If you are not realizing a return on your investment, that is obviously not desirable—but it is not a death knell, either.

If you are launching a new accounting business or adding products and services, negative revenue and negative cash flow are not unusual. You have to expect that with the added marketing costs alone, it will be a while before you turn a profit. When you see negative figures where you would prefer to see positives, do not get discouraged. Go over your pricing to make sure you gave yourself enough profit. The most probable cause is that the sales revenue did not reach the forecasts, which put an excessive burden of support and service costs on the revenue that was achieved.

Breakeven Point Analysis

No business can permit a negative return situation to continue indefinitely. If other parts of the business are not strong enough to support the loss, the business will run itself out in time. By determining how much revenue must be achieved to reach the breakeven point, an estimate can be made as to how much and how long the core business will have to subsidize any new investment.

The breakeven analysis formula is as follows:

$$U = NP + FC \div SP - VC$$

where:

U = number of units (hours, etc.) sold
NP = net profit
FC = fixed costs
SP = selling price
VC = variable costs

Here is an illustration: The firm wants to create a new accounting systems application that will sell for $5,000. The variable costs (labor, maintenance, etc.) are $2,000 per copy. Annual fixed costs are $500,000. When the net profit (usually set at zero) is $0, the breakeven point is U = 167. Adjust the formula slightly to account for any support and service that would be provided, and charged for.

Exhibit 16.1 presents a checklist for improving your business's cash flow. While some may appear too elementary for accountants, they nevertheless provide valuable insights into building a liquidity consciousness.

EXHIBIT 16.1
Checklist: Improving Cash Flow

- ☐ 1. *Do not wait to send an invoice.* Deliver it as soon as you are entitled to payment. Instead of billing at the end or beginning of the month, bill the minute you complete the project.
- ☐ 2. *Deposit the check.* This might sound too elementary, but many businesses wait several days to deposit payments. As a rule, deposits should be made daily.
- ☐ 3. *Do not wait to collect.* If your terms are net 10 days and it is now 11 days, call the client. Do not wait, trying to be nice. It is your money being held up. Besides, you will often find that payment has not been made because of a bookkeeping or other error.
- ☐ 4. *Create new profit centers.* Accounting firms often experience seasonality because of the nature of their target niche markets. To tide the firm over dry periods, set up a subsidiary service bureau to provide payroll and write-up services. These operations are set up to operate on a pay-as-you-go basis and have an excellent cash flow, sometimes better than the parent accounting firm. If the accounting firm is subject to lulls, create new revenue streams, such as for-profit seminars, that can generate fees in addition to marketing applications. Rental and service agreements for accounting software systems provide monthly cash flow and are not driven by hourly demand.
- ☐ 5. *Get the best interest.* Do not keep too much cash in your checking account. Decide when you might need it and

then place it in a certificate of deposit or a money market fund that allows withdrawals when necessary.

- ❑ 6. *Monitor past due accounts.* At least every week, generate an accounts receivable aging report that shows which clients are past due, for how much, and for how many days.
- ❑ 7. *Use your lines of credit.* When big orders for hardware and software systems are at hand but you do not have enough cash to finance it, a line of credit at the bank is invaluable. Remember, banks like to extend credit when you do not need it. Do not wait until a major project hangs in the balance.
- ❑ 8. *Collect deposits.* Usually, ask for a 40 percent deposit before starting a project. If you are relatively unfamiliar with the client, ask for 50 percent or more. Consider asking all clients for deposits, especially on projects with high upfront expenses.
- ❑ 9. *Settle all client disputes fast.* Unhappy clients often hold up payment until they are satisfied, which is why it is important to settle disputes quickly.
- ❑ 10. *Prioritize collection efforts.* It costs the same to call or write a client that owes you $1,000 as it does one that owes you $10,000. Put the bulk of your efforts towards the accounts that owe you the most.
- ❑ 11. *Use multiple suppliers.* A single distributor may give the firm a $100,000 line of credit, while three may each extend the same, making the firm's credit line, in effect, three times as large.
- ❑ 12. *Do not maintain an inventory.* The costs and risks of carrying inventory, including the cost of borrowed money, storage space, materials handling, staff, and fixed costs, can be as high as 30 percent of the inventory's value. Use distributors for just-in-time, on-demand, drop shipping direct to the client and never handle the physical products. In effect, the distributor is an extension of the accounting firm.
- ❑ 13. *Limit spending.* Among accounting firms, fast growth is the most common reason for cash flow problems. Conserve resources as much as possible during periods of

high growth. Later, after a cushion of cash has been accumulated, discretionary expenses can be financed.

❑ 14. *Use leasing.* Several leasing companies specialize in arranging lease financing for clients to purchase, install, and service client–server computer hardware, accounting system software, and the accounting firm's professional services. The leasing firms pay for the entire project and also pay the accounting firm a fee for the client introduction. The lease is based on the creditworthiness of the client without any guaranty or liability on the part of the accounting firm. A monthly support plan can be incorporated into the lease agreement.

❑ 15. *The Accounting Guild.* The Accounting Guild provides strategic collaboration between accountants and the distributors, manufacturers, leasing companies, and other affiliates that provide better than usual terms and programs because of the combined purchasing power of the accountant members of the Guild. (Contact the author and founder of the Guild, Jack Fox, at jfox1961@aol.com with questions or requests for more information on the Guild or any aspect of this guide.)

PRACTICE MANAGEMENT SOFTWARE

GoldMine Software Corporation has been active in the personal information manager (PIM)/contact management market since this type of software first appeared. The software is available in a relatively inexpensive single-user version and in a five-user enterprise version. The enterprise version adds an extensive compatibility with d-BASE, and also integrates very well with Microsoft SQL and Microsoft BackOffice.

An E-mail Center with added features is designed to enhance workgroup use of the data maintained by the application. Synchronization of data is maintained throughout the network as a user logs in, and data can be automatically converted to download into the 3Com Palm Pilot.

Among the GoldMine features is its "multiple-window" presentation capability. For example, the "address book" shows standard information such as company name and up to three phone numbers, but it can also display more detailed information that users specify, such as the type of client, market niche, responsible staff member and other information relative to administering the client relationship. A set of tabs in the bottom window provides one-click access to client history, notes, contacts, profiles and the like.

GoldMine's Enterprise will benefit accounting firms of any size. The program's forecast and profile features can substantially improve an accountant's marketing efforts.

GoldMine Software can be reached at (800) 654-3526, www.goldminesw.com.

TAKING CARE OF BUSINESS

Studies have shown that more than 95 percent of CPAs give no or little thought to practice development. This is a strange finding in today's environment of consolidation and integration of the CPA/accounting industry, with many pundits predicting that for many, the choices seem to be to either merge or go out of business. There are, of course, a variety of possible business combinations and alliances. The reality is that there are many choices, and many firms are experiencing phenomenal growth—both internal and external—while expanding into new areas and specialties.

It is interesting that some CPAs are so ingrained in the "old ways" that they are ignoring the vast opportunities that are available. When CPAs "box themselves in" with traditional modes of thinking, they cannot solve many of the business technological problems that keep surfacing in today's fast-changing business marketplace.

For accountants to stay in business and prosper, individuals need to acquire and provide services to clients. The process of accounting business development is rapidly changing, from both a strategic and tactical perspective, while the composition of practitioners is changing from CPAs to non-CPAs and accounting computer software consultants and technicians. Moreover, CPAs are less interested in and are doing less business development activities with each passing year.

CPA firms have seen continuing increases in volume over time, especially since 1995. Many CPA firms have lost valued employees due to the high demand for CPAs and staff accountants in the public accounting profession, in private industry, and the establishment of independent practices by a growing number of entrepreneurial CPAs. Paradoxically, at a time when the CPA firms should concentrate more on practice development, due to the inroads of consolidators such as American Express and H&R Block, CPAs are turning their backs on growth and concentrating only on getting work out.

HISTORICAL ORIENTATION

The major block to accounting business development begins with accounting training. CPAs are not trained as visionaries but instead are trained as business historians. As a result, they do not plan their own businesses. Because of this, the entire profession is at risk to those who do understand the dynamics of business, such as American Express and the many entrepreneurial professional accountants (with or without a CPA certificate) and accounting services consultants.

Besides the "CPA mentality," other factors put CPAs at additional risk. These include a lack of vision, minimal or zero business planning, lack of running the accounting firm as a business, looking at only the bottom line, and concentrating on the technical aspects to get the work out. Firms that remain stuck in this rut continue to lose good employees and clients due to lack of communication and responsiveness.

Activities that CPAs can do to reverse the cycle are the same activities that non-CPAs should do to establish and expand their business:

- Lock up relationships with existing clients.
- Establish a marketing beachhead based on value and location.
- Market into niches.

NICHE MARKETING

It is much more effective to market when the firm has one or more niches, yet most CPA firms niche themselves by accident and some do not even recognize that they have a niche. One way to identify your niche is to ask and answer these questions about your clients: "What do they have in common?" and "Who are our best clients?" When you have the answers, try to find more clients with those characteristics rather than mass market to the entire business community. At the very minimum, an accounting firm of any size needs collateral marketing materials so that prospective clients will know what they are buying. Brochures and brochures highlighting each service are the most basic types of tools that turn the intangible services the firm sells into tangible products.

ENCOURAGEMENT FOR ENTREPRENEURIAL ACCOUNTING PROFESSIONALS

The future of the accounting profession lies with the entrepreneurs of the profession. The rest of the profession will either wind up working for the big firms or leaving it for greener pastures.

The bottom line is: (1) be a visionary; (2) niche yourself; and (3) market into that niche where other firms' mass marketing cannot penetrate.

GLOSSARY

Accelerated depreciation: A depreciation method that provides for high depreciation expense in the initial years of use of an asset and a gradual declining expense thereafter. Compare with **straight-line depreciation.**

Account: An alphanumeric identifier used to record additions and deductions for each individual asset, revenue, expenses, and liability.

Accountability: The obligation to accept responsibility for and to justify one's organizational behavior.

Accounting: The process of identifying, measuring, and communicating economic information to permit judgments and decisions by users of the information. Accounting is a system an organization uses to track and report on its financial condition to determine how much money it makes, where that money comes from, where it goes, and where it is kept. In practice, the accounting process also draws on management skills, especially budgeting, to define those costs that must be incurred to operate the business from day to day.

Accounting method: The method(s) and procedures used by an organization to record and report its income, expenses, assets, liabilities, and taxes.

Accounting period: A period in which an organization's accounting information is designated.

Accounts payable: What an organization owes to its suppliers and other creditors for inventory, goods, and services. Compare with **accounts receivable.**

Accounts payable turnover: Credit purchases divided by accounts payable; a measure of the number of times accounts payable are paid over the accounting period.

Accounts receivable: What is owed to an organization for the sales of its goods and services. Compare with **accounts payable.**

Accounts receivable turnover: Credit sales divided by accounts receivable; a measure of the number of times accounts receivable are collected over the accounting period.

Accrual-basis accounting: A method of accounting in which income and expenses are posted on the basis of when they are earned or incurred, not when the funds actually transferred. Although the accrual method generates a more accurate description of an organization's financial condition, it also creates the need for adjusting entries at the end of an accounting period. For example, a company purchases a year's worth of office supplies six months into its fiscal year. The purchase would be recorded immediately as an asset; but at the end of the accounting period, an adjusting entry would have to be made to reflect the value of the supplies still remaining unused. Compare with **cash-basis accounting.**

Accrued expense: An expense that has been incurred but not paid. Sometimes called **accrued liabilities.** Compare with **actual expense.**

Accrued income: Income that has been earned but not collected. Sometimes called **accrued assets.** Compare with **actual income.**

Accumulated depreciation: The total amount of depreciation claimed to date on an asset.

Acid test ratio: Cash and other short-term assets (accounts receivable and marketable securities) divided by current liabilities; a measure of an organization's ability to meet its current obligations. Also called **quick ratio.**

Acquisition: Generally, the purchase of an asset; often, the term is used to describe the purchase or takeover of a controlling interest in one business by another business.

Activity-based accounting: A method of accounting for revenue and expense based on activities.

Activity-based costing: A cost allocation method for identifying activities incurring costs and allocating these costs to products (or other cost objects). An accounting framework based on determining the cost of activities. The activity cost is then related to products for product costing.

Activity ratios: Measures of the effectiveness with which an organization uses its assets. See **accounts payable turnover, accounts receivable turnover, asset turnover, days' sales outstanding,**

inventory turnover, and **property and equipment turnover ratios.**

Actual expense: The money an organization actually pays out for an incurred expense. Compare with **accrued expense.**

Actual income: The money that is actually received in an organization for sales of products and services. Compare with **accrued income.**

Actual vs. budgeted values: A comparison in an accounting period of what was spent in the period with the budgeted amount to be spent for that period. The analysis should identify differences between actual and budgeted costs and should also explain the differences (an increase in the price of raw materials for instance, or an increase in shipping costs) so that they can be factored into future budgets.

Adjusted income method: A budget method that adjusts net earnings to a cash basis by adding all transactions that affect actual cash and subtracting those that do not.

Administrative budget: A budget that reflects all the expenses of departments or segments of a business classified as administrative.

Administrative expenses: Expenses incurred in the administration or general operations of a business. An expense not associated directly with manufacturing or sales.

Allocation: The proportional assignment of income or expense to different accounts.

Allowance method: A method of accounting for receivables that cannot be collected. Also referred to as **bad debt.**

Amortization: The gradual reduction of a debt, for example, a mortgage reduced through scheduled payments. Also, writing off the costs of acquiring a patent, goodwill, or some other intangible asset over the useful life of the asset.

Annual report: A formal financial statement that describes an organization's operations, income, expenses, assets, and liabilities over a fiscal year.

Annuity: A series of equal payments made over a specified number of periods (usually years).

Applets: Client–server programs that can be imported and recompiled across a wide range of system applications. They can be downloaded from the Internet to perform specific tasks.

Appreciation: An increase in the value of an asset over time.

Artificial knowledge management system: A computer system that assists a knowledge manager in measuring and managing the knowledge processes of an organization.

Asset: Physical items (tangible) or rights (intangible) that are owned by an organization. Anything an organization owns that has monetary value, including inventory, accounts receivable, equipment, and cash. An asset can be valued at historic cost (less amortization or depreciation), actual cost, or fair market value. Compare with **liability.**

Assets to sales ratio: Total assets divided by total sales; a measure of how efficiently an organization utilizes its assets.

Asset turnover ratio: Net sales divided by average total assets; a measure of the efficiency with which an organization uses its assets to produce sales. The higher this ratio, the more effectively the organization is using its assets.

Assignable costs: Costs incurred by or for a specific product or project.

Audit: Verification of the accuracy of an organization's financial records and the appropriateness of its accounting methods; often performed by an external (independent) auditor.

Average cost method: The method of inventory costing that is based on the assumption that costs should be charged against revenue in accordance with the weighted average unit cost of the items sold.

Bad debt: A debt that is not collectible.

Balance sheet: A formal financial statement that shows an organization's assets, liabilities, and net worth as of a specific date. The statement is divided into two parts—assets on the left, and liabilities and owners' equity on the right—which must equal each other (assets = liabilities + owners' equity).

Batch posting: The act of posting a batch of transactions. Most low-end accounting programs offer "real-time posting" so that the transaction is posted to the general ledger as soon as it is saved. This ensures that all transactions get posted in the appropriate month. Mid-range accounting programs offer batch posting because it is anticipated that several people will be involved with data entry, and the transactions may need to be reviewed before they are posted to avert errors.

Book costs: Costs in which accounting allocations of prior expenditures are treated as an expense in the current period.

Book value: The actual cost of an asset less its accumulated depreciation. The book value of a business is the same as its stockholders' equity.

Bottom-up method: A budgeting method that starts from the lowest operating level and is based on the goals and objectives for each segment of the company.

Break-even analysis: Using the break-even point—in dollars or units—to determine the level of sales at which the organization begins to turn a profit. Shows the effect of changes in sales on cash flow and profitability.

Break-even point: The level at which revenues equal total costs (fixed costs and variable costs). Any revenue earned above the break-even point is profit.

Budget: An outline of an organization's future plans, stated in financial terms. A budget is used to plan and control operations and allocate resources for achieving maximized efficiency. At a minimum, most businesses develop a budget for the coming fiscal year and divide that budget into quarterly reports so that they can monitor actual performance against budgeted **performance** and, where possible, adjust for significant differences.

Budgeted cost: The expected cost of an activity.

Budgeting: Refers to all the processes of preparing a budget: coordination, control, reporting of variances, and all policies and procedures needed to accomplish a company's objectives.

Budgeting process: Brings together all of the planned activities of a company into a meaningful set of actions.

Burnout: A phenomenon of exhaustion and lack of motivation often experienced by accountants working long hours without the proper rest and relaxation.

Business: An entity—a for-profit or nonprofit enterprise, profession, or trade—that sells a product or performs a service.

Capital: Owners' equity plus debt; the money and other property that owners have invested in a business.

Capital asset: A long-term asset, usually a physical facility or equipment. See **fixed asset.**

Capital budget: A financial plan that describes the expected investment in fixed assets over the budget period to support sales and production facilities and opportunities for cost reduction and new-product development.

Capital expenditure: Costs that add to the usefulness of assets for more than one accounting period.

Capital structure: The manner in which an organization uses debt and other sources of capital to finance its operations.

Cash-basis accounting: A method of accounting in which income and expenses are posted when money is actually collected or paid. A sale would be posted, for example, when the goods are paid for, not when the order is made or shipped. Although cash-basis accounting is the most traditional method of accounting, it is not as descriptive as **accrual-basis** accounting. For example, a company could have a record-breaking sales quarter and, as a function of the production and billing cycles, have no income to show for it. Compare with **accrual-basis accounting.**

Cash budget: An estimate of cash flow over a future accounting period.

Cash flow: The movement of cash into and out of an organization over an accounting period. A positive cash flow means more money is coming into the company than is going out. A negative cash flow means more money is going out of the organization than is coming in. A consistently large positive cash flow could indicate that expansion is not only possible but is necessary. It can also indicate that it is time to pay off outstanding debt. However, a consistently large negative cash flow could very well indicate that the business is in serious trouble and that drastic measures (reorganization and reductions in overhead and expenses) need to be taken.

Cash flow statement: A formal financial statement that shows the effect of all operating, investing, and financing activities on an organization's cash flow over a specific accounting period (usually the fiscal year). Also called the **statement of cash flows.**

Cash management: Process of (1) having enough cash on hand to meet day-to-day expenses and (2) investing as much cash as possible in longer-term investments so that its money is working for the company.

Cash ratio: Cash and marketable securities divided by current liabilities; a measure of an organization's liquidity.

Central processing unit (CPU): The computing part of the computer. A personal computer CPU is a single microprocessor chip that is the "brain" of the computer.

Chart of accounts: The system of accounts that make up the ledger for an organization.

Closed-ended question: Used to elicit a specific ordered choice.

Closing: The act of consummating a sale or scheduling an appointment over the phone.

Clustering: The ability to make multiple servers appear as one server to network clients.

Collateral: Property (or assets) pledged as security for a loan. If the loan is not repaid, the title of the property passes to the lender.

Commodification: This occurs when distinctions between the quality and performance of products blurs in the clients' minds, reducing even the most sophisticated equipment and service to the status of being mere commodities.

Consolidated financial statement: The combined financial statement of the parent company and its subsidiaries.

Content server: Shares data in HTML (Hypertext Markup Language) and other Internet-compatible formats for dissemination to Internet/intranet users.

Contingent liability: Potential obligation that will materialize only if certain events occur in the future.

Contra accounts: Accounts that are offset against other accounts.

Contribution margin: The difference between total sales and variable costs at a given volume of sales. The measure of the net contribution that any product, division, or subsidiary makes to paying off an organization's fixed costs.

Convertible debt: A security—usually a bond or preferred stock—that can be exchanged for another form of a corporation's securities (usually common stock).

Corporate cost: Any cost associated with activities in a corporation's headquarters. Corporate costs are allocated to divisions and product lines.

Corporate structure: The organization of a corporation's departments and agencies, and the distribution and delegation of functional responsibilities within the organization.

Cost: A disbursement of cash for the purpose of doing business.

Cost accounting: A method of accounting that accumulates and reports the costs of materials, labor, and overhead associated with production for financial reporting and decision making purposes.

Cost allocation: The assignment of indirect cost to a cost object (product) or a job.

Cost-based pricing: A method of pricing goods or services based on the purchase price or the cost of raw materials, plus the cost of delivering the goods or services to the customer.

Cost–benefit analysis: A comparison of the expected costs and benefits of a decision. Before making an investment decision, for example, an organization should carry out a cost–benefit analysis to determine whether the investment is the most effective use of its resources.

Cost center: A decentralized entity in which the manager has responsibility for the control of costs incurred and the authority to make decisions that affect these costs. The term for any non–revenue producing department or entity within an organization.

Cost of goods sold: The cost of manufactured product sold; usually includes the cost of raw materials, utilities, labor, and overhead.

Cost of money: The interest paid on funds borrowed and any amount less than the best rate of return on funds invested.

Cost of sales (COS): The cost of the goods or services sold plus the cost of selling and delivering those goods or services. In the case of goods, the COS also can include follow-up service or maintenance.

Cost pool: A collection of costs that have been allocated to or identified with particular cost centers, products, or services. The common cost pools include overhead costs, general and administrative costs, and corporate costs.

Cost principle: The generally accepted accounting principle that the value (purchase price) of any asset must be recorded at the time ownership of the asset is transferred.

Current assets: Cash, accounts receivable, and other assets an organization owns that can be liquidated within a year.

Current liabilities: Accounts payable and other debts that an organization is expected to repay within a year.

Current ratio: Current assets divided by current liabilities; a measure of a company's ability to pay its current obligations using its current assets.

Database server: Runs the DBMS (database management system) that stores and manages accounting data.

Database 2 (DB2): A relational database management system from IBM.

Data warehousing: A method of accessing the potential of numerical accounting data and harnessing its power in a single query-oriented database to provide decision support and business management functions.

Date of declaration: The date on which a corporation announces that a dividend will be paid.

Date of payment: The date on which a corporation actually distributes a dividend.

Date of record: Following an announcement that a dividend will be paid, the date on which ownership of the shares is determined, anyone who purchases shares after the date of record does not receive the dividend.

Days' sales outstanding (DSO) ratio: Accounts receivable multiplied by 365, divided by credit sales; a measure of the average number of days a company waits for payment of its credit sales.

Debt: Any liability and, more commonly, money borrowed from and owed to another person or institution.

Debt ratios: Measures of an organization's debt. See **debt-to-equity** and **debt-to-total-assets** ratios.

Debt security: A security that represents an obligation between a creditor and the business issuing the obligation.

Debt-to-equity ratio: Total liabilities divided by total owners' equity; a measure of an organization's debt structure: how much of that debt is owed to shareholders versus creditors. This is an important distinction. Obligations to creditors are fixed; they must be repaid at agreed times in agreed amounts or the organization could be forced in bankruptcy. Dividends and other distributions to equityholders are not fixed; they are made at the discretion of the organization's board of directors. The larger the debt to equity ratio, the greater the organization's fixed debt and risk.

Debt-to-total-assets ratio: Total liabilities divided by total assets; a measure of an organization's capital structure.

Decentralization: The separation of a business into more manageable operating units.

Decision Support System (DSS): Presents summary data and provides true modeling capabilities, i.e., the answers to "what if" questions. See also **executive information system**.

Deferred expenses: Items that are initially recorded as assets but are expected to become expenses over time. Sometimes called **prepaid expenses.**

Deferred revenues: Items that are initially recorded as liabilities but are expected to become revenues over time. Sometimes called **unearned revenues.**

Depreciation: The gradual decline in the value of an asset because of use or age and the expense arising from that loss in value. The expense of depreciation is tax deductible.

Diagnostic selling: This is the technique of listening to discover the problems clients have and the types of solutions they are searching for, and then determining how and if a product or service will help them toward their goal.

Direct cost: A cost of labor or materials that can immediately be traced back to a product. See **indirect cost.**

Disbursement: Cash paid out to a creditor.

Disbursement method: The method by which annual expenses and revenues are disbursed throughout the year.

Discounted cash flow: The present value of a series of future receipts and disbursements, at a specified interest rate.

Distribution: Cash paid out to an organization's bond and shareholders.

Distribution channel: A means used to transfer goods from a manufacturer to the end user.

Dividend: A disbursement—usually in the form of cash or additional shares—of a corporation's earnings and profits to its shareholders.

Double-entry accounting: A system for recording transactions, based on recording increases and decreases in accounts so that debits always equal credits.

Drill across: The ability to compare data from different sectors of corporate activity at the same scale of detail.

Drill down: The ability to pursue a database query through successively finer-scale views, from a general overview to a specific item or cell.

Dynamic data exchange (DDE): An early Windows protocol allowing communication between applications, so that when a document is updated in one application, related information will be updated in other documents linked to it.

Dynamic link library (DLL): Collection of functions (program sections that perform specific tasks) that can be used by several applications at the same time.

Earnings per share: The profitability ratio of net income to the number of shares outstanding.

Earnings statement: A financial statement that reflects how much profit was made during a given period by recording all income and expense transactions.

Economies of scale: The per-unit savings realized as the total number of units produced or purchased increases.

Employee's earnings record: A detailed record of each employee's earnings.

Equity: Total assets minus total liabilities; shareholders' interest in a corporation; the book value of the organization. Also called **net asset value** and **net worth.**

Executive Information System (EIS): Consolidates and summarizes ongoing transactions both internal and external to the organization, then allows some "what if" analysis, but does not have the true modeling capabilities of a **Decision Support System**.

Expense: A cost of doing business over a past, present, or future accounting period; a decrease in owners' equity produced by a cost in operations.

Expense recognition principle: The generally accepted accounting principle that expenses can be recognized only when an organization's resources are being used to generate revenue.

Factor: A company that buys or accepts title to an organization's accounts receivable and then acts as principal to collect those receivables.

Factory overhead cost: All the costs of operating the manufacturing facility except for direct materials and direct labor.

Fair market value: The price a willing buyer would pay a willing seller for goods or services. Especially in the case of real estate and other valuables that are not easily converted to cash, fair market value is not determined by the original price of the object but by the price it can command on the open market.

Fault tolerance: Duplicating resources, such as fans, power supplies, and network interface cards, to ensure high levels of system availability.

Federal Reserve System (Fed): A system established in 1913 to regulate national banking and monetary practices. The Fed uses its authority to regulate the nation's money supply (by setting the prime interest rate), to act as a clearinghouse for the transfer of funds between banks, and to oversee practices in the nation's banks.

Federal Trade Commission (FTC): An agency established in 1915 to enforce antitrust laws in the United States.

Fibre Channel: A network transmission standard specifying signaling and data handling techniques for a variety of connection media including coaxial cable and fiber-optic cable. This standard provides high reliability in connections and assured delivery of the data at speeds up to one gigabit per second (GPS).

Financial Accounting Standards Board (FASB): An independent board established in 1973 (it succeeded an organization formed in 1959) to develop and interpret accounting principles, procedures, rules, and regulations for all entities except state and municipal governments.

Financial statement: A formal report on the financial status of an organization or the results of its activities. See, for example, **balance sheet, cash flow statement,** and **income statement.**

Finished goods inventory: The cost of finished products on hand that have not been sold.

First-in, first-out (FIFO) method: A method of inventory costing based on the assumption that the costs of merchandise sold should be charged against the revenue in the order in which the costs were incurred.

Fiscal year: Any continuous 12-month period defined by an organization for financial, accounting, planning, or tax purposes; the period over which an organization prepares and reports its financial results. An organization's fiscal year often is different, by choice, from the calendar year.

Fixed asset: Equipment, machinery, a plant, a building, land, or some other property that an organization owns and does not expect to sell in the normal course of business. Fixed assets are long-term assets. Their useful life should extend beyond the current accounting period.

Fixed cost: Costs that tend to remain the same in amount, regardless of variations in the level of activity. The property tax an organization pays on its factory, for example, is a fixed cost; it does not vary over the year with the volume of production or the hours worked. Compare with **variable costs.**

Fixed expense: Any operating cost that does not vary with the volume of sales or production. Fixed expenses include depreciation and supervisors' salaries. Compare with **variable expense.**

Forecast: A projection of sales or some other activity based on past performance, knowledge of the marketplace, and an understanding of the business dynamics of the organization.

Franchise: The right sold by the franchiser to the franchisee to an exclusive territory or market.

Free on board (FOB): The point at which the title of goods transfers from the producer to the buyer. For example, FOB-origin means that the title to the goods transfers when the goods leave the producer's loading dock (and that the buyer pays for shipping).

Fringe benefit: Insurance, day care, health club membership, or any other benefit an organization pays for that has value to and will be used by its employees.

Front-end query tools: Stand-alone desktop tools that allow "what if" and other analysis through a graphical user interface (GUI). The software then sends the query to a server where the relational database is stored, which processes the query and returns the answer.

Full-disclosure principle: The generally accepted accounting principle that financial statements must reveal—in the document, in notes to the document, or in supplemental documents—any information that could influence the decision making of the individuals who see and use those financial statements the accountant has prepared. The failure to disclose relevant information usually results in legal action.

Functional organization: An organizational structure based on the functions performed within an organization, for example, finance, marketing, and personnel.

Gain or loss recognition principle: The generally accepted accounting principle that gains should not be recorded until they are realized, but that losses must be recorded as they become known or unavoidable.

Gateway server: Provides users of legacy systems with access to accounting data on mainframe or minicomputer platforms.

General and administrative (G&A) expense: Any cost necessary to operate a business that is not associated directly with production or sales.

General expense: An expense that is not directly associated with administrative or selling expenses or with the cost of goods sold.

Generally accepted accounting principles (GAAP): The rules, regulations, and guidelines that define accepted accounting practice and make audits and comparisons of businesses possible.

Goodwill: The difference between the purchase price of a business and the book value of its assets. Goodwill is an **intangible asset** that can be depreciated.

Granule or module: Units of system functionality in accounting software. Where a given accounting task—for example, inventory, job costing, invoicing—might have been handled by a module of software, increasingly, they are being broken down into granules to allow for even finer-scale customization.

Gross margin: See **gross profit.**

Gross national product (GNP): A measure of the performance of a national economy over a specified period.

Gross profit: Sales less the cost of goods sold; a measure of profitability. Also called **gross margin**. Gross profit is different from net profit, which is gross profit net of other income or expenses and taxes.

Gross profit ratio: Gross profit divided by sales. The resulting fraction is applied to periodic sales to determine the taxable gain from each sale.

Growth capital: Funds an organization sets aside to meet specific needs—a planned expansion or market outreach, for example. See also **working capital.**

Head count: The actual number of people working in a company, division, or business, or needed to work in a company, division, or business.

Highlights: A report that shows revenue, gross profit, operating expenses, net profit, and cash over an accounting period.

Holding company: A corporation operated for the purpose of owning common stock in and managing other companies.

HTML: HyperText Markup Language, a standard for defining hypertext links between documents. It has become the standard language of the World Wide Web.

HTTP: HyperText Transfer Protocol, the protocol used by the World Wide Web to communicate over TCP/IP. All addresses on the World Wide Web begin with the prompt "http."

Human resources budget: Reflects the human resource requirements of an organization.

Income statement: A formal financial statement that summarizes an organization's earnings and expenses over an accounting period. Also called **profit-and-loss statement** and **operating statement.**

Indirect cost: A cost—for example, rent or insurance—that cannot immediately be allocated to an organization's product. Usually, indirect costs accrue regardless of the number of goods manufactured or the amount of services provided. Compare with **direct cost.**

Inflation: A period when prices in general are rising and the purchasing power of money is declining.

Intangible asset: A long-term asset that derives its value not from its physical substance (it has none), but from the rights or privileges it accrues to the organization; leaseholds, copyrights, patents, goodwill, market dominance, and brand names are all intangible assets. Compare with **tangible asset.**

Interest: The cost of borrowing money or the return for lending it.

Interest coverage ratio: Net income before taxes plus interest expense, divided by interest expense; a measure of the degree to which creditors are protected should the organization default on its interest expenses. The higher the ratio, the greater the coverage.

Interest expense: The cost of borrowing money.

Interest income: The return from lending money.

Internal controls: The detailed policies and procedures used to direct business operations and assure accurate reports and compliance with laws and regulations.

Internal rate of return (IRR): A method of analysis of proposed capital investments that focuses on using present value concepts to compute the rate of return from the net cash flows expected from the investment.

Internet accounting: Distributed access, using custom applets appended to users' Web browsers, permitting use of core accounting software from remote locations. This enables reports to be written as HTML pages and data files to be transmitted via e-mail or FTP over the Web. A way of exploding the traditional corporate accounting department in time and space.

Internet server: Manages the connection of Internet users to the accounting database and process servers.

In the black: Operating with a positive cash flow. The expression dates back to the time when accountants worked in ink and used black ink to show a surplus of operating capital.

In the red: Operating with a negative cash flow. The expression dates back to the time when accountants worked in ink and used red ink to show a negative balance in operating capital.

Inventory: An organization's stock of raw materials, work in process, and finished goods.

Inventory control: The process of managing inventory to maintain a balance between too much inventory (which ties up cash, space and other assets) and too little inventory (which could lead to stock-outs), and to prevent the loss and theft of inventory.

Inventory turnover ratio: The cost of goods sold divided by average daily inventory; a measure of the times a company's inventory is sold and replaced over an accounting period. A low turnover rate usually indicates that an organization is carrying too large an inventory.

Inventory valuation: The process of placing a value on inventory by physically counting it and then determining its cost (which includes the cost of raw materials, assembly, insurance, transportation, and storage). Accuracy in this process is critically important. The value of inventory is a key component in determining the cost of goods sold.

Investment tax credit: A federal income tax credit allowed on certain capital assets.

Investor: An individual or institution who puts up cash or other assets to fund the operations of a business organization and who, in return, receives some ownership interest in the organization and a right to a share of its profits.

Job costing: A fixed-asset analysis tool included in some accounting packages, available as a third-party add-on for others. Job costing often lets you compare individual job costs with revenue to identify profitable jobs. It also lets you break costs into components such as equipment and labor.

Job order cost system: A type of cost accounting system that provides for a separate record of the cost of each particular quantity of product that passes through the factory.

Just-in-time (JIT) manufacturing system: Systems of manufacturing in which a primary emphasis is on the manufacturing of products only as they are needed by the next stage of production or by the marketplace.

Knowledge engineer: Communicates with experts to acquire relevant knowledge.

Knowledge management processes: The management of a set of processes occurring in an organization to create, refine, use, retrieve, extract, transfer, and exercise control over and manage knowledge.

Knowledge system: A computer system that represents and uses knowledge to carry out its task.

Last-in, first-out (LIFO) method: A method of inventory costing based on the assumption that the most recent costs of merchandise sold should be charged against the revenue.

Lead time: The time required for the manufacture of a product from receipt of an order until it is shipped to the customer.

Lease: A contract allowing the use of a fixed asset—a machine or a vehicle, for example—over a stated period in exchange for payment. Although in the long run a lease can be more expensive than a purchase, lease payments usually are lower than installment payments and they give the organization the flexibility to "trade up" if technology changes significantly.

Leaseback: The sale of property through an agreement in which the seller leases the property from the buyer.

Legacy data: Historical information, usually from many sources within the organization, that goes into building multidimensional databases.

Lessee: The organization that leases an asset from another organization.

Lessor: The organization that owns an asset that is being leased to another organization.

Leverage: The use of long-term debt (as opposed to owner's equity) to generate profits; assumes that the cost of borrowing funds will be less than the return earned on using those funds. The higher the ratio of debt to equity, the greater the leverage.

Liability: Any debt owed by an organization (including accounts payable, notes payable, and loan payments). The value of a liability generally is the value of the loan payments. Compare **asset.**

Line of credit: An arrangement whereby a financial institution commits itself to lending up to a specified amount of funds over a specified time.

Liquid asset: Cash or some other asset—a bank deposit or a U.S. Treasury bill, for example—that is readily convertible to cash. The longer it would take to realize money from an asset, the less liquid the asset.

Liquidity ratios: Measures of an organization's ability to pay its short-term debt. See **acid test.**

Loan: Money borrowed (from a bank, lending institution or other source) that must be paid back with interest (the cost of the loan).

Long-term asset: Property that an organization expects to own for more than one year. See **fixed asset.**

Long-term debt: Any obligation scheduled to be paid off in a year or longer. Also called **long-term liability.**

Long-term loan: Any loan scheduled to be paid off in a year or more.

Low end: Costing less than $300 and built for small businesses with less than 50 employees and typically less than $1 million in revenue.

Management by objective (MBO): A method of organizational planning and control in which managers and employees agree on performance goals, which later become the criteria against which performance is evaluated.

Management process: The five basic management functions of (1) planning, (2) directing, (3) controlling, (4) improving, and (5) decision making.

Manufacturing overhead: Manufacturing costs of producing a product over and above direct materials and direct labor.

Margin: The difference between the price received for an organization's goods or services and the cost of producing them. See **contribution margin** and **profit margin.**

Marginal income analysis: An examination of the cost of producing a product at different volumes and the expected effect on revenue of different levels of sales to determine how the product contributes to the organization's profit margin, overhead costs, or variable costs.

Market: A clearly defined group of people who want and are able to buy a product or service. Also called **demand.**

Market-based pricing: A method of pricing goods or services in a highly competitive environment that considers competitors' pricing as well as the cost of producing the goods or services.

Marketing: The process of identifying and selling to the needs of a market.

Market share: An organization's sales divided by total sales in that industry; usually expressed as a percentage.

Markup: In pricing a product for retail sales, the percentage of increase over the wholesale cost. For example, if a furniture store chooses a 50 percent markup on coffee tables, it would charge $150 for a coffee table that wholesales for $100.

Matching principle: The generally accepted accounting principle that revenues must be assigned to the accounting period in which they are earned and that expenses must be assigned to the period in which they are used to produce revenues.

Merger: A voluntary reorganization in which one corporation absorbs another.

Messaging server: Manages the routing of messaging traffic such as e-mail and packages of workflow-related data.

Metric: One dimension or type of measurement within a **multidimensional database (MDD)**.

Mezzanine financing: Short-term borrowing that is replaced by longer-term financing when a transitional phase—for example, the construction of a building—is complete.

Middleware: Software providing a link between applications that do not use the same programming language.

Mid-range: Accounting programs costing more than $1,000, usually sold by module and built for medium-sized businesses with more than $1 million in revenue and with 50 to 100 employees.

Modem (Modulator-DEModulator): A device that connects a computer to a telephone line, thus allowing the computer to talk with other computers through the phone system.

Module: The pieces of an accounting program that address separate financial departments. Some programs offer several main modules as a bundle and then additional modules cost extra. The main modules for mid-range accounting programs are system manager, general ledger, accounts receivable, and accounts payable.

Multidimensional database (MDD): Also called "data cube," a database that organizes data across many dimensions, e.g. region, products, and sales volume.

Needs analysis: Listening to clients talk about their needs and goals before presenting a product or service.

Net: The income (or sales, profit, or worth) remaining after expenses are paid.

Net asset value: See **equity.**

Net income: Sales minus all expenses—including federal and foreign income tax—for a specific accounting period; in common usage, profit after taxes. Also called **net profit.**

Net of: Remaining after; for example, profit net of income taxes is profit after taxes.

Net profit: See **net income.**

Net profit margin: See **profit margin.**

Net sales: Revenues received from customers in exchange for goods sold or services rendered, less any returns or allowances; a company's prime source of revenues.

Net working capital: Current assets minus current liabilities. See **working capital.**

Network server: The servers and clients are connected together with ethernet cables and network hardware. Other devices that can be attached and shared in the common network include printers, modems, and tape drives.

Net worth: See **equity.**

Node: The term for servers in a cluster configuration.

Object linking and embedding (OLE): 32-bit extension of DDE. OLE provides services that make it easy for applications for data sharing. Allows direct editing within another application, where one program appears to be an extension of another.

Object server: Manages application object components that provide specific application services and functions.

Online analytical processing (OLAP): Business intelligence using multidimensional analysis; builds a multidimensional data cube from information stored in relational and other two-dimensional databases. DOLAP is the desktop version of OLAP, ROLAP (relational OLAP) is the same as OLAP.

On the fly: The ability to enter data for one area of the program from a different area of the program (usually by clicking a button) without losing your place. For example, entering a new customer while in the Invoice Data Entry window.

Open database connectivity (ODBC): The ability of a database to be incorporated into a data warehouse for use in **multidimensional databases (MMDs)**.

Operating expenses: Expenses that are incurred during an organization's day-to-day operations.

Operating profit (loss): The difference between sales and cost of goods sold (which do not include financing expenses or taxes).

Operating statement: See **income statement.**

Operational planning: The development of short-term plans to achieve goals identified in a business's strategic plan; sometimes called **tactical planning.**

Opportunity costs: Represents a benefit that is foregone as a result of choosing one alternative over another.

Organization: The framework of roles and responsibilities that allows a business entity to meet its objectives.

Organizational chart: A graphic presentation showing the interrelationships of positions within an organization in terms of authority and responsibility.

Organizational planning: The process of developing management strategies and tactics to meet the organization's objectives.

Organizational structure: The distribution of responsibility and authority among the members of an organization.

Other expense: An expense that cannot be traced directly to operations.

Other income: Revenue from sources other than the primary operating activity of a business.

Outstanding stock: The stock that is in the hands of stockholders.

Overhead: The indirect cost of running a business; includes the cost of utilities and insurance.

Overhead pool: A cost pool for a particular type of overhead. See **cost pool.**

Overhead rate: Estimated overhead costs divided by an estimated measure of production activity. In budgeting, the rate is used to assign estimated overhead costs (which are indirect costs) to some measure of production activity, among them machine hours, labor hours, and units of output.

Owner's equity: The owner's right to the assets of the business after the total liabilities are deducted.

Paid-in capital: The capital acquired from stockholders.

Par: The monetary amount printed on a stock certificate.

Patent: The legal right to exclude others from making or selling an invention for a specific number of years.

Payables: An organization's current liabilities; its legal obligation to pay workers, rent on property owned by others, interest and payments on loans, and invoices for materials and supplies. Compare with **receivables.**

Percentage of completion: A method used to recognize income over the course of a long-term project.

Period cost: Any cost that is expensed over the same period in which it is incurred. Also called **period expense.**

Personnel: An organization's employees. Also called **human resources.**

Planning: Identifying a sequence of actions needed to meet an organization's objectives.

Portability: When an operating system may be moved from one hardware platform to another with minimal recoding, it is said to be portable.

Posting: The act of transferring information from an individual module to the general ledger. In most cases, items that are not posted may be deleted. Once the transaction is posted, it must be voided or reversed, but it cannot be removed from the general ledger.

Prepaid expense: An amount paid for products not yet received or services not yet rendered; considered an asset.

Prepaid income: A payment received for products or services not yet delivered; considered a **liability.**

Prescriptive selling: Telling clients about a product or service that cures a particular problem, without listening to clients first to find out what their problems are.

Present value: The amount that must be invested today at a given rate of interest to produce a given amount in the future.

Price: The amount an organization charges for a product or service.

Price–earnings ratio: The ratio, often called the **P/E ratio**, computed by dividing the market price per share of common stock on a specific date by the company's earnings per share on common stock.

Pricing strategy: The factors an organization considers in setting a price for its goods or services. Key factors are the cost of producing the product and supply and demand for the product.

Proactive: Anticipating problems and taking steps to deal with them.

Procedural knowledge: In a word, know-how. Knowledge that is in the form of procedural rules and is the most fundamental form of knowledge.

Proceeds: The money the seller of an asset receives after sales commissions have been paid.

Product costs: Production costs that relate to unit output and are charges to the cost of the product when it is sold.

Product line: A group of closely related (in terms of use, production, and marketing) products manufactured or sold by an organization. The depth of a product line refers to the number of products in the line.

Product mix: The variety of goods or services an organization sells.

Profit: Sales minus expenses; an organization's earnings.

Profitability ratios: Measures of a business's operating efficiency and profitability; include gross profit ratio, profit margin, return on assets, return on equity, and return on invested capital rates.

Profit after taxes: See **net income.**

Profit-and-loss (P&L) statement: See **income statement.**

Profit-based pricing: A method of pricing goods or services that adds a standard percentage of profit to all of the costs (direct and indirect) of producing, selling, and distributing the goods or services.

Profit center: An organizational unit in which the manager has the responsibility and the authority to make decisions that affect both costs and revenues. Also called **revenue center** or **source.**

Profit contribution ratio: Computed by dividing the contribution margin by net sales; reciprocal of the relationship of variable costs to net sales.

Profit margin: Net income divided by net sales; a measure of the net income produced by each dollar of sales. Also called the **net profit margin.**

Pro forma financial statement: A financial statement that includes hypothetical or projected information; used within an organization to facilitate decision making and planning. A pro forma income statement, for example, might show how a merger that has not been completed would affect the financial statements.

Programmed costs: Costs that result from specific decisions without any consideration of volume activity or passage of time.

Project or job costing program: The module that maintains project information. This module usually integrates with the other modules as a reference during customer invoicing, employee time sheet processing, and vendor payment processing to manage the profit and loss of a project.

Property: Any object, benefit, or right owned by an organization.

Property and equipment turnover ratio: Net sales divided by average property and equipment; a measure of the efficiency with which an organization uses its property and equipment to produce sales. The higher the ratio, the more effectively the organization is using its property and equipment.

Quick ratio: See **acid test ratio.**

Random access memory (RAM): The computer's primary workspace. The "random" means that the contents of each byte can be directly accessed without regard to the bytes before or after it. This is also true of other types of memory chips, including ROMs and PROMs. However, unlike ROMs and PROMs, RAM chips require power to maintain their content, which is why you must save your data on disk before you turn the computer off.

Ratio analysis: Using the relationship between figures found in the financial statements to determine, among other conditions, the organization's liquidity, profitability, and long-term solvency.

Raw materials inventory: The portion of inventory that consists of the materials that have been purchased and that will be used to make revenue-producing products; the value of raw materials inventory is the cost of the materials themselves.

Rebate: A portion of the money paid on a purchase that is returned to the buyer. Rebates are often used in promotion, to make prices temporarily or conditionally lower.

Receipt: An amount of cash received.

Receivables: Current assets; the money owed an organization for rent on property it owns, interest and payments on loans it has made, and invoices it has sent out for goods or services supplied. Compare with **payables.**

Recourse: The right of a lender to claim money as well as any collateral pledged when a borrower defaults on a loan. Recourse can be limited by contract to none, some, or all of the borrower's assets.

Redundant array of inexpensive/independent disks (RAID): Several disk drives are grouped together and data is mirrored over multiple disk drives. If one drive fails, the data may be retrieved from the other drives for redundancy and fault resilience.

Refinancing: The process of borrowing from lender B to repay lender A; also can be used to extract cash from an asset or to restructure an existing loan.

Reforecast: A plan that incorporates new information.

Reporting server: Stores data specifically organized for efficient decision support or other reporting tasks.

Residual value: The value of an asset at the end of its useful life. Also called **salvage value.**

Restructuring a loan: The process of changing the terms of a debt — the amount owed, the date the loan must be paid off, and the interest rate. Owners' equity can also be restructured.

Retained earnings: A corporation's net profit after dividends have been paid to shareholders.

Return: The income a lender or owner receives as compensation for the loan or investment; usually expressed as an annual rate (percentage).

Return on assets (ROA) ratio: Net income divided by average total assets; a measure of the profitability of an organization's assets.

Return on equity (ROE) ratio: Net income divided by owner's equity; a measure of how effectively owner's money is being used.

Return on investment (ROI): Investors' earnings on their original investment; usually expressed as a percentage.

Return on sales ratio: Income before taxes divided by sales; a measure of an organization's operating efficiency that is used not only to analyze performance in different accounting periods, but also to analyze the organization's performance in relation to the performance of its industry. (Return on sales varies markedly from industry to industry.)

Revenue: The total sales earned and recorded in an accounting period; usually used to refer to sales of services rather than goods. Compare with **sales.**

Revenue centers: Centers where performance is measured in terms of sales revenue.

Revenue forecasting: Using current and projected data to predict revenue in some future accounting period.

Revenue recognition principle: The generally accepted accounting principle that a business must have the legal right to earn revenue before it can record that revenue.

Revenue source: See **profit center.**

RFI: Radio frequency interference.

Risk management: The process of identifying possible sources of loss and measuring the financial consequences of loss to minimize the impact of loss on an organization.

ROLAP: OLAP tools designed to work with relational databases and their data.

Rules server: Stores business rules and logic or application metadata for regulating access to accounting data.

Sales: The total revenue earned and recorded in an accounting period; usually used to refer to revenue earned from goods rather than services. Compare with **revenue.**

Sales budget: An estimate of sales allocated by product, territory, or individual and prepared weekly, monthly, quarterly, or annually.

Sales volume: The accumulation of all sales made by an organization.

Salvage value: See **residual value.**

Scalability: If a system is built so that additional components may be easily added, it is known as scalable. Scalability also refers to the system's "adaptability" to increased demands.

Scanner: A device that can convert printed pages and color pictures into editable, usable computer files. With optical character recognition (OCR) software, the scanner can convert printed pages and forms into word processing text.

Schedule: A written or printed statement of accounting information—for example, a schedule of inventory or indirect costs.

Semivariable costs: A cost that has both fixed and variable cost components. A phone bill is a semivariable cost: The monthly charge is fixed, but the charges for long-distance calls are variable (they reflect actual use).

Shareholders' equity: See **stockholders' equity.**

Short-term assets: Any property that an organization expects to convert to cash within a year.

Short-term debt: Any obligation that must be paid off within a year. Also called **short-term liability.**

Short-term debt-to-total-liabilities ratio: Current liabilities divided by total liabilities. Measure of the organization's level of debt coverage.

Short-term liability: See **short-term debt.**

Short-term loan: Any loan scheduled to be paid off in less than one year.

16-bit: The number of bits of data that can be processed at once. With 16-bit Windows programming, one program must wait for another to finish processing its tasks before proceeding.

Slice and dice: "Drill down" abilities afforded the OLAP end user, the processing of queries about large amounts of data to provide multidimensional views of the data by relying on built-in algorithms and programmable business rules. Moving, during a database query, from top-down, bottom-up, or across functional areas to determine performance on key variables.

Small Computer System Interface (SCSI): The SCSI bus and parallel interface standard allows components such as hard disks and tape drives to communicate with a peripheral device that uses embedded intelligence. The interface supports one master host and seven or more slave peripherals, connected in a daisy chain through a cable to an SCSI expansion board known as a host adapter. SCSI interfaces can move data at rates ranging from 5 to 40 megabytes per second (mps).

Small Office/Home Office (SOHO): Refers to the small business or business-at-home user.

Source and application of funds: Indicates how much money flows through a business by highlighting where the cash was from and how it was used.

Standard cost: The estimated cost of producing a product based on engineering and accounting studies. A standard cost can be used as an expense when the sale of a product is recorded on the income statement.

Starting balance: The balance in an account at the beginning of an accounting period.

Statement of cash flows: See **cash flow statement.**

Stock: Ownership shares in a corporation.

Stockholders' equity: The value of stockholders' ownership in a corporation.

Stock option: The right to buy or sell common stock at a predetermined price within a specified period. Stock options are often used as an incentive or as compensation for an organization's employees.

Stock warrant: The right of an existing stockholder to buy additional shares of stock at a predetermined price within a specified period.

Storage area network (SAN): A network architecture and system that pools resources for centralized data storage. A SAN system may include multiple servers working against a centralized data store built with redundant hardware, such as a RAID.

Straight-line depreciation: A method of calculating depreciation in which the amount of the annual deduction stays the same over the useful life of the asset. Compare with **accelerated depreciation.**

Strategic planning: Determining the long-term objectives of the organization and developing strategies for reaching them.

Strategic value: The value of the organization as perceived by a potential investor or a competitor.

Subordinated debt: In the case of default or foreclosure, debt that has a lower-priority claim on assets than does other debt.

Substitutive innovation: Creation of new products, technologies, processes, or procedures to take the place of, or eliminate, old ones.

System manager: The module that maintains the whole system's options, such as company name, address, tax ID, other general company information, user IDs and passwords, and various other options that are the foundation of each module.

Tacit knowledge: Unspoken knowledge manifested in individual skills, routines, and experience.

Tangible asset: A long-term asset whose value is a function of its physical substance. Machinery, equipment, land, and buildings are all tangible assets. Compare with **intangible asset.**

Target market: The most likely group, based on any number of criteria, determined to have the highest potential to buy a product or service.

Tax table: A table that lists tax liabilities for a range of taxable incomes.

32-bit: The standard number of data bits used by most current operating systems; 32-bit Windows programs allow preemptive multitasking, appearing to perform more than one task at a time.

Top-down method: A budgeting method that utilizes a central staff to determine corporate goals.

Total assets-to-current-debt ratio: Total assets divided by current debt.

Total quality management (TQM): A management practice that relies on cooperation, teamwork and employee training to improve that quality of an organization's overall performance.

Trade association: An organization formed to benefit members of the same trade by informing them of issues and developments that could affect their operations or sales.

Trade credit: An open-account arrangement between a seller and a buyer; an organization's record of payment with its suppliers.

Trademark: An insignia or logo that distinguishes one organization's products from all others.

Transfer price: The price charged by one department or unit of a company for products or services supplied to another department or unit of the same company.

Turnover: The number of times inventory or some other asset is replaced over an accounting period; the rate at which inventory or some other asset is used and replaced over an accounting period. (In Britain, *turnover* is the term used to describe what Americans call revenue.)

Unassignable costs: Costs that cannot be directly traced to a specific product and/or segment of the business.

Unified modeling language (UML): A language used for object-oriented software development. It was pioneered by the Object Management Group.

Uninterruptible power supply (UPS): Backup power used when the electrical power fails or drops to an unacceptable voltage level. A UPS system can be connected to a file server so that, in the event of a problem, all network users can be alerted to save files and shut down immediately.

Unit cost: The cost of a single item that is either produced or acquired by an organization.

Useful life: The period over which an asset is depreciated.

Value-added reseller (VAR): The person or company from which mid-range accounting programs are purchased. The VAR has paid for the code in which the accounting software was written. By knowing how the software was built, they can customize it to better fit a client's needs. The VAR will usually be certified to install the software on the system and to train the users to use it.

Value-added tax (VAT): A tax imposed at each step in the production process, in the value added to the asset in that step.

Variable cost: A cost that varies in direct proportion to a change in volume or activity. The cost of materials, for example, is a variable cost: It goes up in defined increments with each additional unit produced. (Notice that variable costs are constant per unit, unlike fixed costs, which go up or down per unit as the number of units produced falls or rises.) Compare with **fixed cost.**

Variable expense: Any operating cost that varies with the volume of sales or production. Variable expenses include the costs of raw materials, labor, and sales commissions. Compare with **fixed expense.**

Variable-interest loan: A loan whose interest rate can change at specific intervals over the life of the loan.

Variance: The amount by which an actual financial parameter, a cost, for example, differs from its standard or budgeted value.

Working capital: Current assets minus current liabilities; the cash an organization keeps on hand in order to meet its day-to-day needs.

W3C: An industry consortium that monitors, reviews, and develops standards for the evolution of the World Wide Web. W3C works with the global community to produce specifications and reference software.

INDEX

ABOUT THE AUTHOR

Jack Fox is Executive Director of The Accounting Guild. This unique Internet-based membership organization assists computer-knowledgeable accountants to acquire and advise clients in establishing and maintaining accounting, recordkeeping, and other business systems. The Guild networks the accountant in a strategic alliance of other professional accountants, computer distributors, integrators, computer hardware manufacturers, and accounting software publishers, who serve as associate members.

This virtual online organization provides the individual-affiliated accountant/consultant the ability to provide small to medium-sized business consultation and implementation of automated business accounting systems through the wholesale purchasing of resale products and cooperative services, such as configuration, installation, and service, with other Guild members when additional expertise is required.

A dialogue service is available at www.onelist.com/subscribe/accounting business, which enables the sharing of collective experience and diminishes one's sense of professional isolation.

Mr. Fox is an unforgettable speaker and results-producing author/consultant who has assisted accountants and consultants in starting and building their own successful businesses during the last 20 years. His other books include *Accounting and Recordkeeping Made Easy for the Self-Employed* (published by Wiley), *Accountants' Guide to Budgetary Automation, GOD's Business Gamebook and Business Planning Guide,* and *How to Obtain Your Own SBA Loan.*

All communications from readers are welcome and acknowledged. Personal experiences about your own accounting or consulting business hurdles and successes are particularly encouraged. For any and all comments, questions, plaudits, information requests and seminar or consultation inquiries, please e-mail the author at jfox1961@aol.com.